Aging Angry

Aging Angry

Making Peace with Rage

AMANDA SMITH BARUSCH

OXFORD
UNIVERSITY PRESS

Oxford University Press is a department of the University of Oxford. It furthers
the University's objective of excellence in research, scholarship, and education
by publishing worldwide. Oxford is a registered trade mark of Oxford University
Press in the UK and certain other countries.

Published in the United States of America by Oxford University Press
198 Madison Avenue, New York, NY 10016, United States of America.

© Oxford University Press 2024

All rights reserved. No part of this publication may be reproduced, stored in
a retrieval system, or transmitted, in any form or by any means, without the
prior permission in writing of Oxford University Press, or as expressly permitted
by law, by license, or under terms agreed with the appropriate reproduction
rights organization. Inquiries concerning reproduction outside the scope of the
above should be sent to the Rights Department, Oxford University Press, at the
address above.

You must not circulate this work in any other form
and you must impose this same condition on any acquirer.

Library of Congress Cataloging-in-Publication Data
Names: Barusch, Amanda Smith, author.
Title: Aging angry : making peace with rage / Amanda Smith Barusch.
Description: New York, NY : Oxford University Press, [2024] |
Includes bibliographical references and index. |
Identifiers: LCCN 2023030154 (print) | LCCN 2023030155 (ebook) |
ISBN 9780197584644 (hardback) | ISBN 9780197584668 (epub) | ISBN 9780197584675
Subjects: LCSH: Anger in old age. | Anger—Social aspects. |
Aging—Psychological aspects.
Classification: LCC BF724.85.A54 B37 2024 (print) | LCC BF724.85.A54
(ebook) | DDC 155.67/147—dc23/eng/20230817
LC record available at https://lccn.loc.gov/2023030154
LC ebook record available at https://lccn.loc.gov/2023030155

DOI: 10.1093/oso/9780197584644.001.0001

Printed by Integrated Books International, United States of America

*To grumpy, cantankerous, and obstreperous elders everywhere.
Long may you rage.*

Contents

List of Illustrations — xi
Preface: Who's Angry Now? — xiii
Acknowledgments — xvii
A Note on Memory — xix

1. Aging While Angry — 1
   What's Anger? — 1
   Simple Truths versus Scientific Proofs — 4
   Death by a Thousand Cuts — 6
   They're Just Going to Die Anyway — 8
   Ageism at Work — 8
   Family Matters — 9
   Mad as Hell — 10
   Don't Put a Lid on It — 10
   Anger Unbound — 13

2. Speaking of Anger — 14
   Telling It Slant — 15
   I Just Exploded — 15
   Disgusting Idioms — 17
   Metaphors from Other Lands — 18
   Hold Your Tongue — 20
   Cantankerous, Crotchety, and Grumpy — 21

3. Anger Through the Ages — 23
   Contemplating Aristotle — 25
   If a Thing Is Bad — 26
   Vengeance Is Mine — 29
   Was Jesus Angry? — 31
   Is Anger a Sin? — 32
   My Nightmare — 33

4. Angry Bodies — 35
   Inside the Lizard Brain — 36
   The Survival Circuit — 37
   Late Life Variability — 38
   Bad for Us or Just Plain Bad? — 39
   Context Matters — 41

5. Women Cry / Men Rage — 44
   - Anger Makes You Ugly — 46
   - Real Men Don't — 47
   - I Need Another Happy Pill — 49
   - A Lot to Be Angry About — 52
   - Are Men Really Angrier? — 53
   - A Gender Paradox — 55

6. Race and Anger in Later Life — 57
   - Angry Times in American Streets — 58
   - Of Life and Time — 60
   - The Tiresomeness of It All — 61
   - A Legacy for the Grandchildren — 64
   - Anger Builds Character — 66

7. Elders on Social Media — 69
   - The Rage Contagion — 70
   - Cyberspace for Rants — 71
   - A Duty to Die? — 72
   - Seniors Trapped in YouTube — 74
   - Meanwhile, Back in the U.S.A. — 75
   - The Anger Project Online — 75

8. Lessons on Anger and Love — 79
   - Homes Full of Anger — 79
   - A Panoply of Family Anger — 81
   - The Lovers' Quarrel — 82
   - The Sulk — 83
   - Serpents' Teeth — 84
   - Kick the Dog Syndrome — 86

9. Aging, Angry, and Armed to the Teeth — 90
   - A Very Big Year — 91
   - Yeah, It Fits — 93
   - War on the Government — 96
   - People Talking Down to Me — 96
   - A Regular Old Neighbor — 97
   - Santa's Coming — 98
   - A Family Annihilator — 98
   - What Was Wrong with This Man? — 99
   - That Nagging Sense of Unfairness — 101
   - Rage-onomics — 101
   - Not Again — 102
   - Beyond Disgruntled — 103

10. Taming the Rage — 105
    - Intermittent Explosive Disorder — 107

    Helping People Manage Anger   108
    Stop Dictating to Us   110
    Destroy That Monster   112
    Sometimes Therapy Works   112
    Time's Passage   114

11. Embracing the Anger   116
    Chemical Restraint   117
    A Dose of Hope   118
    American Cool   119
    A Word from the Wise   121
    Turning toward Anger   122

12. Changing the World   123
    Anger Constrained?   126
    Great Old Broads and Raging Grannies   129
    Choosing Anger   131
    Striking a Light   131

Conclusion: The Eye of the Heart   134

Appendices
    Appendix 1: The Anger Project   139
    Appendix 2: The Interview Protocol   151
    Appendix 3: Internet Survey Instrument   153
Notes   161
Bibliography   181
Index   197

Illustrations

Figures

3.1. *Achilles dragging the body of Hector around the walls of Troy* by Pietro Testa, 1648–1650.   24
5.1. Detail of *Raging Medusa*, 1998, by Cristina Biaggi.   45
6.1. COVID Lowers US Life Expectancy.   61
6.2. Regal Theater and Savoy Ballroom in Bronzeville, Chicago, IL, 1941. Farm Security Administration—Office of War Information Photograph Collection, Library of Congress.   65
7.1. "What makes you angry" post from The Anger Project, April 8, 2021.   76
7.2. "Anger in Love" post from The Anger Project, April 15, 2021.   77
8.1. Amanda and Larry were glad they didn't cancel the trip.   88
9.1. Mass Murders in America 1982–2022.   95
12.1. Carol pointing a rifle. Reproduced with permission.   125
C.1. We might need to march for our grandchildren. Photo by Roya Ann Miller on Unsplash.   137

Tables

A1. Pseudonyms, Demographics & Themes for Interview Respondents (n = 32)   143
A2. Internet Sample (n = 239) Demographics   145
A3. How Has Your Experience of Anger Changed with Age?   147
A4. What Do You Feel in Your Body When You Get Angry?   148
A5. Reflecting On What You Did during the Incident that Made You "Really Angry"   148
A6. What Advice Would You Give to Someone Younger about Anger? (n = 197)   149
A7. Do You Consider Yourself an Angry Person?   150
A8. Type of Incident that Made Respondents Angry (n = 209)   150

Preface: Who's Angry Now?

> Old age should burn and rave at close of day.
> —Dylan Thomas, *Do Not Go Gentle Into That Good Night*[1]

We were all on our best behavior for the first faculty meeting of that fall. The beginning of a new school year is always exciting and this time we had a new dean to welcome. Dressed for success, we jockeyed for position at the huge rectangular conference table. I stationed myself mid-table, behind a fresh clean notebook and a cup of herbal tea. The cast of characters had grown larger and more diverse during my thirty-four years on the faculty. Looking at my colleagues, I felt a surge of pride. I had chaired the committees that hired most of these bright young faculty members. I smiled as I watched the usual suspects, armed with laptops, tablets, and phones, huddle at the head of the table as close as they could get to the seat reserved for our new dean, almost as if some of his power might rub off on them.

The man himself strode in wearing a well-tailored suit and a brisk air of authority.

Following introductions, he launched into his plan to establish new standards for publications—standards that would apply to all faculty.

"But not if you're, like Amanda, in the twilight of your career."

All eyes shifted to me. I sat up straighter, cheeks burning, heart racing. I shrugged and gave a sheepish grin while the dean went on to detail his exciting new agenda.

"The twilight of your career." *Did he just say I was old?* At 62, I liked to think I had a few good years left. It was almost funny; just a tasteless joke. Or could it be a coded threat? My stomach clenched. Did he think I was senile? Did he think I would go quietly? If so, he had a lot to learn.

So did I.

A full professor with tenure, I had researched and taught about aging for four decades, but the dean's remark was my first experience of overt ageism. It left me feeling threatened and confused. I had already experienced my share of ageist microaggressions and had even learned to appreciate the cloak of invisibility that descends upon older women. But this was different. This was at my university. This was only the beginning.

In the weeks that followed, colleagues bustled into my office one by one and carefully closed the door. "You know, he's still making that joke about your twilight years." "Why is he singling you out?" "You aren't the oldest one here." I had no idea why the dean was targeting me; why he kept repeating that phrase.

Sure, there was "deadwood" on the faculty and I knew the administration expected the new dean to root it out. There's deadwood in many academic settings: teachers who refuse to do research, researchers who can't teach, tenured professors who never show up for meetings, people who use incompetence to avoid work assignments. In my days as an administrator, I had attempted to rejuvenate or remove some deadwood myself.

Could I be deadwood? I directed the largest program in the college, engaged in research, taught classes, mentored students, wrote books and published articles. I saw myself as productive, competent, and (for the most part) well-liked. I certainly had no intention of ending my career. But, in the following weeks, the dean made it increasingly clear that he wanted me gone.

A pattern developed. In meetings, our new leader ridiculed my suggestions and ignored my accomplishments. In private, he complemented me on my appearance. This combination of dismissal and objectivication created a bizarre discordance. Meanwhile, staff who worked under me were transferred to other units. Paperwork and administrative demands consumed more and more of my time. Some days it felt like I was under siege. Colleagues sympathized but were not in a position to help lest they too become targets. Frustration eventually spilled over into my personal life and I found myself snapping at my husband and waking at 3 AM to ruminate over my mistakes. Finally, I had to admit that I wasn't aging well, I was aging angry.

And that is how this book was born.

One day, Margaret Morganroth Gullette sent an e-mail to members of the North American Network of Aging Studies reporting that growing numbers of older faculty members with tenure were being pushed out of their positions. They couldn't be fired, but administrators could make their lives miserable by changing their job assignments and fostering a culture that was hostile to older adults.

Partly, it's about the money. Cost-conscious administrators figure they can save by trading a highly paid older adult for a less expensive novice. Also, at least in academic settings, an untenured faculty member is likely to be more malleable— less confrontive—than someone who enjoys the job security conferred by tenure.

After two years, I was on the verge of suing the university. Instead, like so many older adults, I decided to leave voluntarily. I didn't want to spend my "golden" years in endless and (let's face it) probably futile litigation.

In 2019, the year I retired, over 15,000 older workers filed age discrimination complaints with the federal Equal Employment Opportunity Commission (EEOC), most related to discriminatory discharge and age-based harassment.[2]

That's just the tip of the iceberg when it comes to age discrimination. It doesn't include state-level data and, apart from that, most older adults don't pursue legal remedies. A more accurate measure of the extent of this problem comes from a 2017 survey conducted by AARP, which found that 61 percent of older adults reported having seen or experienced age-based discrimination in the workplace.[3]

Age alone is no reason to push a person out of a job. During the twentieth century the rate of illness and disability among older adults declined steadily as longevity rose. As a result, millions of Americans are as capable as ever in our sixties, seventies, and (for the lucky ones) even in our eighties.[4] We can certainly do the job.

But, despite our best efforts, we can't prevent age-related changes in our appearance. While our minds and bodies may be perfectly healthy, our faces slowly collapse into wrinkles, our hair steadily turns grey, and our profiles become . . . well . . . ample. These signals lead others to see us through the lens of their own fear of aging. In a process known as "social aging," their responses tell us repeatedly that we are unattractive, incompetent, or irrelevant. In time, we may come to believe them.

Most older adults are unprepared for the assaults on our dignity that wear us down and erode our confidence. They make us angry. Sometimes, we displace that anger toward those we love. Sometimes, we direct it back toward ourselves in fits of self-loathing that can increase our risk of suicide. Some of us, lost in bouts of impotent rage, commit murder or mayhem. Still others serve as role models, channeling their anger into efforts that improve the world.

Graduation day is one of the real delights of academic life. At our university, it was invariably sunny and hot. I dressed lightly under my heavy regalia and paraded across campus smiling at parents and their robed graduates. That year, my usual joy was tinged with sadness. It would be \ my last graduation.

After the final set of handshakes and hugs, I went to my near-empty office. Theplants and books were all gone; the recycling bin full of old reprints. I abandoned the award plaques: "Teacher of the Year." "Dean's Award for Research." "Leadership Award." But I did save the thank you notes from students. Those, along with their silly gag gifts, would go home with me.

I refused all offers of help. I couldn't stand the pity in my colleagues' eyes. Muttering mantras of strength and resilience, I borrowed a hand cart and hauled the last set of boxes out to my car.

A treasured glass plate still sat in the middle of the table where my students and I used to meet. Made of clear glass with tiny bubbles by an artist in New Zealand, it was square with a perfect sprig of lavender embedded in its center and a beautiful navy blue border. Our long-dead family dog (a lab) used to retrieve smooth stones and I kept her collection on the plate. Students liked to handle the cool rocks while we talked. It seemed to help them stay calm and centered.

That plate was the last thing I packed. On my way out, I picked it up from the table, slipped the stones into a paper bag, and set it carefully into the top box on the cart. When I stopped at the curb, that box slid ever-so-slowly-and-inevitably to the ground, spilling the plate onto the asphalt. It shattered. Of course. Hot tears filled my eyes as I clenched my fists and swore like a sailor. Someone offered help, but I shook my head.

It was up to me to pick up the pieces.

This book grew out of that process. I began by asking other people about their experiences of anger. Then I conducted in-depth interviews and developed an online survey that would be completed by hundreds of older adults. I talked to experts. I read. I observed. I thought a lot.

The lessons I gleaned while assembling these pages deepened my understanding of both anger and age. I came to recognize the tight weave of culture, history, and identity that shapes our experience and expression of anger. I learned about the enormous contribution neuroscience has made to our understanding of human emotions; and yet, how tightly we cling to antiquated notions about both anger and aging. I learned how anger norms vary across time and cultures and even among families. I came to see how the expression of anger can be used to control others and how its suppression can threaten both personal and public well-being. I began to understand how age, gender, and race interact to shape our experiences of anger. Most importantly, I learned that in later life, when our emotional intelligence is at its peak, we can tap into the power and wisdom of anger to fuel the changes that we and our world so desperately need.

Acknowledgments

I am grateful to hundreds of older adults, who shared their experiences, lessons, and insights about anger. Through long conversations with laughter and tears they provided the threads for this surprising and complex narrative. Then, specialists in fields from medicine and law to mythology and philosophy lent their expertise, answered even my dumbest questions with patience and generosity. Many thanks to John Baxter, Jerry Buie, Rob Butters, Miriam Dexter, Warren Farrell, Michael Kimmel, Ari Mermelstein, Rich Pfeiffer, June Oh, Allie Savage, Dan Spencer, and Liz Van Voorhees.

Thanks to the brilliant sculptor, Cristina Biaggi, for her raging Medussa. An image of this piece oversaw the writing from a bulletin board in my office and Cristina generously agreed to let it grace the cover.

Huge thanks to the team at Oxford University Press: Dana Bliss, Acquisitions Editor, for believing the project could work and telling me when it didn't; and Mary Funchion, Project Editor for loving Medusa and finding a path through endless details. On the production end, Joyce Helena Brusin served as copy editor extraorinaire. Her light touch gave the final polish to these pages. Finally, Sharana, of Newgen Knowledge Works shepherded the book through production.

The book had its own marvelous team. From day one to the very end, Max Regan, my miracle-worker/developmental-editor at Hollowdeck Press, always knew what the work and I needed. Students and colleagues at the Universities of Otago and Utah helped shape my half-baked ideas and threw in a few of their own. My talented beta readers included Sarah Canham, Mona Delavan, Cheryl Hunt, Amanda Hart Miller, and Sara Sanders. Their feedback lit my way through the dark days of revision. My critique group with the Women's Fiction Writing Association, Kit Hodge, Karen Kroll, and Pat Grissom reviewed most of these pages, lending suggestions and encouragement. Angela Newman made those feisty end notes toe the line. Finally and fortunately, the brilliant poet, Lisa Birman, and her intrepid line edits made the book a more lovely read.

For me, it all comes down to my astonishing family. Larry, Nathan, Ariana, Sarah, Zach, and Isaac. They reeled me in from the book's turbulence. Always and ever, they make it all worthwhile.

A Note on Memory

Each time we touch a memory we reshape it according to our mood, our attitudes, and our ongoing discovery of new truths. This certainly applies to the personal recollections I offer in this book. Although I have checked basic facts with others who were present, my own perspective no doubt colors the narratives you will find in these pages. Those looking at these events from other points of view might describe them differently.

1
Aging While Angry

> The Land of Faery . . . Where nobody gets old and bitter of tongue.
> —William Butler Yeats, *The Land of Heart's Desire*[1]

Never before in the history of humanity have so many people lived to be so very old. Throughout our past, a few individuals might have made it to old age but "mass aging" is a new concept for the human species.

Premodern life expectancy was about thirty years.[2] Global life expectancy has more than doubled since the beginning of the nineteenth century and today is approximately seventy years, exceeding eighty years in most of the developed world. Since 2018, the number of adults sixty-five years or older has outnumbered the number of children under five for the first time ever. This rapid change is reshaping our social landscape in ways we can only begin to fathom.

Even as we speak of older adults as a group, we must acknowledge their tremendous variety. For one thing, their ages span half a century. Some like to distinguish between the "young old," aged between fifty-five and seventy-five and "old old." who are seventy-five and older.[3] Sixty-five is a traditional marker of late life, set as a retirement age by the architects of social security programs around the globe. Some claim that "60 is the new 40." Most of us think that old refers to someone at least five years older than us. I use fifty years of age as the beginning of late life, because this is the time when we generally begin to show signs of aging.

We all have a vague idea of what it means to be old, but the aging process is uneven and multidimensional. It can be accelerated by social pressures and is profoundly influenced by dimensions of positionality, such as gender, class, and race. In many ways, older adults are more unique than the young; our personalities, like our bodies, honed by a lifetime's experiences. Some insist that "an old dog can't learn new tricks." Of course, millions of older adults disprove this as they begin new careers, heal old wounds, and transform their lives and the world.

What's Anger?

Anger is included on lists of primary or core emotions. The scope of these lists varies. When there are four items, we might see happiness, sadness, fear, and

Aging Angry. Amanda Smith Barusch, Oxford University Press. © Oxford University Press 2024.
DOI: 10.1093/oso/9780197584644.003.0001

anger. When there are ten items: fear, anger, shame, contempt, disgust, guilt, distress, interest, surprise, and joy. But anger is always on the list.

Although pervasive, anger is neither simple nor basic. This ancient emotion is complicated, messy, and uniquely value laden. It's more like a constellation than a continuum because it varies in so many ways, among them: its cause (sometimes called the "trigger"), our physical reactions (and our awareness of them), and our response to provocation (which can vary from self-silencing to mass murder).

Given this complexity, it's hardly surprising that experts disagree about anger. Some even suggest that anger isn't what it seems. These people, including some therapists, see anger as a mask or shield that hides the "real" feelings, such as fear, disappointment, or grief. They call it a "secondary" emotion, which implies it is less important or central. Philosopher Martha Nussbaum writes, "Anger becomes an alluring substitute for grieving, promising agency and control when one's real situation does not offer control."[4] This feels like gaslighting to me. Why does anger have to be a substitute? Can't we be angry and sad, vulnerable or afraid at the same time?

There's a tendency, even among gerontologists like myself to disregard the anger of older adults. This was very apparent when I started looking into research on late-life anger. The lion's share of work on anger focuses on young adults.[5] Even experts seem to hold the mistaken assumption that anger is not especially relevant or dangerous in later life. Chapter 9 should disabuse us of that notion.

When I told colleagues I was writing about anger among older adults, their responses were telling. "That's . . . *interesting*." "I thought people were *less* angry in old age." "What do they have to be angry about?" One academic questioned the need for a book of this kind, pointing out that, "the bulk of psychological aging . . . work shows that older adults actually have significantly increased emotional stability and control." Does increased emotional stability mean we don't get angry? Might greater emotional control mean we stifle our anger more effectively?

The past fifteen years have seen a large body of cross-sectional research that some believe indicates late life brings a decline in so-called "negative" emotions, including anger. A seminal article on the topic came out in 1997. Titled "Emotion and Aging: Experience, Expression, and Control," it was published in *Psychology and Aging*, widely considered a leading journal on the intrapsychic landscape of later life.[6] The authors were a dream team of leading gerontologists, including, James Gross, Laura Carstensen, and Monisha Pasupathi (all from Stanford University) as well as collaborators from the University of California, Berkeley and the University of Trondheim. Carstensen, a colleague of German gerontologist Paul Baltes, is quite well known as the lead researcher who developed the theory of socio-emotional selectivity, which argues that over time we learn to optimize our happiness by avoiding settings, people, and experiences that make us unhappy.

The team conducted four separate studies. First, they surveyed 127 African Americans and European Americans aged nineteen to ninety-six years. Second, they surveyed eighty-two Chinese and European Americans in two age groups: young (20 to 35 years) and old (70 to 85 years). The third study involved a sample of forty-nine Norwegians from two age groups (20 to 25 and 70-plus). Finally, they surveyed 1,080 American nuns aged twenty-four to 101 years. In each study, older participants "reported fewer negative emotional experiences and greater emotional control" (590). They also reported expressing their emotions less frequently.

The American studies didn't look at anger, but in the Norwegian study, both groups reported experiencing anger between "rarely" (scored as a 2) and "sometimes," (scored as a 3) with the mean score for older adults 18 percent lower than younger adults. With the nuns, the team found a modest negative correlation (−.32) between the experience of anger and age.

I inflict these numbers on you because they help us interpret what researchers mean when they say, "With age... individuals report greater emotional control and lesser negative emotional experience." Translated, that means, "If you survey a lot of people, you'll find that the average seventy-year-old *reports* experiencing a bit less anger than your average twenty-year-old." (Italics are added.)

That doesn't necessarily mean people become less angry as they age. It could reflect what we call "cohort differences" or historic changes in the norms governing anger. When they were young, today's older adults may have internalized prohibitions on anger that are not imposed on young people today. Their survey responses may also reflect a desire for approval. In a society that equates passivity and contentment with wisdom, the angry elder is likely to face disapproval.

Science is a powerful way of learning truths; narrative is another. I developed the Anger Project, the precursor to this book, to access the tools of both science *and* story.[7] After reviewing the research, I conducted a nationwide Internet survey open to anyone over age fifty. More than 260 older Americans completed standardized questions and shared their stories in an open-ended format. In addition to interviewing twelve experts, I conducted in-depth interviews with thirty-three adults over age fifty. This book draws heavily on their stories. I have assigned pseudonyms and sometimes changed other details to protect my respondents' privacy.

Although other researchers may be interested in describing how older adults respond, "on average," I am interested in their stories and how they interpret their experiences. Among other things, I asked, "Has your experience of anger changed since you were younger?" Seventy-six percent said, "Yes," agreeing with the bulk of research on negative emotions. But 25 percent said it had not. Here we see the variability that is a hallmark of later life.

People who responded affirmatively were asked to describe how their anger had changed. The most common response, described by 15 percent was that the way they express anger had changed. A few said they had become "more outspoken about it." For the rest, things had toned down. These results are summarized in Table A3, Appendix 1 (page 146).

With social aging, permissions and expectations about anger shift. Most of us, either consciously or unconsciously, realize that we have less permission to express anger in later life. "When I was younger, I said more things. Now I've learned to keep quiet... I don't talk when I'm angry," Tomas, fifty-nine, told me, adding that he did find it hard to keep quiet. One fifty-seven-year-old woman wrote, "I don't yell as much as I used to." A fifty-one-year-old man said, "I don't break as much stuff."

Ten percent of respondents reported experiencing less anger in later life; four percent said they experienced more. Some (7%) described how their experience of anger or their awareness or understanding had changed. One fifty-two-year-old woman said, "I have learned to process my feelings before acting on them and identify my triggers and focusing inward rather than outward for resolving conflicts." An eighty-nine-year-old man said, "Age brings understanding and acceptance." A sixty-five-year-old woman wrote, "I get angry more because I understand things better." A fifty-four-year-old trans respondent reported, "I am better able to appropriately direct it where deserved and not just internalize it."

Simple Truths versus Scientific Proofs

In 2014, *Psychology Today* published an article called, "The Simple Truth about Anger." Written by clinical psychologist Dr. Robert Firestone, it presents the classic psycho-dynamic argument that suppression of emotion creates tensions that later manifest in ailments ranging from headaches to cancer. Firestone suggests that stifled anger is behind forgetfulness, procrastination, and other irritating behaviors. He coins a clever adage, "A thought murder a day keeps the doctor away."[8]

This, like so much advice we receive about anger, is based less on research than on what some call "folk psychology." That doesn't mean it's wrong; folk or "naïve" psychology draws on observations and beliefs that reflect common human experiences. Indeed, one way we learn about emotions is by observing the people around us.

Careful observation has a lot to recommend it. Darwin's entire Theory of Evolution grew from his detailed observations of the natural world. One major set of these observations had to do with anger. Darwin noticed similarities in emotional expression among humans and between humans and other animals. He observed that babies recognize angry faces from an early age and humans can tell when other mammals are angry. In 1872 he wrote *The Expression of Emotions in Man and Animals,* with illustrations of humans expressing various core emotions.

Based on these similarities, he argued that emotional expression was genetically determined. His work supported the notion advanced by the Stoics of ancient times that emotions stem from our "animal" origins, that they aren't inherently human. Unlike the Stoics, Darwin acknowledged that emotional expression can be helpful. For example, our universal understanding of emotions comes in handy for interpreting children's cries and avoiding angry predators. However, other than communicating needs and states, Darwin didn't see any deeper function for emotions. He saw them as souvenirs of our evolutionary past or "vestiges of evolutionary history."[9]

On the other hand, John Dewey, the "great pragmatist," considered emotions from the perspective of the person experiencing them. He concluded that emotions were "useful" and that their function is "serving life." Put simply, Dewey concluded that emotions help keep us alive.

Though its approaches may be imperfect, research is one of our best tools for locating truths that aren't readily accessible through observation. Methods with their origins in the scientific revolution of the seventeenth century have helped access some very important, albeit partial, truths.

In pursuit of precision, psychological research has been accused of reductionism; of answering questions that are so small that they are hardly relevant to everyday life. Social and psychological researchers have a hard time dealing with human complexities. This is partly because so many of us embrace what I call "the myth of a single identity;" the notion that one aspect of our identity (such as age or gender) can possibly define us. Each person lives at the intersection of multiple identities. In addition to being a sixty-seven-year-old woman, I am a mother, a grandmother, a wife, a friend, a retiree, a teacher, a researcher, an author, an American, and a kiwi. At any given time, a unique array of these identities might govern my actions. Our multiple identities and histories make each of us unique in ways that research methods can hardly capture.

Research tells us that, on average, aerobic exercise is good for our cardiac health and that the average score on an anger measure is higher for men than for women. This speaks to probabilities that can be applied to populations but does not capture the range and complexity of an individual human experience. After all, some joggers have heart attacks and, as we will see, some women are very angry.

Any given average is primarily made up of people above and below it. Remember Lake Wobegone, where all the children are "above average?" When I say that "there is no such thing as an average person," I am not speaking statistically. We may be average on some dimensions—height, weight, pulse—but we are usually above and below average. (My husband says I'm well above average on stubbornness.)

Some researchers measure anger by asking people questions. Charles Donald Spielberger developed the State-Trait Anger Expression Inventory in 1999. Popularly known as the STAXI, this widely used questionnaire distinguishes anger directed inward ("anger-in") from anger directed outward ("anger-out"). That is, it measures both the control or suppression of anger and its expression. It also distinguishes anger as a "state" from anger as a "trait."

Instead of just asking about anger, some researchers induce it then watch what happens. They expose volunteers to insults, films, angry memories, or unjustified criticism. Neuroscientists watch the electrical impulses anger creates in certain regions of the brain and study anger's physical correlates, such as increased heart rate, blood pressure, and inflammatory markers.

Universal truths are hard to find. Even science's best tools only offer provisional truths. As research progresses and attitudes shift, new truths inevitably replace the old. The best social science can do is ask questions and look for associations that enable us to say, "A person who is X is more likely to do Y." It's possible, maybe even likely, that X caused Y. But it's also possible that something else altogether caused both X and Y.

Of course, anger comes at us from many directions. Some people I spoke with were angry about concepts such as racism, poverty, injustice, feminism. Others were angry at people they'd never met: Donald Trump, welfare cheats, those damn Republicans. Some were angry at themselves, for hitting their thumb instead of the nail, or at their families for mistreating them. Some were angry about things they couldn't control. One source of simmering rage is the steady accrual of tiny insults.

Death by a Thousand Cuts

Some of us like to believe that there was a golden era when older adults were universally respected and admired, but historians point out that this respect was reserved for older people with high status and good health. Those who are old and frail or old and poor have long been objects of disdain. Lately, it seems that ageism has gone rampant, extending well beyond the disadvantaged. Robert Binstock, one of the pioneers of gerontology, links the rise of the "greedy geezer" stereotype to the neoliberalism of the 1970s, now a dominant ideology throughout most of the world.[10]

For a long time, we didn't have a word for minor insults that are so hard to recognize and understand. A friend of mine used to call them "death by a thousand cuts." In 1970, Harvard University psychiatrist, Chester M. Pierce, coined the term "microaggression." He was talking about the "insults and dismissals" routinely inflicted on Black Americans for over four hundred years.

In 2010, Dr. Derald W. Sue popularized the term and expanded its definition beyond African-Americans to:

Everyday verbal, nonverbal, and environmental slights, snubs, or insults, whether intentional or unintentional, that communicate hostile, derogatory, or negative messages to target people based solely on their marginalized group membership.[11]

Once we had a name for it, the conversation could begin. Academics could study microaggressions, teachers could sensitize their students, and poets—like MacArthur genius, Claudia Rankine in her 2014 book, *Citizen: An American Lyric*—could use their magic to help us understand.

Although microaggressions are most often discussed in relation to racial prejudice or homophobia, the term equally applies to the experiences of older adults. If confronted, the person who says, "You look good for your age," just like the one who says, "You're smart for a girl," will insist that they don't mean to offend. That's why, at least initially, it's so hard to respond. No one likes to be seen as a whiner. But left unchecked pervasive ageism is internalized and may mushroom into harmful behaviors.

Microaggressions have corrosive impacts. Researchers argue that they are damaging precisely because it is so difficult to respond directly. Most victims downplay or ignore them, unsure whether an insult was intended and telling themselves that they are being "over-sensitive."[12]

In a marvelous book called, *Ending Ageism*, Margaret Gullette documents the microaggressions that result from the culturally imposed invisibility of older adults. Gullette writes about a man who made the mistake of descending subway stairs while old. He went slowly and carefully and most people streamed around him. Perhaps some muttered under their breath. Then someone got impatient and shoved him from behind. Down he went and, while the damage was not permanent, it took surgery and months of rehabilitation to recover. If confronted, the person who bumped into him might deny any intention of hurting him, but one has to wonder about the attitude that enables this type of assault.[13]

They're Just Going to Die Anyway

The US Centers for Disease Control and Prevention reports that over 75 percent of U.S. deaths from COVID-19 have been among those sixty-five years of age and older. This holds true in high-income nations around the world. In France, for instance, 91 percent of 2021 COVID-19 deaths were of people sixty-five and older.[14]

In part, this is no doubt due to the physical vulnerability that comes with age. But ageism doesn't help. Ambulance drivers in Belgium administered morphine to nursing home residents and left them to die rather than taking them to hospital. One is reported as saying, "They're just going to die anyway."[15]

Likewise, during Hurricane Katrina 75 percent of the people who died were over sixty. As Bill Blytheway explains, older adults suddenly became "unmanageable burdens for the authorities." One group of seventy-, eighty-, and ninety-year-olds was taken to a school and abandoned for two days. Vehicles dispatched to evacuate nursing homes were commandeered for other purposes. At Memorial Hospital, a doctor and two nurses took it on themselves to euthanize frail elderly patients.[16]

Ageism at Work

Ageism also contributes to workplace discrimination. During the 2008 recession, baby boomers were among the most vulnerable workers, as many found their prime earning years cut short. In fact, baby boomers like myself are the hardest working elders in decades. According to the Pew Research Center, in 2018 nearly a third (29%) of Americans aged sixty-five to seventy-two were either working or looking for work. This rate of labor force participation exceeds the rates of the "Silent Generation" (21%) and the "Greatest Generation" (19%).[17] While some work for personal fulfillment, many simply don't have the resources to fund their retirement.

In 2018, ProPublica and the Urban Institute analyzed data from a nationally representative sample of 20,000 Americans who responded to the Health & Retirement Study.[18] They found that over half (56%) of workers who entered their fifties with stable full-time jobs experienced "employer-related involuntary job separations" after age fifty that reduced their earnings for years or led to long-term unemployment. Only one in ten ever earned as much money as they had before. As Gary Burtless, a labor economist with the Brookings Institute put it, "We've known that some workers get a nudge from their employers to exit the work force and some get a great big kick. What these results suggest is that a whole lot more are getting the great big kick."[19]

"But that's illegal," those aware of the Age Discrimination in Employment Act (ADEA) passed in 1967 may complain. The act states that: 'It shall be unlawful for an employer to fail or refuse to hire or to discharge any individual or otherwise discriminate against any individual... because of such individual's age.'" Yes, age discrimination is illegal. But it's hard to prove.

Julianne Taafe and Kathryn Moon of Ohio State University hit the jackpot when an e-mail from their new boss went astray. In it, he described, "an extraordinarily change-averse population of people, almost all of whom are over 50, contemplating retirement (or not) and it's like herding hippos." They pursued a successful age discrimination complaint that forced the university to address these ageist attitudes.[20] But that's just one win out of thousands of workers subjected to age discrimination.

Some argue that older workers crowd younger workers out of employment and promotions. Alicia Munnell and April Wu, of Stanford University's Institute for Economic Policy Research, conducted an exhaustive study using Census data from 1977 to 2011. They found "no evidence that increasing the employment of older persons reduces either the job opportunities or wage rates of younger persons."[21]

Family Matters

Family is another potent locus of anger in later life. Researchers Susan Brown and I-Fen Lin suggest that America is experiencing a "gray divorce revolution."[22] Reviewing Census and vital statistics data for 1990 to 2010, they learned that the rate of divorce had doubled among those fifty and older and tripled for those sixty-five and older. They also found that those over fifty who were employed full-time were significantly more likely to divorce than those who had exited the labor force (aka retired). This was not the case for younger adults. Maybe part of our generation's high divorce rate is caused by the stress of dealing with ageism in the workforce. It's difficult to identify the reasons for late-life divorce using this kind of data but we've got to figure that some, if not all of those divorces left at least one party aging angry.

Caregiving can also be a source of late-life anger. Caring for an older adult, particularly one with dementia can be infuriating. Sometimes dementia patients are, themselves, overwhelmed by anger and frustration. Their behaviors can range from bizarre to aggressive. Caregivers, most of them wives of the patients, are often overwhelmed. Very few abuse or neglect their loved ones, but it's no wonder they get angry.

Dr. Linda Ree Phillips (University of Arizona Center on Aging) set out to determine what differentiated those who did engage in abuse or neglect from those who did not.[23] She conducted in-depth interviews with caregivers and care recipients in two groups. The first had "good relationships," while the second had "abusive/neglectful relationships." Phillips found that levels of anger, hostility, and stress were "remarkably similar between the groups." The key differentiating factor was social isolation. Left alone and unsupported, caregivers failed to manage their anger and abused their loved ones.

Mad as Hell

The scene is unforgettable. People of all ages and colors leaning out of high-rise apartment windows screaming and throwing things—a hairbrush, the newspaper, an undershirt. They're shouting and pounding on their windowsills. In the midst of this cacophony the camera pans back to reveal blocks and blocks of New Yorkers ranting into thin air. "I'm mad as hell and I'm not going to take it anymore!"

When the lights came up, my classmates agreed that the movie captured the essence of our times. This was 1976. The endless war was finally over. Nixon had resigned, but he'd left us with a president some said couldn't walk and chew gum at the same time. Some corporations, like the newly founded Apple and Microsoft, seemed to be taking over the functions of nations. The country faced the unheard-of combination of economic stagnation and double-digit inflation. My friends and I were about to graduate from college. We were angry and scared.

Network won four academy awards and is preserved in the National Film Registry in recognition of its cultural significance. But forty-four years later, all I remember is that scene in which the masses release their payload of anger. Mass catharsis, some might call it. A collective explosion of pent-up rage.

All that 1970s anger seems quaint in this era of mass murder, trolling, and unabashed rage. To say that we live in angry times is an understatement. Perhaps the extreme violence of our era reinforces the prohibition against any expression of anger. Certainly, it frightens us. For some, it may seem like a slippery slope from yelling at a meeting to whipping out an AK-47 and ripping your colleagues to pieces. As I write this, the world holds its breath in hopes that Vladimir Putin won't launch a nuclear weapon.

Don't Put a Lid on It

There is a syndrome known in Korea as *hwa-byung*, or fire disease. Believed to result from suppressed anger, this illness afflicts middle-aged and older adults, particularly women. Its symptoms include feelings of suffocation, disappointment, betrayal, and rejection. It's cause: "intolerable life problems" such as family conflict or economic hardship.[24]

Those who study *hwa-byung* say that it can lead to a condition known as *hahn*, which has been described as a "unique depression-like affective state" that results from the "chronic suppression of anger and frustration." It's fascinating that a culture known for its emotional reserve has identified a syndrome caused by pent-up rage.

Psychodynamic theorists developed a similar understanding of the relationship between anger and depression. Freud argued that depression was the result of "anger turned inward," which festers until it becomes self-loathing. Perhaps, in yet another act of cultural appropriation, researchers in the United States might borrow the Korean concepts of *hwa-byung* and *hahn* to articulate the hazards associated with pent-up anger.

"Today my neighbors and I made a snowman, a snow owl, and a snow fox. It was fun and amazing." That was the first thing fifty-eight-year-old Valerie said when I asked how she was. Building a snow owl is hardly consistent with our stereotypical expectations of age, but then, Valerie is something of a maverick.[25]

Valerie and I were introduced by a colleague who knew I wanted to talk to older activists. As an advocate for Black Lives Matter, she is vocal on Facebook and Twitter and helps set up safety and coping plans for demonstrators. With a background in trauma therapy, she has a great deal of experience with dialogue and mutual aid. She describes her activism as "a powerful outlet for when I'm irritated or frustrated."

When I ask if she feels like she's making a difference, she says, "No. I did lots of work on this, but I have no sense of pride and satisfaction. Only a few good outcomes." adding, "We don't do it to win but because it's the ethical thing to do."

Valerie has lived in a tiny cottage in an isolated beach community on the Pacific coast for twenty-three years. Her neighbors are integral to her existence. At the time we spoke, they were helping her navigate a crisis. Valerie and a neighbor who was a single mother of two small children had just received eviction notices. Valerie has lupus and relies on disability for her income. Neither she nor her neighbor had been able to keep up on their rent payments, and housing options in the area were extremely limited. Valerie was, as she put it, "scared and angry—raging." It wasn't clear how much she was angry on behalf of her neighbor, who had lost her job in the pandemic, and how much she was angry for herself. Thinking about how the anger felt in her body, Valerie says, "My voice got loud. Thoughts were limited. Some paralysis... My heart pounded."

True to their hippie roots, Valerie and her neighbors organized a "nonviolent communication circle" to facilitate conversation with the landlord. Valerie planned her comments carefully. She spoke in a way the landlord could hear. "I framed it as, 'The situation we find ourselves in . . . has created lots of discomfort . . . our needs are in conflict.'" She was able to direct her anger toward the capitalist system, rather than toward individuals. Her neighbors set up a GoFundMe page that bought her and the single mom a few months' reprieve, but Valerie knew sooner or later she would be living in her car.

Valerie attributes her interest in appropriate expression of anger to growing up in a large Italian family whose members "were really comfortable expressing anger . . . anger was easily resolved through loud communications. We had permission to be highly communicative." She feels that "poorly expressed and unexpressed anger are super harmful. Suppressed emotions in the body create illness, depression, malady."

Valerie was the first person I met who described a connection between anger suppression and bad health. She argues that if we don't "embrace our anger," it becomes a form of poison. "I'm interested in helping people get in touch with their anger and disrupting the disruptor [anger]."

"Embrace the anger." At the time it sounded like an interesting play on words. I would soon come to see it as a coping mechanism in these angry times—particularly for older adults.

Rather than suppress anger, some older adults do learn to embrace and channel it. Rage becomes outrage and, instead of internalizing their anger, they focus outward to eliminate the intolerable conditions that might otherwise make them ill. In the process, these activists teach and inspire.

Maggie Kuhn (1905–1995) was one of the most effective angry retirees you're likely to come across. Like me, Maggie thought of herself as an exception. She describes her experience of social aging in her autobiography, *No Stone Unturned*, "I didn't think of myself as about to enter the ranks of the nation's old . . . I was just me—neither young nor old . . ."[26]

Maggie "was ordered to retire" when she turned sixty-five, shortly *after* the 1967 passage of the Age Discrimination in Employment Act. She could have fought the order but instead, like me, she elected to "opt for a graceful exit." But Maggie was fuming. She decided to organize meetings with others who had experienced age discrimination. Together, they founded the Gray Panthers, an activist organization that unites age and youth to fight for peace and social justice.

Other seniors have also chosen organizing and protest over docile acceptance. Tish Somers, cofounder of the Older Women's League (OWL) became "activated" after witnessing the horrors inflicted on German Jews.

Irina Savostina, of Kazakstan, said she became politicized when "she became a pensioner and found she couldn't live on the income." She was jailed for a week in 1997 when she led an unauthorized demonstration against utility fee hikes.[27]

Bill Ryan, a ninety-seven-year-old American, has been jailed a half dozen times and continues to fight environmental degradation with Extinction

Rebellion. Of his climate change activism Bill says, "At this stage of life, I think I'd be wasting my time if I didn't take action against this."[28]

Vancouver's "Raging Grannies" also take their outrage to the streets, spawning a movement of older women who protest environmental degradation and injustice. Emily Carr echoed Bill's sentiments when she said, "I don't want to trickle out. I want to pour 'til the pail is empty. The last bit going out in a gush, not in drops."[29]

* * *

Anger Unbound

Late life can bring a whole new slate of things to be angry about and, for some, it brings insights and strategies for coping with anger. Historically, the direct expression of anger was a privilege reserved for the powerful. But that is changing.

Perhaps, this unbinding of obsolete strictures is what makes our times so angry. Maybe the anxiety and anger that keep us up at night are the result of multiple existential threats like climate change, global pandemics, nuclear war, terrorism. Either way, it is more urgent than ever that we access the lessons anger can offer and harness its energy for good. It's time to take our anger seriously; to get beyond anger suppression and learn to embrace and channel its wisdom. It's time for a new worldview that treats anger as legitimate unless and until it is proven otherwise.

2
Speaking of Anger

> The difference between the *almost right* word and the *right* word is really a large matter—'tis the difference between the lightning-bug and the lightning.
>
> —Mark Twain, in *The Art of Authorship*[1]

When I ask my first question, "How often have you experienced anger in the past month?" seventy-one-year-old Connie replies, "That's not in my nature." She explains that she might get frustrated with the vicissitudes of age, and she does have some losses to grieve, but, "I don't get angry. I get incensed with passion at things that are important."

Connie sees anger as pointless and destructive. She learned this from her mother, who she describes as "Graceful. Beautiful. A dutiful loving consummate hostess, wife, and mother." She taught Connie everything she knew. I wonder if the "incensed" metaphor comes from her mother. It does have an old-fashioned ring.

About an hour into her performance of the older woman who never gets angry, Connie lets slip that she is "experiencing a slow burn." Only yesterday she got angry, maybe even furious. She had an argument with her daughter-in-law, who is pregnant with Connie's first grandchild. At last, we are getting real. As Connie describes her experience, she and I laugh until our eyes water.

It seems Connie's daughter-in-law is a difficult person. She's "direct to the point of being insensitive." Connie, on the other hand, has learned to "stomach" things, a visceral metaphor that rings true as she describes her efforts to get along using politeness and tact. On the day in question, she took some croissants to her son's house (as she thinks of it). Her daughter-in-law insisted that Connie wear a mask in *her* house. That was mildly irritating. Then conversation turned to COVID precautions for the new baby. That's when Connie "blew."

Although she was welcome to come to the hospital, she would not be allowed to hold the newborn. She said, "Does that mean I'll have to meet my grandchild through a window? That fucking sucks." When the daughter-in-law asked if they could talk about it, Connie said, "I just did." and stomped out of the house.

Connie's word choices are instructive. Her earlier insistence that anger isn't part of her nature puts the emotion at a distance from her innermost self. Then,

Aging Angry. Amanda Smith Barusch, Oxford University Press. © Oxford University Press 2024.
DOI: 10.1093/oso/9780197584644.003.0002

a "slow burn" led to a moment of explosive agency. Shortly after "the explosion," Connie apologized twice to her daughter-in-law. Then she went to her daughter's house and told her all about the "come to Jesus talk" she had just had. I recognize that metaphor. My mother used "come to Jesus" to describe conversations that veer close to the bone.

Telling It Slant

As I conducted more interviews, I became fascinated by the very process of talking about anger. It wasn't always easy. Like Connie, most of the older women I spoke with took some time before they could really open up about their anger. They often hedged. "I wasn't angry. I was miffed" or "frustrated" or "incensed." I think the taboos around anger are such that people, particularly older women, only speak frankly after a certain trust has been established. This is why I put little faith in surveys that suggest older people experience anger less frequently than the young. It's quite possible that older adults are just less willing to *admit* they experience anger to some stranger.

Once we start talking, we are all poets when it comes to articulating our anger. Our word choices reflect our identities and personal backgrounds as well as the historic moment and cultural context in which we swim. We resort to figurative language and, as Emily Dickinson suggests, we "tell it slant."

Speaking directly about anger can be fraught. Even, or maybe especially, in this angry age, many of us would rather just walk away. By looking at how others language their anger we can sensitize ourselves to the deep meanings beneath our own expressions. As sociologist Jorie Hofstra (Princeton University) explains, "Metaphor is more than just a poetic device; it's at the heart of how we comprehend and communicate our experiences."[2]

I Just Exploded

A friend described seventy-six-year-old Kay as an expert on anger. Kay spent her entire career promoting conflict management in public schools. Her grandparents came to the United States from Korea and settled in Seattle, where she lived when we met via zoom. Kay struck me as particularly strong and tall. She spoke of anger with authority and insight using rich, complex metaphors.

Kay described a life-changing moment of rage she experienced in college. An instructor was explaining the dynamics of institutional racism and a white female classmate took exception to something he said. "The anger started to well up inside me. I saw my whole life go before me. . . . A weight lifted from my shoulders [and] I just exploded." Kay shouted at the student, spewing out her own experiences with racism. As events in Kay's childhood came into focus, she understood why her parents had had such a hard time purchasing a home in a good neighborhood. "All of a sudden, I had a different perspective on what they went through. . . I saw images of my parents telling me if you go into the neighbors' houses don't touch the walls; make sure you don't have sand in your shoes. I grew up with these horrible feelings of inferiority."

I imagine Kay exploding; angry shards of racism bashing into the walls of the classroom. She can't remember what she said during or after the explosion but, half a century later, she sees it as a turning point in her life: the moment when a quiet withdrawn girl started to become the assertive, mindful woman she is today.

She describes the experience as "a catharsis. Such a realization. This light bulb went off." A moment of insight is more traditionally described as a light bulb going on, its glow symbolizing new ideas or understanding. But Kay isn't the only person who describes anger as a light going "off." Perhaps, following a blinding insight, the bulb goes out, allowing our vision to adjust.

"Catharsis" captures the clarifying influence of extreme anger. Originally from Greek, the nineteenth century English version was used to describe "the purgation of the excrements of the body."[3] This was seen as a cleansing process with beneficial health effects. Freud also used the term to describe the calm or emotional release we feel after a strong emotional experience. Ferdinand de Saussuer, the father of modern linguistics, argued that words don't shed their earliest meanings. They carry them along like boxcars on a train.[4] Perhaps there was a trace of excrement in Kay's catharsis.

Some phrases evoke the destructive capacity of anger: "I just exploded." Others suggest the discomfort or disgust we feel about anger: "I had a shit fit." Still others mimic the physical experiences associated with the emotion, as when we "blow off steam." Often, without even being aware of it, we let anger claim a part of our identity, "I *am* furious." By peering beneath the surface of our language, we can generate insights into how anger, particularly late-life anger, is conceived and experienced.

Heat is one of the most common ways that people around the world speak about their anger. It serves as a "metonym" for the anger. This literary term refers to a figure of speech that stands in for something else, as when the word "crown" is used to refer to a king or queen.

Connie's metonymic use of heat as a stand-in for anger illustrates a strategy that, as South African scholar Zacharias Kotzé points out, lets the effects of anger stand in for the emotion. This approach focuses on the physiological experience of anger—accelerated heart rate and blood pressure often produce a hot flush.[5] The converse is also true. A sixty-eight-year-old woman says, "I kept my cool," to tell me that she did not lose her temper.

Zoltan Kövecses and others argue that "hot liquid or gas under pressure" as universal metaphors for anger stem from the heat we often feel when we are angry.[6] This is seen in a wide range of languages, including English, Hungarian, Japanese, Chinese, Zulu, Polish, Wolof, and Tahitian. Typically, these hot liquid metaphors treat the person who is angry as a "pressurized container" about to burst. In French, a hot temper is compared to *soupe au lait,* hot milk boiling over. Consider the implications: Anger doesn't just stay on the surface. Pressure builds inside the angry-person-as-container. As long as the anger remains contained or unexpressed, it is under control. But if the person doesn't "blow off steam" or "vent," an annihilating explosion may ensue.

Disgusting Idioms

Scatological idioms are often used in speaking about anger. Three of the people I interviewed used urine to describe their anger saying, "I was pissed off," or, "I was so pissed."

This expression is believed to have originated with the U.S. military during World War II[7] and is now used around the globe. Writing on Wordwizard, one user speculates that it described an "ignominious" method for getting rid of a morning erection. Authorities on Grammarphobia suggest the phrase might have evolved from the practice of "pissing on" someone as a display of disgust. "Piss off" is also used (primarily in the United Kingdom) to tell someone to scram or go away.[8] "Pissed off" adds a distinct "flavor" to the hot-liquid metaphor, evoking bodily waste that must be discharged.

Today, "pissed off" is considered only mildly vulgar. Those of us who grew up during the 1960s may recall an even milder variant, "PO'ed." My elementary school classmates and I were often "PO'ed" at one another. We didn't even know what it stood for.

While "pissed off" usually describes a state of mind, "throwing a shit fit" implies action. A sixty-nine-year-old member of the Raging Grannies used "threw a shit fit" to describe Jeff Bezoes's reaction when Seattle passed a "tiny tax" on businesses like Amazon to fund low-income housing. Shit is more visceral than urine, so it serves as an apt metonym for the anger of people we despise.[9]

Linguist Carolyn O'Meara, from Universidad Autonoma de Mexico, reports that in the Seri language "anger stinks." Hunter gatherers of Northern Mexico, the Seri use odors in healing and to perfume homes and people. Of a person who is angry, they say, *iisax cheemt,* which O'Measra and Mahid translate as "its spirit stinks." She argues that "spirit" serves as a metonym for a person and the "stink" stands in for their anger.[10]

Some people describe being "beside themselves" with rage. Jorie Hofstra links this notion of the doubled self to Seneca's comment in *De Ira* that anger is "utterly inhuman." In the Senecan perspective, the sane, rational self of the mind lives in constant conflict with the irrational, chaotic self of the emotions. If anger cannot be stifled, the emotional self has taken over. In this event, Seneca suggests that suicide must be considered. Hofstra offers two vivid examples from literature: *The Strange Case of Dr. Jekyll and Mr. Hyde* and *The Incredible Hulk*. Another example can be found in Randal H. Flutur's accounts of uncontrollable rage following a Traumatic Brain Injury in his 2013 memoir, "The Stranger Inside of Me."[11]

Six of the people I interviewed, all women, hold their anger apart from themselves when they speak of "having a relationship" with it. Sixty-four-year-old Shauna says, "My relationship with anger is tentative . . . It has its own life force. It's this thing that can take over a human." Dinah says, "I'm fortunate; especially when compared to people in this culture because I don't have a negative relationship with anger." Allie Savage, a life coach who focuses on women's empowerment, argues that "Conflict is necessary. Without it, we get violence. Messed up relationships with anger produce unwanted byproducts." This kind of externalizing is often used in both Rogerian and Narrative therapy to render a problem more manageable, but it does reinforce the notion of a person divided against themself.

Metaphors from Other Lands

Sometimes our language confines our imagination. We can broaden our conceptual possibilities by considering the metaphors used in diverse cultures to describe anger.

What if, instead of explosive and scatological metaphors, English-speaking people adopted the approach of the Zulu of South Africa? In Zulu, anger can be a hunger that consumes everything. It can be an elemental force of nature, described in metaphors of thunder, wind, and lightening. The Zulu language also uses liquid heat metaphors for anger, but "one can [metaphorically] extinguish somebody's anger by pouring water on them." Kövecses calls this a "metaphorical entailment."[12] That is, a new metaphor that serves as a logical extension of the original metaphor.

The Chinese also use nature imagery to describe anger. "I violently discharged thunderbolts" captures a high-intensity expression of anger even as it links anger to the inevitability and unpredictability of the natural world.

Chinese speakers have access to a wide range of compound words to express various types of anger. Judy Woon Yee Ho, of Lingnan University, did a careful reading of stories written by bilingual speakers of English and Chinese in Hong Kong. She notes how difficult it can be to express nuanced emotions in a second language. She also sheds light on how the Chinese language enables the description of anger through the use of compound words, metonyms, and metaphors.[13]

Ho explains that Chinese is fundamentally monosyllabic. Each syllable has a character, and concepts are expressed by combining syllables (morphemes) to express constructs such as "hatred-anger" *(fennu)*, "vexation-anger" *(naonu)*, and "grievance-hatred" *(yuanhen)*. Chinese metonyms for anger include "a long face," "blind eyes," and "zippered lips." For instance, one of Ho's respondents wrote, "Kathy was irritated so *she was blind to me* in school." Another said, "[My] friend was already pulling a long face." Sometimes when a person is angry, they choose not to say anything. One of Ho's respondents captured this when they said, "I even zipped my lips." Notice the sense of agency here. The speaker is not "tongue-tied," their self-silencing is deliberate and complete.

Chinese metaphors illustrate a specific cultural understanding of anger's physical effects. As Ho explains, the word *qi* refers to vitality, life force, or "the motive force or impetus for all processes of change and transformation in the universe."[14] The concept of qi is mapped onto anger in the expression, *qi jie* or "breath tied." In this situation, the vital qi is blocked by anger, a condition that, when fatal, is called *qi si* (dying of anger). The Chinese traditionally consider anger to reside in the liver. When a person is angry the qi of the liver rises. This can manifest in abdominal swelling and indigestion, which can be relieved by *fa pi qi*, or "releasing the qi of the liver."

The locus of emotions—that is, their location within the body, varies among diverse cultures. The Chewong, an indigenous group living in the Malaysian interior, also consider the liver to be both the seat and cause of emotion. Paul Heelas writes about their "liver-talk" as an idiom for explaining emotions.[15] "My liver is fine" might be used by someone who is feeling happy; "my liver is small," by someone feeling shame.

The Chewong see emotions as destructive forces that must be suppressed. Anger, in particular, is taboo and seldom discussed. By relegating anger and other negative emotions to the liver, the Chewong distance them both from a person's behavior and from their "self."

There's no adjective for anger in Gaelic, a language indigenous to Ireland that is also spoken in Scotland and the Isle of Man. A person doesn't say, "I am angry." Instead, they say, "Anger is upon me:" *Tá fearg orm*. The same applies for sadness: "Sadness is upon me." *Tá bron orm*. The structure of Gaelic insulates the self from these emotions holding feelings and self linguistically apart. They might be like the monkey on our backs, but they can't consume our very identity.[16]

Anthropologist Grace Gredys Harris (University of Rochester) conducted extensive fieldwork among the Taita tribe of Kenya. There, anger of either a living person or one who has died is seen as a major cause of misfortune. Anger-removal rites are used to "cool" or "clean" the heart of the angry person and restore well-being to the group. Misfortune caused by a living person's anger requires anger-removal rites to cast the anger out of their heart. The rites might involve slaughter of a goat and consumption of beer and porridge. In smaller instances, it might include gifts to the angry person to placate them or cool their heart. These rites are said to be "cutting the curses" and are used even if the person has not expressed their anger.[17]

Hold Your Tongue

Cultures differ, not only in the words they use to express anger, but also in the norms that govern anger expression. Two immigrants I spoke to mentioned American prohibitions on anger expression.

Tomas says, it's "hard to be an immigrant, especially in the U.S." He had to develop an American persona to navigate a whole new set of sometimes conflicting emotional rules. "Don't express anger." "Do represent your culture."

> I come from a culture where people are crazy. On the corner people stand up on blocks and argue about politics. Then when they're done, they kiss each other and leave. Here, if you express anger, people think you need therapy. They think because you get mad you aren't friends anymore. We fight all the time with friends and then we kiss each other goodbye.

Tomas says he "was shocked at how not okay it was to express anger; how judgmental people could be about anger. I was often perceived as angry when I was not." He had to train himself to say, "In my opinion . . ." and to speak slowly and calmly. At times, he felt that his job depended on it.

He also has to moderate his body language. He told me about a time he and a friend from Uruguay arrived early for a meeting with some American colleagues at a restaurant. They sat in the car talking while the others assembled. When Tomas went in to join his colleagues they asked if he was okay. At first he was puzzled, then he realized that he and his friend had been talking and gesturing passionately. The Americans thought they were fighting.

Dinah, the sixty-seven-year-old daughter of Russian Jews who migrated to Israel, enjoys anger's rush, "It makes the energy—like a flame versus a drip—I like the flame. It has an addictive quality to it. An intensity." She feels no pain, just strength and focus. Like Icharus, Dinah says she flies toward the heat. "But I don't like the falling." The after-effects of her anger can be unpleasant. For one thing, her partner of over twenty years has difficulty with it. "My anger impacts her health. I feel horrible. Like I'm abusive." So Dinah tries to avoid blow-ups, tries to pause before she vents.

She says her later life is "strewn" with regrets, but she has become more accepting. "Otherwise, I could crumble under the weight of regret. I've hurt people. But I say, We all do the best we can and I accept the consequences." She has become more reflective, more sad, less patient. "It does get harder to just be chipper."

Dinah has lost friendships by violating American anger norms. "It was my anger, my directness. Bluntness. It took me twenty years to understand the cultural differences, the social etiquette." She tells me that in America, "anger has one of the worst social stigmas. It's a kind of rudeness in this culture; an intrusion into others' personal space. 'Oh my gosh! Such shocking rudeness!'"

Dinah still finds this challenging because she is angry every single day about "the politics in this country during the past four years; the shocking stupidity, the shocking cruelty of nearly half—of millions of people in this country."

Cantankerous, Crotchety, and Grumpy

Old age has its own anger vocabulary. "Cantankerous" has roots in Middle English. It evokes both cankerous ("a chronic, non-healing sore or ulcer") and rancorous (having a "deep-rooted and bitter ill feeling"). Used primarily for older people, the word dismisses their anger as relatively harmless, vaguely disgusting, and incurable.

Another dismissive term for late-life anger is "crotchety." It technically refers to someone who has "crotchets." According to the Oxford English Dictionary, a crotchet is a blunt hook, but in this context, it likely means "a peculiar notion on some point (usually considered unimportant) held by an individual in opposition to common opinion."

Then there's "Grumpy Old Men," a phrase popularized in a 1993 comedy in which Jack Lemmon and Walter Matthau play retirees competing for the affections of an attractive woman and inflicting practical jokes on each other. Although we might chuckle at their antics, no one wants to grow up to be a grumpy old man.

These age-specific terms reveal that English-speakers are disinclined to take the anger of older people seriously. This is problematic on multiple fronts. Treating the frustration of older adults as trivial or comic can be deeply insulting. Ignoring it can be perilous. In the weeks before I wrote this section, the United States saw three mass murders committed by individuals aged sixty years or older. Noticing and eliminating our use of these terms may be a first step toward recognizing late-life anger as a force to be reckoned with.

3
Anger Through the Ages

Life can only be understood backwards;
but it must be lived forwards.

—Søren Kierkegaard, *Journalen*[1]

One sunny day a few decades ago, my three-year-old son was playing peacefully with his baby sister. When she picked up his favorite toy train and started to walk away with it, he reared back and slapped her on the cheek. A classic family scene went into motion. Dad picked up the baby and yelled, "No dessert for you, kid. You don't hit your sister."

"But she stole my train!"

"That doesn't mean you can hit her. You know what happens now."

Now, our son was angry at his sister *and* his father.

"I hate you!" he screamed, making his way to the time-out corner. As he pouted and kicked the wall, struggling to process what had happened, he decided his anger was perfectly justified. Next time he would take his revenge in a way that wouldn't get him punished.

Pietro Testa's *Achilles dragging the body of Hector around the walls of Troy* is only ten inches high and sixteen inches wide, just one of many black and white etchings in the chambers of the Metropolitan Museum of Art in New York City (See Figure 3.1). Achilles rears up muscular and arrogant to gaze down at Hector's body. Hector's muscles are shrunken in death, his bones exposed, arms flung back. In the background, his wife Andromache faints into the arms of a grieving servant. Onlookers wave, point, and judge Achilles for desecrating the body.

Only minutes before, Hector had stood tall; the blood of Patroclus (beloved of Achilles) dripping from his hands. Then he faced Achilles, who appeared "as a serpent of the mountain . . . dread wrath hath entered into him, and terribly he glareth." Hector was a great warrior, but facing such a massive wall of rage, he ran. The pair circled Troy three times before Hector turned to face his enemy. After a brutal battle, Achilles stabbed Hector in the neck, and he died. Slowly. Even this did not satisfy Achilles's appetite for revenge. After he slaughtered Hector, he pierced the tendons in his ankles with ox hide and dragged the body behind his chariot; its head bouncing on the cobblestones.

Aging Angry. Amanda Smith Barusch, Oxford University Press. © Oxford University Press 2024.
DOI: 10.1093/oso/9780197584644.003.0003

Hector's terror is part of our literary heritage. We feel it in our bones when we face a massive rage. We experience it as toddlers when our parents explode with anger, as teenagers when the class bully looks our way, as workers when a boss threatens us with disciplinary action. Like anger itself, the fear induced by another's rage can briefly destroy our ability to reason.

Voices from the past echo through our psyche: "Turn the other cheek." "Revenge is sweet." "If you can't say something nice, don't say anything at all." A close look at the history of these and related ideas enables us to re-examine truisms that might otherwise go unquestioned. It enables us to stretch beyond knee-jerk reactions and draw upon the thoughts of some of the world's greatest minds to access a deeper, more examined approach to anger when we discipline our children.

This chapter examines insights from Western philosophic and theological traditions. Other schools of thought emphasize the role of transcendence and avoidance of worldly attachments. In fact, a substantial body of work in gerontology adopts the theory of "gero-transcendence," sometimes presented as a reformulation of disengagement theory.[2] Letting go of attachment when efforts at change are futile is certainly a viable alternative. For some, transcendence may also enhance well-being.

Figure 3.1. *Achilles dragging the body of Hector around the walls of Troy* by Pietro Testa, 1648–1650.
Courtesy of The Metropolitan Museum of Art. Figure reproduced under a Creative Commons Zero license.

Contemplating Aristotle

Gregory Sadler, editor of *Stoicism Today*, notes that he was once a pretty angry guy. Something as minor as missing a turn on the freeway could send him into a tailspin. Since studying Aristotle, he says he has become less angry. He still gets mad but is able to keep his anger within reasonable bounds. As he explains,

> Aristotle's position on anger is that it is one of the most complex and distinctive of the human emotions, that it involves bodily, psychological, social, and moral dimensions, and that anger can and ought to be felt and acted upon in a number of right ways.[3]

With my abrupt retirement two years behind me, I agree with Sadler. Contemplating anger from an Aristotelian perspective helps me understand it, diminishing my sense of impotent rage and easing my thirst for revenge.

In the *Nicomachean Ethics*, Aristotle compares anger to a hasty servant, saying: *Anger seems to listen to argument [reason] to some extent, but to mishear it, as do hasty servants who run out before they have heard the whole of what one says, and then muddle the order, or as dogs bark if there is but a knock at the door, before looking to see if it is a friend; so anger by reason of the warmth and hastiness of its nature . . . springs to take revenge.*[4]

This quote reveals three key elements of Aristotle's understanding:

▷ that anger serves a purpose,
▷ that it may be amenable to reason,
▷ and that it seeks revenge.

Aristotle accepts anger as an inevitable part of human nature; a natural reaction when we perceive that someone has slighted us. Anger gives us courage and motivates us to let others know when they've wronged us. Thus, anger serves a social purpose by reducing injustice. Anger is unique among the emotions in that it is informed by our understanding of justice. It also motivates us in ways other emotions don't, giving us the energy and heat, what Sadler calls the "emotional raw material," to take action.

Although anger may be amenable to reason, "the warmth and hastiness of its nature" sometimes causes us to do things we regret. We might slap our little sister. Later, when we have a chance to quietly ponder the situation (and what is time-out for if not that?) we grapple with the moral dimension of anger as we ask, "Did I really do wrong?"

Thus, anger becomes a moral issue. Aristotle might use the concept of "proportionality" to decide whether my son's anger and my response to it were right or wrong. As the philosopher himself explained, "moral virtue is . . . a mean between two vices, the one involving excess the other deficiency . . . ."

Applied to anger, this suggests, and Aristotle concludes, that vice lies in either too much or too little. He argues that those who put up with insults and humiliation are deviating from the path of virtue every bit as much as those who are quick to anger.

"Wait a minute!" Some might exclaim, "How can too little anger be a vice? What happened to turning the other cheek?" We'll look at this a bit later when we turn to Christian perspectives on anger.

Aristotle insists that reason be applied to moderate the effects of anger. "Anyone can get angry—that is easy. . . but to do this to the right person, to the right extent, at the right time, with the right motive, and in the right way, that is not for everyone, nor is it easy" (Ethics, Book 2:9). Future scholars would label the ability to keep our anger within moral boundaries a form of "emotional intelligence."

Aristotle treats anger as one of the many "appetites" associated with being human. Anger brings the desire or appetite for revenge. As is true of the satisfaction of any appetite, the expectation of revenge is sweet. Imagine Wiley Coyote chuckling and rubbing his hands as he plots another disaster for the intrepid road runner.

In Rhetoric, Aristotle writes, "Revenge . . . is pleasant, it is pleasant to get anything that it is painful to fail to get, and angry people suffer extreme pain when they fail to get their revenge; but they enjoy the prospect of getting it." He cites *The Illiad*, in which Homer describes Achilles' wrath: *Sweeter it is by far than the honeycomb dripping with sweetness.*[5]

Here, I find one of the weaker parts of Aristotle's argument. He suggests that "no one grows angry with a person on whom there is no prospect of taking vengeance, and we feel comparatively little anger, or none at all, with those who are much our superiors in power." This doesn't square with anger I have experienced; nor does it explain the outrage we sometimes direct toward our political leaders. This may be a cultural issue. Perhaps what Americans experience as impotent rage manifested itself differently in the strictly stratified culture of ancient Greece.

If a Thing Is Bad

We often use the word "stoic" to describe people who endure pain without complaint. But this doesn't entirely capture the philosophical tradition of the Stoics.

A Stoic understanding of the good life rejects Aristotle's emphasis on moderation as a virtue ("the golden mean"). They don't buy his notion of "right anger."

For them, reason is *the* essential feature of humanity, and all animal passions lead us toward vice; wrong morally and wrong because they stem from mistaken beliefs or flawed reasoning.[6]

You might think the lives of the Stoics revolved around ascetic isolation. That wasn't the case. Many were men of the world, and some died in particularly gruesome ways.

Marcus Tullius Cicero (106 to 43 BC) spent much of his career as a Roman politician, though he studied Greek philosophy and wrote on a wide range of topics. Like most affluent Romans, he had an arranged marriage. His wife, Terentia, was from an affluent family and evidently took some interest in his political career. The couple had two children: a son (Marcus Minor) and a daughter (Tulia). After thirty years of marriage, Cicero wrote a friend that Terentia had "betrayed" him. Following their divorce, Cicero took up with a young woman who had been his ward. This marriage did not last long. When Tulia died in childbirth, her father was bereft. Then Cicero really fell on hard times. After Julius Caesar died, Mark Anthony declared him an enemy of the state and had him beheaded.

In his writings, Cicero advised Romans to avoid emotions altogether. In direct refutation of Aristotle's golden mean, he said, "If a thing is bad, it is bad also in a moderate amount."[7] There's no question that Cicero considered anger morally wrong. He stated his case plainly: "the defining characteristic of the angry person is that he desires to inflict as much pain as he can on the one he believes to have harmed him... which means that he is rejoicing over someone else's misfortune... the wise person never does that."[8]

For Stoics, reason is key. Cicero asks, "Is there anyone who can get angry without having his mind disturbed by emotion?" He suggests that when we are angry, we lose touch with the faculty that makes us human. One hundred years later, during the lifetime of Christ, Seneca took the same position.

Lucius Annaeus Seneca lived from roughly 4 BC to AD 65, receiving his training in Stoic philosophy when he was a teenager. His early career as a Roman senator was quite successful, but one of his speeches so offended Caligula that the emperor ordered him to commit suicide. Luckily, Seneca was seriously ill at the time and friends told the emperor there was no need for suicide as he would die soon anyway.

A few years later, someone accused Seneca of adultery and he was once again condemned. The sentence was commuted to eight years of exile in Corsica. In his forties, Seneca married a younger woman named Pompeia Paulina. He became an advisor to Emperor Nero, a role that enabled him to amass a huge personal fortune. Accused of participating in a plot to kill Nero, Seneca was again ordered to commit suicide in AD 65. He slit several veins and slowly bled to death in his bathtub.[9]

In his treatise, *De Ira,* dated to the mid-forties AD, when he was a successful senator, Seneca made his case against anger, going beyond abstract argument to offer practical advice on preventing and controlling the vice. He acknowledged that in a world full of cruelty and injustice anger is likely to arise, but he argued that the tasks of the wise man are threefold:

- to resist anger whenever possible,
- to lay it aside or restrain it when it does arise,
- and to "heal the anger of others."

Seneca believed that the tool for accomplishing these three tasks is reason. First, the wise man reminds himself of the suffering that comes with anger. He knows that a person who slights him will always be either stronger or weaker. "If he be weaker, spare him: if he be stronger, spare yourself."[10]

He argues for a lofty stance and a placid mind. This is accomplished in part by avoiding tasks that are too ambitious as well as the burdens "which others' hands lay upon us." He seems to be writing exclusively to Romans of leisure when he advises modest ambitions, "Let us attempt nothing which if we succeed will make us astonished at our success." He also recommends risk avoidance: "Since we know not how to endure an injury, let us take care not to receive one."[11] Noting that life is short, he reminds us that there are, quite simply, better ways to spend our time. "Let us rather pass the little remnant of our lives in peace and quiet."

Seneca offers specific and practical recommendations for avoiding or managing anger:

(1) He expands on an old saying, "a weary man is quarrelsome" to include those who are hungry, thirsty, or "suffering from any cause whatever." To avoid anger, he suggests you "know what your own weak point is, that you may guard it with special care." That is, avoid situations that will make you uncomfortable or stressed so you will not fall into the vice of anger.

(2) He recommends avoiding people who are likely to make you angry: "Choose straightforward, good-natured, steady people, who will not provoke your wrath." (*De Ira*, Book 8)

(3) He advises standing in the shoes of those who offend you and considering their intentions. "Let us put ourselves in the place of him with whom we are angry." Then we can either ignore offenses or allow time for anger to subside.

(4) He argues against revenge in two separate books: "How far better is it to heal an injury than to avenge it?" (Book 27) "How much better it would be to win friends, and disarm enemies; to serve the state, or to busy oneself

with one's private affairs rather than to cast about for what harm you can do to somebody." (Book 28)
(5) On soothing the wrath of others, he recommends letting the initial burst of anger pass, because "it is deaf and frantic (39)," then distracting the angry person to "lead him to forget his passion." Alternatively, you might try deceit or persuading the angry person to "quash his passion." If the angry person is incurable and you are very strong, you can simply "crush it out of existence."
(6) Finally, Seneca reminds you to keep things in perspective, "Believe me, the things which cause us such great heat are trifles." (Book 34)

For Seneca, the bottom line is to minimize the risk of becoming angry by avoiding stress, ambition, fatigue, hunger, and related ills. If that's not possible, learn to ignore irritations or hide your anger. Don't act on it. "If you cannot conquer anger, do not let it conquer you" (Book 13).

As a contemporary American, I was initially unimpressed by the Stoic argument. It felt stilted and unrealistic, and Seneca's much-lauded language seemed arrogant in translation. But I did find his thoughts on anger management intriguing. Strangely enough, his advice forms the basis for key elements of many contemporary anger management interventions. More on this in Chapter 10.

Vengeance Is Mine

Many modern Christians haven't read the Old Testament. According to the Pew Foundation, less than half even open the Bible more than a few times a year.[12] Some might believe it was replaced by the New Testament and that the original thirty-nine books are no longer relevant. But these documents form the basis of key Christian teachings.

The God of the Old Testament is full of wrath. In Deuteronomy, God says, "Vengeance is mine," claiming anger as his dominion and counseling against human attempts at judgment. This is exemplified in a powerful sermon delivered by Jonathan Edwards in 1741, titled, "Sinners in the Hands of an Angry God." Edward tells sinners, "The God that holds you over the pit of hell, much as one holds . . . some loathsome insect over the fire, abhors you and is dreadfully provoked. His wrath towards you burns like a fire. . . . You have offended him infinitely more than ever a stubborn rebel did his prince. And yet it is nothing but his hand that holds you from falling into the fire . . . ."[13]

Reading the Old Testament, God's anger feels both terrifying and remarkably human. Consider the flood. Looking upon humans, the best and most important of his creations, God was furious. They didn't listen to him. They ignored his commandments. They committed sin after sin until God was consumed by red hot rage and bent on destruction. But when all was said and done, God experienced a twinge of regret and promised never to do it again.

Leading theologians have argued that it is dangerous, possibly sinful, to equate the wrath of God with human anger. John Stott outlines the differences between the two: For one thing: "[God's wrath] is never unpredictable but always predictable, because it is provoked by evil and by evil alone."[14] For another, God's anger can be understood as a force of nature rather than as a puny emotion. It is the inevitable consequence of human sin. Feelings and emotions, in this view, are the purview of mortals and God alone stands in judgment.

The Old Testament offers advice similar to Seneca in relation to human anger. Readers are told to "Cease from anger and forsake wrath (Psalm 37:8) and avoid those with angry dispositions (Proverbs 22–24). In responding to the anger of others, Proverbs 15 reminds us that "A gentle answer turns away wrath, but a harsh word stirs up anger." Proverbs 29:22 warns, "An angry man stirreth up strife, and a furious man aboundeth in transgression."

Reminding us of Aristotle's hasty servant, Ecclesiastes 7 advises, "Be not hasty in thy spirit to be angry; for anger resteth in the bosom of fools." Similarly, Proverbs 16 emphasizes the power that comes from controlling our anger: "He that is slow to anger is better than the mighty; and he that ruleth his spirit than he that taketh a city."

Although this advice leaves us well-equipped to cope with the wrath of other humans, there seems little we can do but tremble before God's fury. Fortunately, Lactantius offered a unique and, I think, brilliant interpretation of divine rage.

Lucius Caecilius Firmianus Lactantius (250–325 AD) was born in North Africa to a non-Christian family. He went to school in the kingdom of Numidia and became a successful teacher. Emperor Diocletian invited him to Nicomedia, an ancient city in what is now Turkey, where he served as a professor of rhetoric. Following his conversion to Christianity he resigned his post just in time to avoid being purged by the Emperor's "First Edict Against the Christians." He lived in poverty until his old age, when Constantine appointed him to tutor his son, Crispus.[15]

In his treatise, *De Ira Dei* (On the Anger of God), Lactantius argues that anger and kindness are flip sides of the same coin: "it follows that God is angry, since He is moved by kindness."[16] (Possibly remembering the involvement of ancient Greek gods in human affairs, Lactantius rejects the notion that any god simply enjoys their immortality "with supreme repose, far removed and withdrawn from our concerns." Instead, he emphasizes that God cares about human transgression. Although God may be immune to lesser emotions, like fear and envy, Lactantius feels that "in truth, favour and anger and pity have their substance in God, and that greatest and matchless power employs them for the preservation of the world." Further, he suggests, "God becomes angry at evil and wicked things and when he takes his vengeance on them, he is doing this "to promote the interests of all good men." Thus, "even in anger itself there is also contained a showing of kindness."[17] In rejecting the notion of an indifferent God, Lactantius reminds us of an important point: *We (like God) become angry because we care.*

Lactantius argues that people who are angry are, in some ways, superior: "They who are liable to anger are less timid, and they who are of joyful temperament are less affected with grief" (Chapter 15). He nonetheless counsels against rage, emphasizing the need to curb our anger. On one point he clearly agrees with Aristotle: "the restraining of one's anger in the case of sins is faulty." He notes that God "enjoined us to be angry, and yet not to sin." This sets the stage for the concept of "righteous anger."

Was Jesus Angry?

Charles Dodd, a twentieth-century New Testament scholar from Wales, draws a strong distinction between the Old Testament and New Testament positions on God's anger. In the New Testament, he explains, "Anger as an attitude of God to men disappears, and his love and mercy become all-embracing. This is, as I believe, the purport of the teaching of Jesus with its emphasis on limitless forgiveness."[18] Indeed, there is very little anger in the New Testament; instead, the teachings of Jesus focus on love and forgiveness.

Jesus delivered a powerful admonition against anger during the Sermon on the Mount. In establishing a new, more demanding set of commandments, Jesus is reported to have said, "Resist not evil; but whosoever shall smite thee on thy right cheek, turn to him the other also; and if any man will . . . take away thy coat, let him have thy cloak also" (Matthew 5:38–40). Here, he establishes a standard that explicitly rejects Aristotle's notion of right anger, commanding his followers: "Be ye therefore perfect."

Perhaps the most memorable example of Jesus choosing forgiveness over anger is his crucifixion. While bleeding on the cross he cried, "Father forgive them, for they know not what they do." This might be why the Apostle Peter, in his first letter to churches under persecution urged them to follow the example of Christ, "who, when he was reviled, reviled not again; when he suffered, he threatened not, but committed himself to Him that judgeth righteously" (Peter 2: 23).

Looking at these teachings, some conclude that Jesus, being perfect, was never angry. And yet at least two instances suggest otherwise.

The Apostle Mark said Jesus became angry when the Pharisees tried to trick him into breaking the sabbath by healing a man with a withered hand. Mark describes the tension of the moment: "And they watched him, whether he would heal on the sabbath days that they might accuse him." Jesus called the man with the damaged hand forward and "when he had looked round about on them *with anger*, being grieved for the hardness of their hearts, he saith unto the man 'Stretch forth thy hand.'" (Mark 3:5–7, italics mine).

Matthew, Mark, Luke, and John all tell the story of Jesus expelling the money changers from the Temple. They describe how he overthrew the money-lenders' table and all but John record that he accused them of turning his father's house into a "den of thieves." These sound like the actions of an angry man, though none of the disciples describe Jesus as angry in that moment. Some suggest that as part of his divine nature Christ did not experience anger, and was simply urging the businessmen to leave. Even if he had experienced anger, it wouldn't be a sin because it was a "righteous anger."

Is Anger a Sin?

Thirteenth-century theologian, Saint Thomas Aquinas (AD 1225–1274) also considered the sinfulness of anger. Born to a family of low nobility in Italy and living to the ripe age of forty-nine, his was a monastic life. He entered a Benedictine monastery at the age of five and later joined a Dominican order. He studied the works of Aristotle when he was thirteen, informing his thinking on many topics. Aquinas wrote prolifically until 1273, when a vision led him to question the value of writing. He never wrote again, devoting the remaining year of his life to teaching. He was canonized by Pope John XXII forty-nine years after his death.[19]

Aquinas argued that "Anger is a venial sin if it does not proceed to action." But "Anger is a mortal sin when the subject is moved to seek retribution and retaliation."[20] That is, Aquinas agrees with the Stoics that all anger is vice; but draws a fine line between emotion and action, suggesting anger is less sinful than taking revenge.

Aquinas reminds us that anger is contrary to charity and that the pursuit of revenge can also be contrary to justice. He seems to equate justice with charity when he counsels that "if the matter cannot be resolved rationally, the injured party is to endure the wrong with a justice that is merciful and kind . . . ."

Taking a remarkably familiar stance, Aquinas references Ephesians 4:26: "Be ye angry, and sin not." He advises that "Righteous anger hates the sin but not the sinner," and he argues against revenge, advising that in the event of righteous indignation or anger you look into your heart, find examples of the injustice or sin in your own life, and pray for yourself.

I value Aquinas's caution that righteous anger can be the most dangerous kind. The violence that has been done under its banner has left whole nations in shambles. But how do we know whether our anger is righteous? One anonymous commentator on the Anger Project Facebook page offered an excellent gauge, suggesting that we judge our anger by its fruits. If it destroys lives, relationships, and our own self-esteem we might conclude that it isn't so righteous after all. In that case, we might find ourselves spending eternity in Dante's fifth circle of hell.

Dante integrates the ancient and biblical sources we've been discussing here in *The Divine Comedy*. A devout Catholic, writing during the medieval period, Dante Alighieri (AD 1265–1321) did not speak Greek, but did have access to ancient writings that were translated into Latin, including those of Homer and Aristotle. He found a place for ancient philosophers in his cosmology, and chose the Roman poet Virgil as his guide through Hell.

In *The Inferno*, Dante consigns the "souls whom anger has defeated" to the fifth circle of hell, where they sink into the muddy river Styx. He describes them vividly in two sections: "I, who was intent on watching it, could make out muddied people in that slime, all naked and their faces furious." (Canto VII, 109–111). "Beneath the surface of the water, the sullen lie "bitter in the blackened mud" (124). He distinguishes between the sinful anger of the damned and his own anger at his enemy Filippo Argenti. While Filippo Argenti is mired in the mud and damned for all eternity, Dante's narrator is rewarded for his anger when his guide gives him a rare hug and blesses his "Indignant soul" (Canto VIII, 45).

Perhaps the hug was necessary so that Dante's fifth circle could encompass the three types of angry people who were of interest to him: the wrathful, who act on their anger and tear each other apart on the river's surface; the sullen, who internalize their anger and remain mired below the surface; and the righteous angry, who float above it all and celebrate with their mentors. In this respect, *The Divine Comedy* foreshadows modern perspectives on anger.

My Nightmare

My departure from the university brought a kind of peace; release from struggle, but after a pleasant week of retirement I still caught myself fantasizing about revenge. Maybe I would key the dean's fancy car or let the air out of its tires or change the locks on his office or put pepper spray in his air conditioner.

Aristotle would have told me this was natural.
Seneca would have urged me to get over it.
Jesus would have counseled me to turn the other cheek.

But I couldn't get over it. I was obsessed. I started enjoying my revenge fantasies. Things were spinning out of control. My righteous anger was morphing into hatred. Raised in a liberal Protestant tradition, I knew hatred was, if not a mortal sin, certainly a violation of the Second Commandment. Besides, this was not the person I wanted to be. I knew what my pastor would say, "Look to yourself; search your own soul. You'll find the problem there." I revisited a frayed catalogue of the injustices I had inflicted on other people. It lived in the back of my mind and was embarrassingly long, and those were just the ones I knew about.

That night a nightmare woke me at two AM; the kind that doesn't let go until you tell someone about it. I dreamt I had just taken a new job running a huge organization. It was a great opportunity and my bosses expected me to accomplish great things. The pressure was on, but I wasn't sure I was up to the challenge. Besides, people kept giving me contradictory information. I had no idea whom I could trust. I felt lost and alone; burdened with responsibility and desperately afraid of failure. I woke up shaking with anxiety.

There I was in my own inferno, quivering and mired, not in mud, but in a new brand of torture: a massive job and no support. When I told a colleague about the dream, she said. "Wow, sounds like you were in the Dean's shoes." My subconscious had delivered a massive dose of empathy to protect me from being consumed by hate.

I wish I could say the dream cured me of my rage. It didn't. I continued to fantasize about revenge with sadistic glee. It was only while reconnecting with the ancients in writing this chapter that I was able to let go of my rage, locate my key beliefs, and walk a few steps in the Dean's shoes.

The paradox of living forward while looking backward had seriously tripped me up. This happens once we grow older. We have so much life behind us and what lies ahead can seem pretty bleak. I hadn't been looking forward to retirement, hadn't focused on its potential as a time of freedom and growth. So, I looked back, expecting to be thanked and respected for what I had done. It took the insights of the ancients to jolt me into looking carefully at what was really making me angry and use it to prepare for life as a retiree.

4
Angry Bodies

> Emotion dissociated from all bodily feeling is inconceivable.
> —William James, *Psychology*[1]

When Tomas volunteered to participate in an interview for The Anger Project, I jumped at the chance to get to know him better. We'd met years ago, and I thought of him as a highly insightful, passionate individual who successfully straddled two cultures—his homeland, Uruguay, and his new home in America. He told me about an experience with anger that unnerved him.

One lovely spring day, Tomas was strolling through his neighborhood, hand-in-hand with the woman he loves, herself an immigrant from Malaysia. He admired the new greenery, the smell of freshly mowed lawns, the huge shade trees, and the tidy homes. It had taken him a long time to achieve his version of the American dream; but that day, he found himself in a perfect relationship with his community. This especially good moment was disrupted when a snarling dog lunged out at his partner from behind a tree. The damn thing was huge. Its snapping jaws frothed with saliva. Tomas said he went from "zero to sixty" and felt "tense, really tense, hot. That heat. I can [sic] feel my heart beating."

Our physical reaction to anger evolved over millennia and sheds light on the intimate convergence of mind and body. Like its close cousin fear, anger alerts us to danger. Unlike fear, anger usually leads us *toward* danger as our bodies prepare to do battle. Maybe that's why the Greeks saw anger as the wellspring of courage. Maybe it's why Aristotle compared anger to "a hasty servant" eager to do our bidding; eager to keep us alive. So eager, in fact, that it starts working on our behalf even before we realize it is there.

When this incident took place, Tomas was fifty-nine years old and just beginning to experience physical aging. He had probably not yet noticed that his reactions were starting to slow down a little, a well-established and universal change that comes with age. This slowing is noticeable when we are driving at seventy miles an hour and less so when we're processing angry impulses.

Aging Angry. Amanda Smith Barusch, Oxford University Press. © Oxford University Press 2024.
DOI: 10.1093/oso/9780197584644.003.0004

Inside the Lizard Brain

Tomas's brain lit up (metaphorically). Electrical impulses triggered the release of hormones and transmitters that boosted his body into what he called "survival mode." It was preparing him to meet the threat before he could even begin to consciously process the event.[2]

The anger impulse begins in a maligned part of our brains. Some people call it the "lizard brain." Those in the anger-management industry like to refer to it as "primitive" or "irrational." But here's the thing: lizards make a living catching flies and flies move really fast. Our lizard brains are remarkably good at making snap judgments. When they say, "Jump!" our bodies don't ask "Where?" They just react.

Threat recognition takes place in two almond-shaped structures called the amygdalae, Greek for almond. Some of the densest and most highly connected parts of the brain, the amygdalae are located toward the front of the temporal lobe, one in each hemisphere. Neuroscientists have observed that the amygdalae's volume does not decline with age to the extent that other regions of the brain do, and their functionality seems to be stable across the lifespan of a healthy adult.[3]

People without functioning amygdalae don't experience or recognize fear and anger in others. People with well-developed amygdalae, on the other hand, are highly sensitive to these emotions in both themselves and others. In one of neuroscience's most interesting studies, Dr. Abigail Marsh and her colleagues at Georgetown University used functional magnetic resonance imaging (fMRI) to scan the brains of people who had committed acts of extreme altruism. They studied heroes who were recognized by the Carnegie Foundation for their selfless acts of bravery and people who had donated a kidney to someone they didn't know.

Marsh and her team found that the amygdalae of these altruists were highly active and about 8 percent larger than average. The fMRI results showed their amygdalae were *less* reactive to anger and *more* reactive to fear than most people's. When Marsh's team examined the brains of children with psychopathic tendencies, they found undersized or damaged amygdalae. These children find it nearly impossible to empathize with the suffering of others.

In a related study, Temple University researcher Dr. Michael McCloskey and his colleagues used fMRI to observe the brains of twenty individuals diagnosed with Intermittent Explosive Disorder (IED),[4] a mental illness characterized by frequent bouts of aggression. Compared to a group of twenty controls, the IED patients showed greater activation to pictures of angry faces. Like altruists and heroes, people suffering from this anger disorder have highly active amygdalae. This finding has also been observed in other studies of people who suffer from problems of "emotional dysregulation."

The brains of angry people perceive and respond to anger more readily. When we seek to locate the cause of this, we run into a bit of a chicken and egg problem. Because of a phenomenon called "plasticity," our bodies are constantly redesigning our brains to equip them for the tasks we need to accomplish. Our thoughts carve neural pathways and our brains expand to provide the structures necessary to meet our demands. So it's hard to tell whether heroes and IED patients behave the way they do *because* of their well-developed amygdalae, or whether their amygdalae are well-developed *because* they behave the way they do.

The Survival Circuit

Tomas immediately put himself between the dog and his partner. Then, "I went nuts. . . . Ran at it screaming." The dog came to a sliding halt and eventually retreated, but not before Tomas "got hoarse, really hoarse from it." Tomas's anger enabled him to frighten the dog away.

New York University researcher Dr. Joseph LeDoux describes the "survival circuit" as a complex collection of neurological structures that keep us alive.[5] Emotions, in his view, are part of the automatic operation of our survival circuits. That's why, at only five to six months, babies can recognize faces expressing anger or fear. And that's why I differ from Seneca and other Stoics who see emotions as deeply dysfunctional mistakes. For millions of years, the circuits that produce anger have kept us alive, so something must be working.

As part of the limbic system, the amygdalae triggers the pituitary-adrenal response orchestrated by the hypothalamus-pituitary-adrenal (HPA) axis. At a signal from the amygdala, the HPA axis sends a message to the adrenal glands located above each kidney and a blast of adrenaline sears through the body.

The adrenaline blast prepared Tomas's body for sudden action. In addition to increasing his heart rate and raising his blood pressure, it adjusted his metabolism to release glucose and send it to his brain. It caused the air passages in his respiratory system to dilate sending more oxygen to his muscles and major organs. This whole cascade happened within two to three seconds of spotting the dog. It converted a human at rest into a fighting machine full of energy with sharp intellectual focus and reduced sensitivity to pain.

Cortisol, an all-purpose stress hormone, is also released by the HPA system. Most cells in our body have cortisol receptors, so, like adrenaline, this hormone affects a range of functions. When an anger trigger is spotted, cortisol prepares us for action by suppressing the digestive and reproductive systems and adjusting our mood, motivation, and fear levels. Although it prepares us to respond to emergencies, long-term exposure to cortisol is widely seen as contributing to the adverse health effects of chronic stress.

It was about here that Tomas's consciousness kicked in and he was able to process his first thought: "What kind of idiot would let that dog run loose?" Perhaps he wondered whether the dog's owner deliberately released the dog when he saw two people of color walking down the street.

Located just behind our foreheads, the cerebral cortex is sometimes considered the "seat of reason." Others call it the "modern" or "evolved" brain. This structure makes thought and language possible. But it's not the first line of defense when danger threatens. It takes time to kick in. That's why an old adage advises us to count to ten before we do anything rash. We need this pause to enable our brilliant but slow cortex to wake up and begin processing.

Neuroanatomists once thought only primates had a cerebral cortex, but the modern view is that all mammals do. It is quite well-developed in primates and enormous in humans, packing loads of neurons for our body weight.

Once the cerebral cortex is activated, we become capable of exercising judgment. At least, most of us do. In several studies, McCloskey and his colleagues observed that people with Intermittent Explosive Disorder display a "reduced coupling" between the amygdalae and the Orbital and Medical Prefrontal Cortex (OMPFC). In lay terms, this means that people with IED recognize threat, but have a hard time reasoning their way through it.

By the time he could reflect on the experience, Tomas was exhausted. It triggered some uncomfortable reflection as he realized that, if something posed "a true threat" to a person he loved, he could kill. This left him, "Scared of what I'm capable of."

Late Life Variability

Late life is a time when people are more unique, more different than ever. Whereas babies tend to do the same thing at about the same time, older adults are much less predictable.

This certainly held true among 214 respondents to my Internet survey when they were asked how anger felt in their bodies. Their answers (summarized in Table A4 in the Appendix page 147) varied widely. Tension and tightness were major themes, reported by 17 percent. The same percentage reported increased heart rate or blood pressure. Thirteen percent experienced anger as general discomfort, "body pains," and feeling "sick." Six percent felt nothing, with the same percentage having the urge "to lash out" or "run away." Four percent located their anger in aches or tension in their face and head, with another 4 percent mentioning their thoughts; either that they were "racing" or that they "couldn't think" when they were angry. A few noticed a rush of energy, some felt sick to their stomachs, others had pain in their throats.[6] Some cried. Some shook.

I was relieved that at least a few people reported shaking when they are angry. That's been my experience. My hands and voice shake and I can't control it. I hate the shaking. It makes me feel and sound like a coward. When I get that mad, I usually shut down.

I was especially interested in the six respondents (mostly women) who experienced anger in their throats or voices. It seemed almost metaphoric. None of them considered themselves angry people. One fifty-eight-year-old said that for her, anger brought the urge to "lash out and yell." A sixty-two-year-old woman said, "My throat closes. I stop talking." Three women agreed with a sixty-eight-year-old who reported "my throat hurts!" This was in contrast to the only man who mentioned his voice: "I think anger acts as a release to me. Scream at someone's idiocy and you feel better."

Bad for Us or Just Plain Bad?

When Americans talk about how "bad" anger can be, we tend to conflate morality with health. When someone with a fiery temper has a heart attack, many are inclined to believe they got what they deserved.

In 1896, a quaint article titled, "On the Physiologic Effects of the Indulgence in Anger" appeared in the *Journal of the American Medical Association*. The article opens with the observation that the words anger and angina have the same derivation; as if that establishes a medical connection between the two. It then turns to a description of "a man in fierce rage: The muscles of his arms are tense, so that his fists are instantly clinched, the muscles of the neck and chest so rigid that breathing becomes difficult and unnatural, and the circulatory system is temporarily congested... It sometimes happens that a man falls dead in a fit of rage." The article suggests that anger is liable to kill you and that resentment and fault-finding cause nervous diseases.[7]

Results of my survey suggest that these antiquated beliefs still hold sway among older Americans. Most of my respondents think anger not only feels crummy but is bad for your health. Over three quarters of those who answered this question agreed or strongly agreed with the statement, "Getting angry is bad for a person's health." In fact, this was the most popular belief about anger that showed up in my study.

This view has tremendous staying power. In December 2022, Gina Cherelus published an article in *The New York Times* suggesting that anger "can play havoc" with several organ systems. As in the 1896 article, she suggested that " moments of extreme anger may leave you more vulnerable to a sudden heart attack."[8]

Bradley, a seventy-one-year-old physician I interviewed, agreed that anger can be bad for our health. "Endogenous chemicals restrict arterial blood flow to the brain and organs and none of that is good. . . . There's lots of research on the harmful effects of cortisol. There's no question that anger can provoke a cascade of chemicals that have short-term and long-term health effects like diabetes." His description is, to some extent, supported by the voluminous research that has been conducted on the health effects of anger; but it glosses over some serious complications.

Thanks to modern imaging technologies like electroencephalograph (EEG) machines, neuroscientists can watch electrical activity in the brain and produce a fine-grained analysis of the mind's physical responses. At the same time, other devices such as electrocardiograph (EKG) machines enable researchers to track cardiovascular responses that accompany anger. This insight into the delicate interplay between mind and body contributes to a complex and nuanced understanding of anger and its effects on our physical well-being.

Most research in this area focuses on anger as a trait because habits are more likely than brief experiences to produce long-term health consequences. Studies often use Spielberger's "State-Trait Anger Expression Inventory" to assess anger tendencies. This enables researchers to distinguish between those who readily express anger and those who tend to suppress it.

There is good evidence that anger, like other emotions, can affect our health through the demands it places on our cardiovascular and limbic systems. However, the effects of anger suppression (anger-in) differ from those associated with anger expression (anger-out).

Contrary to popular belief, considerable research indicates that anger-in is a greater health hazard than anger-out.[9] In 2012, Jameson Hirsch and his colleagues reported that college students who scored high on anger-in thought more often about suicide and harmed themselves more frequently than those who did not. This is consistent with theory and research suggesting that "anger turned inward towards the self is a destructive force."[10]

The authors also reported that self-forgiveness seemed to disrupt anger's influence on suicidal behavior. This was true for both kinds of anger. Among those with high levels of *expressed* anger, those who readily forgave themselves were even less inclined toward suicidal behavior. Likewise, the destructive influence of *internalized* anger was reduced among those with high self-forgiveness. This finding has important implications for clinical work with those who suffer from problematic anger.

It seems that internalized anger may be harmful to younger populations. What about older adults? In 2012, Dr. Gonnie Klabbers and her colleagues at Maastricht University conducted one of the rare longitudinal studies that sheds light on the health effects of anger among middle-aged and older adults.[11] They accessed medical and self-report data from 2,679 participants aged fifty-five years and older in the Dutch Study of Medical Information and Lifestyles. Controlling for health behaviors such as smoking, alcohol consumption, and physical activity, they found that anger did not predict illness or mortality. Neither did aggression or rebelliousness. Only hostility, defined as "negative beliefs about and attitudes towards others," was associated with subsequent mortality. Those scoring highest on hostility had a 57 percent higher risk of premature death.

Although the Klabbers study does not specify the causes of death, other researchers have reported links between hostility and cardiac disease. This led American researcher, Dr. Carol Magai, to note that "There is a considerable body of literature ... indicating a robust relationship between hostility and circulatory disease."[12]

Time and again, researchers have found that hostility and suppressed anger place us at greater risk for illness and death due to heart disorders in later life. Most findings indicate that suppressed anger is the greater potential health hazard, associated with increased resting blood pressure,[13] increased risk of breast cancer, lung cancer, and rheumatoid arthritis.[14]

Like the Hirsch study, other researchers have identified robust health benefits associated with anger expression across diverse samples leading them to conclude that "constructive anger behavior," that is, expressed anger that is goal-oriented, problem-focused and "culturally appropriate," is associated with lower blood pressure and better health.[15] Further, there is some evidence that occasional high-intensity expression of anger may be healthy.[16] Perhaps it has a purging effect on our hearts and minds.

Park, Flores, Aschbacher, and Mendes speculate on the potential mechanism for this effect: "By expressing anger, some individuals might be able to restore a sense of control, maintain self-respect, and compensate for the status challenge following frustrating experiences, through a display of dominance and power."[17]

Context Matters

In some situations, expressed anger leads us to do things we regret. It can mess up our social life, leaving us isolated and riddled with guilt—neither of which can be good for our health. This can be especially complicated for some groups, such as people of color, women, and older adults, for whom anger expression is discouraged or disregarded. Although no studies have focused on gender or age, several have suggested that both anger-in and anger-out may be associated with health risks for people of color in the United States.[18]

Social sanctions against expressing anger pile on top of other stressors experienced by women of color. I was delighted when an eighty-seven-year-old

African American woman I call Ruby agreed to an interview. Ruby has a hard time talking about anger but she acknowledges that "Racism gives you PTSD. It always lingers. To live in constant fear is unbelievable. I'm not afraid for me but for my daughters and granddaughters. They have backbones. I say to the oldest, 'It's OK to be angry but be careful how you display it. You don't know what the other person will do.'"

Ruby says her daughter Sandra, now in her fifties, doesn't tolerate racist microaggressions. When a "rude white woman" at the mall made a racist comment to Sandra, Ruby had to talk her daughter down. Then she said loudly, "Don't you worry about her. She seems a little off. If we need to we'll call the police."

Two studies suggest that anger differentially affects the health of African Americans. In 2015, Dr. Jennifer Boylan (University of Pittsburgh) and her colleagues studied anger and inflammatory markers in 1,200 middle-aged whites and African Americans.[19] Inflammation is widely seen as the mechanism by which stress increases our risk of cardiac disease, which is more prevalent among African Americans.

African Americans reported higher "anger-out" and lower anger control than whites. Among highly educated African Americans, anger-out was associated with elevated inflammatory profiles. This was not true of highly educated whites or of African Americans with less education. The authors speculate that highly educated (high status) whites who express anger "may do so as a symbol of their status and dominance", and therefore may not experience the levels of stress and inflammation seen in highly educated African Americans.

The second study was conducted by epidemiologist Anissa Vines and her colleagues at the University of North Carolina at Chapel Hill.[20] Previous work indicated that Black women were at two to three times greater risk for uterine fibroids and tended to develop them at earlier ages than white women. Other studies have found that Blacks are more likely than whites to suppress their anger. Vines and her colleagues thought these two findings might be related.

They recruited 935 women and conducted pelvic ultrasounds to determine whether they had fibroids. Some 74 percent of the Black women and 50 percent of the white women did. They asked the women, "How often do you feel the need to squelch or swallow strong feelings of anger?" Fourteen percent of Black women said they did so every day, compared to 8 percent of White women. Stress levels among the two groups were comparable, but Black women who reported squelching or swallowing their anger at least weekly had an 8 percent higher likelihood of developing fibroids.

Indeed, as Dr. Nancy Dorr and her colleagues point out, for people of color in the United States, anger expression is a lose/lose proposition, "damned if you do/damned if you don't." While squelching anger might make you ill, expressing anger can get you killed.

Similar effects might be seen among older adults as the health effects of our habits come home to roost. Old bodies are more vulnerable than young ones. If fifteen minutes of suppressed anger raises blood pressure in college students, imagine what fifty years of internalized anger can do to the body of a seventy-year-old.

Additionally, the rules change with the onset of old age, when we are challenged to find culturally acceptable ways to express anger lest we be ridiculed and labeled "grumpy." Fortunately, late life is also a time when our emotional coping resources are at their best. Over the course of a life span we learn to manage our lives and our emotions to minimize discomfort. And, as we will see, most of us find satisfying and healthy ways to channel our anger.

When I ask Tomas, "Why do you think people get angry?" he says, "It's a normal, common emotion—a response to things we encounter—bad weather, bad dogs, nasty people. . . it helped me survive in this culture."

5
Women Cry / Men Rage

> Touch me with noble anger,
> and let not women's weapons, water drops,
> stain my man's cheeks!
>
> —Shakespeare, *King Lear*[1]

Medusa, the ancient gorgon with a headful of snakes for hair, is enjoying a renaissance among contemporary artists. Her story speaks to many issues confronting modern women.

The best-known version is told by the Roman poet, Ovid.[2] Medusa was a beautiful young gorgon sister with long flowing hair serving as a priestess in Athena's temple. When Poseidon raped her in Athena's temple, the goddess watched, burning with jealousy. In a move reminiscent of contemporary rape culture, Athena blamed Medusa for the rape that desecrated her temple. She turned Medusa's beautiful hair into a nest of vipers and cursed the young woman so that any person or animal who gazed upon her face would instantly turn to stone. (Figure 5.1 offers a close look at Crisina Biaggi's sculpture of Medussa's face.)

Medusa's rage was all consuming and her reputation grew. News of her legendary monstrosity reached a Greek warrior named Perseus, who saw an opportunity to enhance his own fame. With Athena's help, he cut off Medusa's head while she was sleeping. The decapitated head became a powerful symbol and amulet. True to her name, (μέδειν) which means to protect or rule, Medusa's head protected its bearer from evil. Perseus and Athena had it painted on their shields and emblazoned on important buildings throughout Greece to ward off misfortune.

The misogyny of Ovid's version becomes clear when we compare it with earlier Greek texts. In Hesiod's *Theogony*, for example, Medusa isn't raped.[3] Instead, she and Poseidon make love in a field of flowers. She conceives twins and, when Perseus cuts off her head, her sons Pegasus and Chrysaor leap out to exact revenge. Euripides also complicated Medusa's protective role in his play, *Ion* where Creusa, another maiden who was raped by the gods, explains that she has two drops of Medusa's blood: one is deadly and the other, a universal cure. Perhaps Creusa's drops of blood symbolize the Janus-faced nature of anger: on the one hand, destructive; on the other, healing.

Aging Angry. Amanda Smith Barusch, Oxford University Press. © Oxford University Press 2024.
DOI: 10.1093/oso/9780197584644.003.0005

Figure 5.1. Detail of *Raging Medusa*, 1998, by Cristina Biaggi.

Medusa's story is especially interesting when we consider how gendered anger was in ancient times. Women's rage was seen as unpredictable, irrational, and extremely dangerous. As Ari Mermelstein writes in *Power and Emotion in Ancient Judaism*, anger was "a gendered emotion whose legitimate expression was reserved for men throughout a vast array of Greek and Latin sources that span a millennium."[4]

Mermelstein studied a fragment of the Dead Sea Scrolls that offered "Community Instruction" to members of an early Jewish sect (*yahad*) living on the outskirts of the Roman empire. In this small community only men enjoyed the right to express anger and even their expression was tightly controlled. This small group of Jews was embedded within a deeply hierarchical Greco-Roman world. Status, or what we might call class, determined which men enjoyed the right to express anger. Judges and other dominant men were seen as having an unconditional right to be angry both in the *yahad* and in the broader social context. For many people, things haven't changed all that much.[5]

In some contexts, gender roles have become less rigid. For Swiss psychologist Carl Jung, the developmental task of later life was "individuation"—becoming our own, authentic and unique selves. For men, this meant getting in touch with their feminine selves (*anima*) and for women it involved accessing their masculinity (*animus*).[6]

More and more people conceive of the gender binary as a fluid continuum rather than an either-or proposition. Some postmodern intellectuals, like Judith Butler, author of *Undoing Gender*, argue that gender is essentially a performance.[7] Butler's work underscores the role of social norms in legitimizing the gender binary. Along with Betty Friedan, author of *Beyond Gender*,[8] Butler argues for conceptualizing identity and structuring social policy in ways that decenter gender.

Some suggest that late life frees us from the binary rigidities of gender. Nonetheless, we often find that norms that seem archaic to the young persist among older adults. Perhaps, once we truly get beyond gender, we will be able to celebrate the attributes that make us uniquely ourselves—including our relationship with anger.

As a modern archetype of feminine rage, Medusa's messages are complex. When Perseus severed her head, he turned her into a monster. Metaphorically, some find that when anger is detached from reason it produces monstrous results. On the other hand, anger can be intimately tied to creativity. As May Sarton pointed out, "fits of rage are like a huge creative urge gone into reverse, something dammed up that spills over."[9] When we focus on the origins of Medusa's name, her anger can be seen as protective. Or like the two drops of her blood, it can either create and heal or destroy.

Miriam Dexter, an independent classics scholar who has published extensively on myths and goddesses, is part of an effort to restore Medusa as a complex and "deeply faceted" being. She traces the Medusa archetype to gods and demons of Neolithic times, observing how ancient authors including Homer, Hesiod, Pindar, Herodotus, Diodorus Siculus, and Ovid molded her story to meet their ends.[10] In the process, Medusa went from beautiful to monstrous and from fertile to lethal, as the story took on an ever-more misogynous tone.

In her unforgettable call to arms for women, Helene Cixous uses Medusa as a touchstone, claiming, "You only have to look at the Medusa straight on to see her. And she's not deadly. She's beautiful and she's laughing."[11]

Anger Makes You Ugly

There's an old Polish saying that roughly translates as, "Anger detracts from beauty."[12] Women of my generation received mixed messages. Urged to pursue the careers of our choice, we were also surrounded by "be nice" messages at home and in school. Of course, nice girls don't express anger.

Today women are writing about their anger in a spate of books that led British feminist scholar, Jilly Boyce Kay, to comment that women's anger is "becoming all the rage."[13] In *Rage Becomes Her*, one of the most popular books in this genre, Sonya Chemaly remembers her mother systematically and silently tossing her treasured wedding china from a second-floor veranda. As she watched the plates soar and crash, the future author could only imagine what had triggered her mother's strange behavior. She knew, without being told, that it would not do to ask. Even now, talking about anger, let alone expressing it, is considered especially unseemly for mothers.

Thanks in part to the #MeToo movement, women who have experienced sexual harassment and assault are now expressing themselves in press conferences, congressional hearings, and courtrooms—venues in which anger must be carefully modulated. To avoid censure, a woman mustn't "lose her temper" in public. Instead, women are advised to behave as Christine Blasey Ford did when she accused Brett Kavanaugh of sexual assault before the Senate Judiciary Committee. In *Vox*, Ezra Klein describes Ford as "calm but demure . . . visibly shaken but steady . . . specific, *credible*, serious."[14] (Italics added) One can only imagine the effort, and therapy, it took to get her to that point. Recently, author E. Jean Carroll successfully brought a civil claim of sexual assault; the first ever against a former president. Carroll's self-presentation balanced vulnerability and calm in a compelling factual narrative. She maintained her composure, never expressing her anger, even while describing the attack in vivid detail.[15]

Real Men Don't

It was relatively easy for me to grasp a woman's experience of anger. It took more work to understand what is going on with men.

I started by reading Michael Kimmel's 2013 book, *Angry White Men*. Kimmel spent time with white supremacists, men's rights activists, and young students, and his book provides a remarkably clear assessment of their rage. He notes that the American dream is out of reach for many white men in America. Raised to expect a certain amount of privilege, they feel that jobs and benefits that should be theirs are being snapped up by others. Kimmel locates the cause of their frustration in "aggrieved entitlement."[16] I find the term a little dismissive, but it did inform my plunge into the men's rights movement.

"You cannot hate what you understand."

Joe, a sixty-one-year-old man, posted this comment on Facebook in response to a recruitment announcement for The Anger Project. Intrigued, I replied, "Well put!" and invited him to an interview.

By this time, I had interviewed a good number of men, ranging from those who were determined to break family cycles of abusive anger to others who were quietly (and not-so-quietly) managing their own rage. But I had not yet met with anyone from the men's rights movement.

Joe sent me a list of topics he wanted to cover: "Anger as pain." "Feminism as hate." "Hungry Lion Syndrome." I was a little nervous. Then Joe explained he wasn't available the following day because he planned to "spend some time in front of the courthouse with a John Mast sign." A quick google search revealed that John Mast lost custody of his four small children when his wife accused him of molesting them. After a four-year court battle Mast was exonerated and awarded unsupervised visitation. He must have been delighted when he pulled into the parking lot to pick them up. Minutes later, Mast's father-in-law fired three bullets into his body. He died and became a cause célèbre for men's rights advocates.

Joe spends a lot of time debating gender issues on social media. He explains, "I'm just the guy who doesn't think there really ever was an oppressive patriarchy." He was the first person to tell me that "For men, pain is behind anger. . . . Angry men are seen as dangerous, not as people in pain. . . . Men can't cry and be men so he [sic] shows it as anger."

Joe's pain stems from a powerful romantic relationship he had in his forties. He describes his wife as "abusive," explaining that she "had unprotected sex with others several times, exposing me to STDs." After he got a restraining order and ended the relationship, his wife accused him of criminal stalking. The charges were eventually dropped, which Joe found disappointing because he didn't get a chance to be exonerated in court.

After our interview, Joe introduced me to other men's rights advocates, including Eddie and Sean.

Moments after he appeared on my computer screen in his t-shirt and baseball cap, Eddie hurried to close the door. He explained that he lived with his mother and didn't want her to listen in. "Men aren't allowed to express their emotions." Then, he told a story that broke my heart.

Eddie lived with an abusive stepfather when he was small. "He would spank me out of anger and took delight in hitting me with a leather belt as hard as he could. I'd get a certain number of lashes—usually twenty. Then if I cried, he'd say, 'If you keep crying, I'm going to keep hitting you.' And he did. He beat the ability to cry out of me."

Now, even when he's overcome with sorrow, Eddie can't cry. There are only two exceptions—in a dark theater during a sad movie or after serving as the bottom in a BDSM (Bondage, Discipline, Sadism & Masochism) session.

In a matter-of-fact tone, Eddie tells me he has an explosive temper. I ask whether he is still angry at his stepfather, and he gives a wry laugh, "We could have a ten-hour conversation about all the anger I've experienced."

People annoy him. "Like the person [at the grocery store] who goes in the door and then just stops. Like they're the only person in the world. 'No Sir! You just take your time!' I'd say. And maybe he'd say, 'Someone's in a hurry.' And I'd shout, 'You go fuck yourself!' He also loves to rage in his car. Sometimes people look at him funny, but at least it's safe.

I Need Another Happy Pill

Joe described Sean as a "reasonable men's rights advocate."

The day before our meeting, Sean e-mailed me an overview of his story. He said he was a fifty-one year-old, "victim of domestic abuse. I have a divorce from my wife on the grounds she was guilty of extreme and repeated acts of mental cruelty." Although he was from the United Kingdom, he'd spent time in the Cook County jail and had slept on the sidewalk in Chicago. He said he had had no contact with his three children since 2015, adding: "I have attached two mugshots . . . so you know I am not some whack job fantasist." One photo showed a pale-skinned man with close cropped brown hair leaning against a grey brick wall. The corners of his mouth turned down and his wide brown eyes stared straight into the camera. In the other shot, he looked away with tight-lipped contrition.

Sean's face pops up right on time with the same wide-eyed expression as in his first photo. He explains that he fell wildly in love with an American woman sometime in the 1980s or 1990s. He isn't sure when. His memory is a little blurry. He never mentions her name, always referring to her as his "ex."

Even in the early days, there were red flags. Her ex-husband had been abusive and she "was not mentally normal." But it was easy to ignore the warning signs. They were young and in love and Sean quickly became "enamored" of her two-year-old son. That was partly why he suggested they get married. They visited her parents in the United States and Sean quickly "fell in love with the place." America was so expansive and there was so much opportunity. The couple and their young son moved to Chicago.

For a while, things were pretty good. Sean got a job making good money in construction. His wife didn't hold down jobs for very long. "There'd be some big drama and she'd quit." They had three children in rapid succession. But his wife's behavior became erratic. "Any stress and she'd go off the deep end." She would become "insanely jealous" and call him at work. They had "silly silly scenes." She smashed a window. She attacked a girl he was talking to in a bar.

Arguments escalated until the night his wife called the police and accused him of physical abuse. Sean had just gotten home, tired from a day breaking cement. When she asked him to clean the kitchen, he refused. He just wanted to rest. Next thing he knew, there were two policemen at his door.

Over the next two years his wife called the police thirteen times, but Sean was never charged. He describes a pivotal incident that occurred after he told her he was going to seek full custody of the kids. He'd been drinking at the time.

> She lunged at my neck. I threw a hand up and it brushed her face. She called the police. They threw me on the bonnet of the car; took my wine key. 'I found a knife!' the one called. It was a fucking wine key! I was cuffed. Spoke with [one of the officers] in the back of the car. She was very nice. All these details I remember. They drove me to the station and charged me with misdemeanor domestic battery. There was no mark on her. And that's how I ended up in the men's rights movement.

Sean pled guilty to reckless conduct and got parole. As he describes the spiraling violence in their relationship, I wonder how the story might be told from his ex's perspective. I also wonder whether police officers and other officials are primed to see men as perpetrators.

Sean is the one who gave me the title for this chapter when he said, "Women cry and men rage. That's just the way it is."

Several men's rights activists I spoke with identified false accusations of domestic abuse and rape as an important men's issue. When I was incredulous, one directed me to a book called *How to Destroy a Man Now,* described as "a step-by-step guide to destroying a man's reputation." I was unable to locate a copy, but I did find sixty reviews on Good Reads, most indicating that the book was dreadful. One reviewer (L. F. Boreol) wrote that "it represents misandry and hatred at its putrid worst."

There is a widespread notion that a false allegation of child abuse, sometimes referred to as "The Silver Bullet," is the weapon of choice for divorcing wives seeking custody, child support, or alimony. Columbia University psychiatrist, Dr. Richard Gardner, coined the term "Parental Alienation Syndrome" to suggest that vindictive mothers pressure children into making false claims against their fathers. Some advocates and professionals believe that a significant proportion, even a majority, of allegations in divorce cases are malicious.

It is important to distinguish between unsubstantiated allegations and malicious reports of abuse. Statistics compiled by the National Child Abuse and Neglect Data system indicate that 60 percent of allegations of child abuse are not substantiated. That means that authorities were unable to establish whether the abuse occurred. Several large-scale studies in the United States and Canada suggest that malicious allegations are somewhat more common in cases where custody is in dispute but, even then, they make up a small fraction (from 6% to 12%) of abuse reports.[17]

The same is true of false rape allegations. In 2010, David Lisak, a clinical psychologist who taught at the University of Massachusetts, reviewed all cases of sexual assault reported at a major U. S. university over a ten-year period. He explains that "To classify a case as a false allegation, a thorough investigation must yield evidence that a crime did not occur."[18] The evidence might, for instance, include physical data or testimony from credible witnesses that contradict key aspects of the victim's story. Lisak found that only six of 136 cases involved false allegations. The team's review of credible studies that use this definition suggests that these cases make up between 2 percent and 10 percent of reported rapes. Despite the fact that victims are considerably more likely to not report an offense, some men are haunted by the possibility that they will be falsely accused.

I spoke with several men who reported this experience, and I came to believe that the false accusations, although rare, may be radicalizing. Even after they were vindicated by the justice system, the men remained angry and bitter. Sean's experiences left him furious.

> It broke me. Talk about anger. I never understood husbands killing wives before that. But I was furious. Homicidally furious. I had never felt violent towards her—after all, she's mentally ill. Nor towards the prosecutors, judges, cops. But a whole social circle formed around her. To several people I said, "Keep away from me or I will hit you."

Sean's wife posted frequently about their disagreements on social media and "her story kept changing." Shortly after she was granted a protection order, Sean was investigated for revenge porn (a Class 3 felony in Illinois) for posting naked pictures of his wife on social media without her consent. Nonconsensual pornography is considered a form of abuse. As of February 2021, it is not prohibited under federal law but is either a misdemeanor or a felony in all but four states.

For Sean, things went from bad to worse after the porn charge.

> Three months later I got a call from the police regarding the order of protection. I said, "I'll be down in an hour." They took me to the back, hand-cuffed me to the wall, then put me in a cell. Took me to court. $15,000 bond. They said I broke the protective order by third party contact.

When he was released, Sean hit rock bottom living on the streets of Chicago. Then he landed back in jail for nonpayment of child support. "I was in jail with two other guys—all of us for child support. Both were mentally ill. One was delusional and the other was a U.S. veteran with dementia. This was a debtor's prison for child support." He was shocked to find a veteran in jail. "They're supposed to be heroes!"

All fifty states have provisions for jailing noncustodial parents who fail to pay child support. At any given time, about 70 percent of child support cases in the United States are in arears and an estimated 50,000 men are incarcerated for nonpayment. Elizabeth Cozzolino from the University of Texas reports that conflict with the mother is a key factor increasing the likelihood that a man will go to jail for nonpayment.[19] Although he didn't mention it, it is likely that Sean's ex-wife reported his nonpayment to authorities.

During the pandemic, Sean lost his job and was living on public assistance at his mother's place. He calls his antidepressants "happy pills" and says they "stopped the nightmares and the rage as well." I ask whether he is content, and he says, "No. I'm medicated."

Sean nurses fantasies of revenge, not against his wife, but against the prosecutor and judge who landed him in jail. When I ask how he controls his anger, he replies, "The meds . . . scheming and planning. If you're going to mess someone over there are 100 ways to skin a cat, to get revenge. Lots of ways are better than thumping them. I remember names."

When I observe that sometimes "fathers discourage boys from crying," he says, "It's natural. I was raised that way. Crying is unmanly. . . . Do you really want a son who'd be crying every two minutes?" His last comment makes me wonder if Sean considers a man's life one of constant sorrow.

He does believe that anger is a man's natural response to pain. "If you're expressing anger consider, 'What's the pain?' Address the pain. . . If she won't sleep with you after an $80 dinner your anger is the pain of not being loved." He also has concerns about the delegitimization of men's anger, adding, "Maybe he's got every right to be angry and he needs someone to acknowledge that."

At one point during our conversation, I say, "You sound angry."

"I need another happy pill."

"Not scary angry."

"You're thousands of miles away."

It almost sounds like a threat.

A Lot to Be Angry About

Joe also suggested that I interview Warren Farrell. He gave me a rare compliment when he said Farrell was, like me, "motivated by love." Still, I was nervous. Warren was the first famous person I interviewed. I prepared a sheet of questions and studied up on his background.

Born in 1943, Dr. Farrell completed his PhD in political science at New York University. He initially came to prominence in the 1970s when he served on the board of the National Organization for Women (NOW). At the time, he explained, he was riding high. His books were on bestseller lists, he was popular on the speaking circuit, and he was even under consideration for a MacArthur grant.

When Warren became interested in the importance of fathers and the challenges they experience during custody disputes, his colleagues at NOW worried that their members would feel betrayed by his shift in focus. He and NOW parted ways. Since then, Warren has organized men's beauty contests, run for governor of California, and published seven books on men's issues. He leads workshops for young men and has become a public face of the men's movement.

Warren's latest book, *The Boy Crisis*, reflects his deep-seated concern that many boys (and girls) are "father deprived." He advocates for gender equality while emphasizing the challenges faced by boys and men.

Like other men who identify with the movement, Farrell locates the cause of gender differences deep in the evolutionary history of the human race. From this perspective, men compete to have sex with women and women compete to attract a man who will protect them and their children. Women prefer alpha men and men prefer what Warren calls, "genetically privileged" (aka beautiful) women.

Warren does not share the hostility other men I spoke with expressed toward feminism. He sees himself as an advocate for gender equality and doesn't like the term "men's rights," finding it inappropriate for men to complain about their lack of rights. He prefers to call it the Men's Issues Movement.[20]

Warren and other advocates I spoke with feel that men have a lot to be angry about. Sometimes this grated on my nerves, as when one man called for "equal rights with women." But as I listened, I came to appreciate some of their concerns.

A pervasive warrior archetype can leave men feeling that their only value lies in their ability to do battle and, if necessary, die for the people or country they love. In the same vein, many men feel valued only to the extent that they provide financially for their families. Farrell speaks movingly of men who choose not to pursue the work they love, often in the arts, because it would not enable them to raise a family. This results in men spending most of their time away from their partners and children, straining bonds and leaving them in the thankless position of working hard to support a family of strangers.

Are Men Really Angrier?

Listening to the arguments of men's activists and watching news coverage of the mayhem perpetrated by angry men (see Aging, Angry, and Armed to the Teeth,

Chapter 9), a person might be inclined to believe that in modern America men are angrier than women. They are certainly more violent. But as social science grapples with gender differences in anger, their results complicate the angry man stereotype.

In 1996, Jerry Deffenbacher, and his colleagues at Colorado State University conducted eight separate studies of diverse populations and concluded that "Men and women are angered by *similar* things and to *similar* degrees, express themselves in *similar* ways, and *suffer* similar consequences."[21]

I wondered whether contemporary studies might yield different results. A careful search revealed twenty-five studies published on gender differences in anger between 2002 and 2019. With some variation, most mirror the results reported by Todd Kashdan in 2016.[22]

Kashdan, director of the Well-Being Laboratory at George Mason University and coauthor of the 2015 book, *The Power of Negative Emotion*, and his team asked 173 undergraduate psychology students to keep daily anger diaries for three weeks, reporting on anger triggers and experiences. They found no difference in the experiences of and reactions to anger, though these young men and women differed considerably in their anger *expression*. Men were significantly more likely to use verbal confrontation than women.[23]

Given that publication is generally biased against reporting negative findings, it is striking that eight of the studies I found reported no significant gender differences related to the *experience* of anger. But most did find differences in anger *expression*, with men reporting more aggressive outbursts and direct verbal expression of anger and women reporting more suppression and internalization of anger.

Another important study was published in 2010 by Robin Simon of Wake Forest University and Kathryn Lively, from Dartmouth College.[24] One of the most persistent findings in the field of mental health is that women are significantly more likely to report suffering from depression. This has emerged in epidemiological studies since the early 1970s. Some explain it with reference to gender role expectations, positing that depression is more acceptable for women than men. Others reference stress, suggesting that women internalize their problems while men act out and abuse substances.

Using a nationally representative sample of 1,125 adults in the United States, Simon and Lively found that the suppression of intense and persistent anger, more common among women than men in their sample, was associated with a higher rate of depressive symptoms. This provides empirical support for a major premise of psychoanalytic theory: suppressed anger morphs into depression.

Although most researchers report that men and women experience anger in similar ways, some do report differing experiences. In one of the few studies that includes older adults, Kira Birditt and Karen Fingerman (2003) interviewed 185 individuals ranging from thirteen to ninety-nine years of age about "difficult situations with their close and problematic social partners."[25] These were categorized into three types of "negative"[26] emotions: anger, sadness, and nonspecific unpleasantness.

In an echo of ancient beliefs that women's anger is especially irrational and dangerous, Birditt and Fingerman found that women of all ages reported having more intense upsets than men. Women also reported staying upset longer, though this effect reversed among those eighty years of age and older.

Women in treatment for anger problems also tend to report more anger than men in treatment.[27] This is particularly true on measures of intense anger. Although it could mean that women experience more intense anger it could also reflect what researchers call "selection bias." That is, women may have to be much angrier than men to get referred for interventions, possibly because of men's greater risk of committing violence (see Chapter 10).

Given the age-old tradition of discouraging women from expressing anger it is hardly surprising that we turn away from our rage. As Audre Lord explains in her essay, *The Uses of Anger*, "Most women have not developed the tools for facing anger constructively."[28] Rather than asking what anger can teach us, we stifle it, misname it, or censor it in order to conform to the gendered expectations of our families, our employers, and our cultures. As we have seen, this habit may be damaging to our physical and mental health.

A Gender Paradox

Gender roles and norms have undergone rapid change, but the results of my national survey point to persistent differences among older adults, perhaps because they have not embraced modern values and expectations regarding gender.

Older women were significantly less likely than men to describe themselves as "an angry person." Only 20 percent of women, compared to 31 percent of men endorsed this descriptor ($p = .045$). (See Table A7 in Appendix I, Page 149).

When I asked people to describe how they usually behave when they are angry, 22 percent of women compared to 13 percent of men said they usually criticized themselves afterward ($p = .049$). This could be a remnant of women's stronger tendency to ruminate following an upset.

Although angry men are more likely to commit violent acts, a significant number of my respondents (21%) endorsed the belief that "when angry, women are more dangerous than men." Perhaps respondents ruminated over their anger focusing, not on their own feelings, but on the effect their actions might have had on other people. Given the ill effects associated with rumination, it may be a good thing that women are significantly more likely than men to tell someone how they feel. Some 34 percent of women endorsed this option, compared to only 17 percent of men (p = .002).

Paradoxically, women are both slightly more likely to say that what they did in response to an incident that made them angry left them feeling better *and* considerably more likely to say they wish they had done something differently. (Please see Table A5 in Appendix I, Page 55).

Interviewing men's rights activists, I felt like Alice in Wonderland. Their world has a topsy turvy logic I can only vaguely comprehend. They often have troubled relationships with women and tend to see themselves as victims of a society that devalues masculinity. Many view feminism as an anti-male ideology that has taken over government policy and American culture. Using the term "gynocentrism," they argue that massive government programs focus on the needs of women to the exclusion of men. Time and again I had to remind myself to just listen.

Still, their concerns often contrasted sharply with mine. For millennia, men have been seen as the defenders of home and family; women, as the nurturers. Men are encouraged to channel their rage into courage in battle and commerce while women are urged to suppress theirs for the well-being of family and community.

But the conditions that may have once made this division necessary for the survival of the species no longer prevail. The more we realize this, the more we chafe at traditional restrictions on our emotional experiences and expressions. Authenticity or being "true" to ourselves has emerged as a key value, one that growing numbers of young people embrace as they shed the constrictions of the past. Older adults, having spent more time in a world of rigid gender rules, may resist change or struggle to catch up. Meanwhile, groups of all ages can find rejection of the old rules and traditional roles deeply disturbing, threatening, even. Perhaps this conflict sets all of us up for what Ursula Le Guin once described as "an orgy of self-indulgent rage."[29]

Many long for a world where we can live together in harmony, where men can cry, and Medusa can laugh. As philosopher Martha Nussbaum points out in her 2016 book, *Anger and Forgiveness*, achievement of this goal will call on all of us to foster "a patient and forbearing disposition to see and seek the good rather than to harp obsessively on the bad."[30]

6
Race and Anger in Later Life

> O human creatures, born to soar aloft, Why fall ye thus before a little wind?
> —Dante, *Purgatorio*[1]

Walking down the city street, we hear voices; a low rumble punctuated by occasional screams or a hysterical laugh. Armored vehicles with tinted windows ooze their silent threat into the warm spring evening. People of all colors, genders, and ages mill past us carrying signs. "My Life Matters" "Hands up, don't shoot" "No justice. No peace."

A few blocks away, a police car wobbles upside-down in the middle of the street. Two men scramble onto the roof of an empty sedan. As they bounce up and down, flames burst from the police car. Officers stand in tight formation. A few souls approach and speak to them while the rest watch, hypnotized. A middle-aged white man with a bandana on his head strides by carrying a rifle.

These scenes, repeated in dozens of cities around the country in June of 2020, are part of a long history of demonstration. They are only one example of the race-based anger so pervasive in the United States. Its corrosive effects stem as much from microaggressions and injustices as dramatic public events. While this anger has its origins in time immemorial, it is based on a flimsy social construct.[2]

The word "race" has its origins in fourteenth-century Norse and Old English words that refer to a contest of speed. It wasn't until the sixteenth century that it came to be used to describe people of shared descent. In his book, *Racism*, political science professor Carter A. Wilson traces the use of the word "race" to describe certain "types" or "categories" of humans to the early days of the British empire.[3] Since then, the term has served as a convenient fiction for those seeking to exploit others, justifying exploitation, murder, inequality, and oppression across the globe. As Kimberlé Williams Crenshaw said in her 2021 lecture, "Race is a fiction. Racism is real."[4]

Aging Angry. Amanda Smith Barusch, Oxford University Press. © Oxford University Press 2024.
DOI: 10.1093/oso/9780197584644.003.0006

Angry Times in American Streets

American streets have been sites of racial anger since well before the country was established. Between the nation's founding genocide, white riots, and contemporary terrorist attacks by white supremacists, we must bear in mind that, as a colleague of mine put it, "White violence is the sea we all swim in." If the dream of *e pluribus unum* is to survive, we must confront and understand racial anger in all its complexity.

In 2010, Dr. Quintard Taylor, a history professor at the University of Washington founded Blackpast.org to provide a central digital repository for documents, bibliographies, and timelines on African American and global African history. The site offers a wealth of resources, including a list of incidents of street violence involving African Americans.[5]

The first incident listed took place in 1526, a year after Spanish colonizers sent a fleet of six ships to settle a place they called San Miguel de Gualdape, the third Spanish settlement north of Mexico. Carrying approximately one hundred enslaved Africans from previous expeditions, the fleet's main purpose was to supply expeditions charged with capturing Native Americans as slaves.

The flagship sank when it hit a sandbar off the coast of what is now South Carolina. Survivors constructed houses and a church. Suffering from hunger, cold, dysentery, and attacks by Native Americans, some of the Spaniards wanted to return home while others favored waiting for fresh supplies. The enslaved Africans set fire to a building and freed the Native American captives before escaping to live with the local tribe. The San Miguel de Gualdape settlement failed and the surviving settlers returned home. According to Blackpast, this was the first of fourteen slave rebellions recorded in North America.

The Antebellum period was marked by urban riots, including the 1834 "anti-abolition riots that broke out in New York City, with clashes among free-born African Americans, formerly enslaved people, working class white men, and an influx of Irish Catholics. In May and June of that year, the Female Anti-Slavery Society was established, which, according to Blackpast, "roiled the racists in the city. The idea of putting women at the front of the abolition movement offended their sensibilities. By October, the rhetoric reached fever pitch and white, working-class mobs attacked. They broke church windows and stormed the homes of abolitionists, smashing fences and throwing paving stones through the windows. The rioters built a street barricade with wood stolen from a church but they proved no match for the National Guard regiment. The troops took up positions across town and the rioters disbursed within a few days.

In western states, Chinese immigrants were frequent targets of white violence, often coordinated by the Klu Klux Klan. On October 24, 1871, a mob of whites stormed the Chinese enclave in Los Angeles, murdering nineteen immigrants and terrorizing an entire community. We must note the role of class here as inflammatory rhetoric from political leaders stoked resentments among working class whites in a pattern that seems familiar today.[6]

It is indisputable that whites have been responsible for a good deal of racial violence. The recent documentary, *Tulsa Burning: The 1921 Race Massacre*, deals with just one horrific instance. By the 1960s, most urban riots in the United States involved African Americans and their allies protesting police brutality or institutional racism. The 1960s also saw the emergence of the Chicano Movement. César Chávez and the Brown Berets organized boycotts, walkouts, and demonstrations in collaboration with Black activists. Speaking to a predominantly white audience two years after the Watts neighborhood of Los Angeles exploded in riots, Dr. King said, "A riot is the language of the unheard." He asked, "What is it that America has failed to hear?"[7]

The Black Lives Matter Movement was founded in 2013 to bring attention to police murders of unarmed black civilians. The 2020 murder of George Floyd galvanized the organization. As of June 6, 2020, about half-a-million people had participated in protests in 550 cities across America, with events taking place in over 40 percent of the country's counties.[8]

The overwhelming majority of these public demonstrations are nonviolent, with some property damage including looting and arson. According to Princeton's Armed Conflict Location and Event Data project about twenty-five Americans were killed during the 2020 Black Lives Matter protests. Most of them were protesters.[9]

Although large protests have become the public manifestation of racial anger, it also surfaces every day in response to subtle or ambiguous microaggressions such as a bank clerk's disrespect, being asked where you're from, or someone asking to touch your hair. In her magnificent book, *Citizen*, MacArthur Foundation fellow Claudia Rankine describes the experience:[10]

> Certain moments send adrenaline to the heart, dry out the tongue, and clog the lungs. Like thunder they drown you in sound, no, like lightening they strike you across the larynx. Cough. After it happened, I was at a loss for words. Haven't you said this yourself? Haven't you said this to a close friend who early in your friendship, when distracted, would call you by the name of her black housekeeper? You assumed you two were the only black people in her life. Eventually she stopped doing this, though she never acknowledged her slippage. And you never called her on it (why not?) and yet, you don't forget.

It's no wonder that people of color, including those who identified as Asian, African American, Latino, multiracial, and Native American in my survey, were more than twice as likely as whites to describe themselves as "an angry person."

Their responses to incidents that made them angry seem more adaptive than those of white respondents. For instance, people of color were three times more likely to say they express themselves "clearly and maturely" and only half as likely to say they criticized themselves afterward.

Of Life and Time

On an emotional level, mortality's approach can signal a time of reckoning. Vulnerabilities associated with racism come home to roost, as the accumulated stress of a lifetime of microaggressions, disadvantages, and traumas hardens the heart and arteries.

Oppression and hatred take their toll on individuals and the collective. This becomes readily visible when we consider the reduced life-expectancy of marginalized groups in the United States.

At the opening of the twentieth century, life expectancy for white Americans was 47.6 years; for African Americans, 33.0 years. During the century's first six decades, this 14.6-year discrepancy declined steadily. By 1960, it was reduced by half. Whites could expect to live 70.6 years; Blacks, 63.6. Progress slowed during the latter half of the century, and by 2000, whites lived on average 5.5 years longer than Blacks. By 2015 the discrepancy was down to 3.4 years.[11]

Then came COVID. Overall U.S. life expectancy plunged by three years during 2020 and 2021; a drop not been seen in over one hundred years. As we see in Fibure 6.1, no racial group was spared during this two-year period. Whites and Asians seem to have been less affected, with whites losing 2.4 years and Asians, 2.1. Other groups lost considerably more years of life, with Hispanics down 3.8 years; African Americans, four years and Native Americans and Alaskan Natives, 6.6 years.[12]

African American men have long had the nation's shortest life expectancy. M. D. Wong and her colleagues found that cardiovascular disease, particularly hypertension, accounts for 34 percent of the difference between African American men and the general U.S. male population. The next greatest influence is infection, particularly HIV, which accounts for 21 percent. The third root cause is trauma, most notably homicide, which alone accounts for 8.5 percent.[13]

In 2019, The National Academy of Sciences of the United States of America reported that "police violence is a leading cause of death for young men." Black, Native American, and Latino men are most likely to be killed. The risk peaks between 20 and 35 years of age, but Black men of all ages face, what the National Academy describes as "a nontrivial lifetime risk of being killed by police." Based on data from 2013 to 2019, the authors predict that approximately one in 1,000 black men and boys will be killed by police. The year 2020 saw 1,021 fatal police

RACE AND ANGER IN LATER LIFE 61

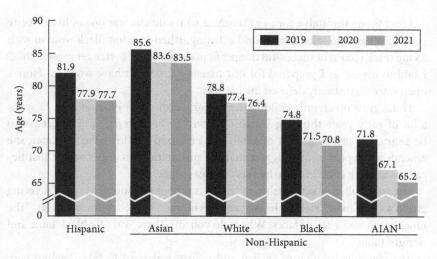

[1] American Indian or Alaska Native

NOTES: Estimates are based on provisional data for 2010. Provisional data are subject to change as additional data are received. Estimates for 2019 and 2020 are based on final data. Life tables by race and Hispanic origin are based on death rates that have been adjusted for race and Hispanic-origin misclassification on death certificates, see technical notes. SOURCE: National Center for Health Statistics, National Vital Statistics System, Mortality.

Figure 6.1. COVID Lowers US Life Expectancy.

shootings. The numbers are still out for 2021, but we know they will be far higher than those of other industrialized democracies.[14]

It can be hard to absorb these numbers. That's why we need to say the names of people who died, and we all need to reach across the divide and have honest conversations about race—a truly difficult task.

The Tiresomeness of It All

In *Sister Outsider*, Audre Lorde writes, "My Black woman's anger is a molten pond at the core of me, my most fiercely guarded secret."[15]

I was delighted when two African American women agreed to meet with me. Fiona and Ruby are radically different women with quite different approaches to anger. At times, I thought some of these differences were generational. Fiona was born into the 1953 post-war boom; Ruby, in 1934 during the depths of the depression. Both were a little uncomfortable speaking to me about their anger. But eventually we got there.

I met Fiona through a former classmate who said she was one of her favorite people. When I googled her I found a distinguished-looking Black woman with a long track record of successful nonprofit management. "Better get presentable," I said to myself as I prepared for our meeting. I needn't have worried. Fiona's open warmth instantly defused my tension.

Fiona grew up an only child in the housing projects of Philadelphia. "I spent a lot of early years thinking I wasn't allowed to be angry. . . kids don't get to be angry. . . I just took a lot of stuff until I realized I didn't have to." Later, she amended her position to suggest that the prohibition on anger wasn't just because she was a child but also because she was a girl.

She got a full-ride scholarship to business school and found herself, "A young girl in a sea of men." Her freshman year was marked by feelings of isolation. "The lunchroom was a sea of faces. Where do you sit? There was one black table and one girl table."

The combined punch of sexism and racism was hard to take. Feeling very unhappy, she spent the weekend with her best friend, who was in college in Massachusetts, just an hour away from her parents' home. When it was time to head back to school, Fiona realized, "I could go back [home] and it would be quiet." Reminding me of Barack Obama's use of the term, Fiona describes this as an "inflection point." She said, "I wanted to go home, but I felt angry at myself for that. Then I thought, I'm not going to be driven away from everything I want in life. I am not allowing this to happen. No one can treat me this way."

At first, we danced around the topic of anger. "I don't spend a lot of time angry—more brief annoyances. . . I'm not speaking for all people of color. . . You know, [but] people want to touch your hair."

Fiona spoke about prohibitions on women's anger and how useless it is to get angry about things you can't control. When she had issues with her bank's security protocols, a friend told her to change banks, but she replied, "They're all scum." Fiona remembers being treated with suspicion when she was twenty-three years old, "bringing in my paychecks to deposit." It wasn't until much later that she realized what was going on: "They treat people of color with suspicion."

Now that she's older, people patronize her. "I try not to get angry. This happened when I was trying to get Medicare sorted out, and the woman I was talking to didn't answer my questions. She just said the same thing over and over only more slowly. Like I was dumb."

She does enjoy some privileges of age. Riding mass transit to work each day, she says, "I don't put up with anything. I'll play the age card, 'Oh no you don't young man.'"

When I ask about historical trauma, she replies, "It does make some people angry. But it's tiresome. It can eat you up inside. It takes up bandwidth . . . The tiresome part is having to wonder, 'Why am I being treated this way?' There is a certain level of gaslighting about being told the person probably didn't mean what s/he said, or you misinterpreted what they said, and hearing this again and again."

Recent coverage of the country's abysmal statistics on Black maternal deaths led Fiona to reflect on her own experiences. "It was like a light went off," she says. Her first birth, in New York, was wonderful; the second, in California, dreadful.

There were red flags at the outset when her obstetrician didn't want to wait for Fiona's husband to arrive for their first appointment. Then, she told Fiona not to gain any weight. When she was due, the physician wanted to use Pitocin to induce labor. Fiona was reluctant, having read that it has serious side effects and wanted to consider an alternative approach. The doctor refused to listen and insisted on using the drug. "But if you go through life, there are layers and layers of interactions—all that second guessing. At the time, I just thought she was a jerk." When she complained to her primary care doctor, she was scolded, "Why are you always complaining?"

"I never thought it was due to race." But then she remembered that her wonderful doctor in New York was Black. "That's the tiresomeness of it. You don't know. Is this OK? Should I take this? Accept this? I don't want to waste my time on it. It's not productive."

Fiona recognizes that not every interaction is defined by race. "But some clearly are and those are often denied when pointed out." She doesn't like the word "racism" because it reduces people to categories, erasing their individuality. But she will speak up if someone says something offensive or inappropriate. "And the response is almost always, 'That person isn't a racist. Saying something offensive doesn't necessarily make one a racist.' But it's still offensive."

We talked about code switching and how people from the majority culture get to choose when they want to enter into a minority culture. People of color don't. They are almost constantly immersed in White culture, where they can be subjected to microaggressions, hostility, and violence just for being themselves. Remembering an African American friend who told me she didn't feel safe walking alone in the post-Trump era, I ask Fiona whether she feels safe on the streets. "Yeah," she says. "I put on my resting bitch face."

Fiona refuses to use tears. "That doesn't work for black women." This helped me better understand the acerbic chapter called, "White-Girl Tears" in Brittney Cooper's book, *Eloquent Rage: A black feminist discovers her superpower*. It emphasizes how white-girl tears draw attention like a magnet, while black-girl tears are usually ignored or disparaged.

Fiona says she has grown less angry with age. "Because I've gained more power and authority as I aged. I've had far fewer situations where things were done or said to me that were infuriating." At the same time, she has come to appreciate the value of anger. "Anger can be helpful, clarifying. It alerts you that something's wrong." I wonder whether she's read the latest research, when she notes that "The pressure to suppress it is unhealthy." Fiona argues that while "uncontrolled anger can be bad... I think it's more unhealthy to never be angry."

A Legacy for the Grandchildren

A friend who had worked with Ruby on the Poor People's Campaign suggested that we talk. It was hard to pin Ruby down. She had a lot going on. We chose a date two months out, but her Internet was down. So we tried again. And again. Finally, Ruby came up on my screen: a petite eighty-seven-year-old African American woman in wire-rimmed glasses who radiated enthusiasm. Ruby's hands flutter gracefully as she speaks and she has a lot to say.

Before our conversation, she was busy preparing a presentation about her college thesis project. "It has always bothered me that African American women who worked at the grassroots level of the civil rights movement have received no recognition. Celebrities received awards and acknowledgement, but not these women. I knew them in New York. I protested in the civil rights movement. I've researched them."

Ruby interviews these women, all close to her age. She videotapes the interviews and makes them available via a website. She also organizes and records a series of panels where they meet with younger women. "This will help the young to understand and the older women to continue....Black women are the foundation of this country.... This will be a legacy for their grandchildren."

Ruby's story gave me the opportunity to learn about the role black enclaves played in late nineteenth- and early twentieth-century America. Like most major cities in the North, Chicago received a large influx of former slaves when the Civil War ended. Then, during "The Great Migration," from 1916 to 1970, over six million African Americans left the rural South and relocated to urban centers like Chicago. During the Jim Crow era, cities and states outside the South passed laws mandating racial segregation.

As a result, black enclaves like Bronzeville (Chicago), Harlem (New York), Little Africa (Louisville), The Greenwood District (Tulsa), Ransom Place (Indianapolis), and the Strivers' Section (Washington, DC) flourished. These were bustling urban communities where African Americans owned businesses, ran churches and schools, and held political office. Class differences endured, with those on relief struggling to feed their children and others growing rich. Figure 6.2 offers an image of a Bronzeville street in this era.

In 2021, Michelle R. Boyd, Assistant Professor of African American Studies at University of Illinois at Chicago published a fascinating book called, *Jim Crow*

Figure 6.2. Regal Theater and Savoy Ballroom in Bronzeville, Chicago, IL, 1941. Farm Security Administration—Office of War Information Photograph Collection, Library of Congress.

Nostalgia. She examines the history and politics of Bronzeville, "a racial refuge, an independent island to which African-Americans had retreated to attend to their economic, social, and political needs."[16] In the context of legal segregation, Blacks created a haven where they could avoid encounters with white supremacy. This "authentic, successful expression of blackness" might have stayed intact but for integration.

Ruby was the fifteenth of sixteen kids but has no recollection of doing without. Her Dad worked as a butcher for one of the nation's leading meat-packing firms. "He received threats for his work against the union. They didn't bother him. He had a strong moral compass." Of her mother, she says, "Mom was emphatic about us dressing well." Even today, Ruby makes a point of dressing carefully. "We never ran into prejudice. . . . Dad took us wherever he wanted . . . symphony concerts, the civic opera house, museums . . . we lived in them."

Ruby started elementary school as the nation emerged from the Depression in the 1940s. Hers was just one of many African American families moving into the middle-class. When integration finally arrived, they moved to "nice middle-class" (white) neighborhoods.

Anger Builds Character

Unfairness was a major theme in our conversation. Ruby has a clear rationale for her advocacy on behalf of others. "If it's happening to someone else it could happen to me." She remembers an incident when a friend of hers was being bullied by six girls. "She had fair skin, almost white." Ruby stood in front of her friend and said, "You are not going to bully my friend or I will bring my brothers." That was enough to discourage them. "Things came up and I couldn't stand back and not be involved."

Both Ruby and her brother faced racial discrimination when they joined the military. Ruby's brother joined the army during World War II and was sent south for training. He confronted so much prejudice and bigotry that he repeatedly went AWOL (i.e., absent without leave). Eventually he was shipped overseas. Insisting that "He didn't want to kill for a country that didn't respect him," he spent most of his tour of duty in confinement.

Ruby followed in his tracks and joined the service. Her Commanding Officer was "a bigot" who took an instant dislike to Ruby, subjecting her to discipline for minor infractions for which white cadets were never penalized.

Her time in the army exposed Ruby to personal violence. "[A] Black man assaulted me and I didn't let him get away with it. I turned him over to the MPs [military police]. MP said report wouldn't do anything and I said, 'file the report anyway.'"

This wasn't Ruby's only experience with violence. Later, when she lived in New York, "I was criminally attacked four times." Random crimes, she says. Then her fourteen-year-old niece went missing for three months and was found shot and cemented into a bathtub. Three of her nephews were shot that same year.

When she was told that her daughters couldn't attend the New York public school of her choice, Ruby went on the warpath. "When the Board of Education said I had to send them to another school, I said, 'No. I want a hearing, I want a variance.'" At the end of the hearing, the Board still said no, it was against policy. "But," said Ruby, "Policy is flexible. My daughters' education is important. Work with me. I'm a taxpayer. I'm asking you nicely." Ruby was angry, but she knew she had to control it in order to accomplish anything. "People don't listen when you show anger." Later, Ruby experienced backlash from other Black people for sending her children to predominantly white schools.

Ruby's struggles with the school board didn't end there. The schools in her "nice middle-class neighborhood" in Queens "weren't up to snuff," so she went to a lawyer. "They recommended mediation but I said, 'This is not about winning. It's about calling attention to the problem.'"

"There is always a fight. You get tired of fighting for equality and now we have to fight drugs," Ruby says, recalling an incident in which a drug dealer shot a child in the park where Ruby and other mothers took their children. "We got really angry and organized a protest in the park and at the police department." Things got better for a while, but when conditions deteriorated again, the mothers organized a protest at the community center. "One day the Black Panthers called me and said, 'We aren't asking you. We're telling you. We are going to protect you.' And they did. For the two days of the sit-in and after that they left someone around to watch over things."

Eventually, the city was just too much for Ruby. She and her husband moved west. Ruby felt her anger was out of control, and she sought counselling at the Wisconsin Veterans Administration, where she was told she had post-traumatic stress disorder (PTSD).

A few days after our first interview, Ruby sent me an e-mail. There was something she hadn't told me, she said. She had some concerns about privacy, so we agreed on additional measures to disguise her identity.

Ruby explained that after her husband died, she moved back to Chicago. Then she got a call from Atlanta. A social worker said her nine-year-old granddaughter was in a children's shelter. The child's mother had been sexually assaulted and was in the hospital.

Ruby decided the first order of business was getting her granddaughter out of the shelter. Her daughter wrote a letter authorizing Ruby to assume custody, but the child was a ward of the state. At a hearing, the judge told Ruby it would take thirty days to get her granddaughter out of the shelter. Ruby said, "Uh oh. That's not going to happen here. Not with me. What's my alternative?" The judge told her she would have to pay for a social worker to travel from Atlanta to Chicago to complete an assessment of her home. "I'll do it." Ruby said, "but I want my granddaughter released immediately." She explains, "I was afraid of the residual effects of what she knew her mother went through. I had to get her out of there."

"All through this process whatever anger I had, and believe me there was a lot, I still had to focus ... I had to shut down and focus on what I had to do." Ruby and her granddaughter moved in with her daughter for a while. The judge who made her pay for the social worker was eventually sanctioned. "That made us feel a little bit better. When you're going through all this you're looking for a little bit of sunshine."

Ruby's granddaughter is doing great now. She recently got her real estate license and her mother is going to law school. "I am so proud of these two women. I am so happy they are utilizing their talents even with all the challenges they've had. They are the winners here."

Though Ruby brims with hope for her country,[17] she found herself crying all the time after the 2020 election. "About COVID; about the killing of black children." She wasn't very hopeful about Biden, but then she noticed that "black and brown people were being appointed."

68 AGING ANGER

Ruby added, "Doesn't mean they'll do right.
I replied, "But at least they're there."
"Thank you."

These days, Ruby uses exercise to control her anger. She had surgery on her knees and her recovery involved long walks. "I go up hills and I breathe differently. It's almost cleansing. I felt on a high." When she gets angry, Ruby always follows the same formula: "Sit down, clear my head, and focus on what needs to be done."

7
Elders on Social Media

> Up! Up! My friend and quit your books;
> Or surely you'll grow double:
> Up! Up! My friend, and clear your looks;
> Why all this toil and trouble?
> —William Wordsworth, *The Tables Turned*[1]

The indomitable Mike Tyson is said to have commented, "Social media made y'all way too comfortable with disrespecting people and not getting punched in the face for it."[2] Seems he might have been right.

During the first COVID-19 lockdown I spent way too much time on social media. One day, in a fit of mindless browsing, I noticed the #OKBoomer hashtag trending. My adrenal glands pumped out their intoxicating stimulants and my heart pounded as I read post after post of inflammatory garbage directed at older adults.

I don't care if they all die of COVID. %*$&^ boomers grew up with a great economy and now they expect us to take the crap jobs they've left behind. #OKBoomers, give it up.

#OKBoomers, you're just going to die anyway. Shut up about it!

Somebody get grandpa off the Internet. It's past his bedtime. Change his Depends give him his Geritol and tuck him in for the night.

#OKBoomers, you ruin our planet and wreck the economy and now you expect us to pay for your Social Security? Give me a break. No more funds for old fogey welfare!

That last one really sucked me in. These presumably young people had a lot to be angry about and they'd found a convenient scapegoat in seniors. Some seemed to genuinely believe that older adults had enjoyed booming economies throughout our lives and didn't give a damn about their future. Hadn't they ever heard of stagflation? How about the Viet Nam war? Or grandparenthood? Quivering with irritation, I wrote:

All this bitterness coming at baby boomers. It's like we're the target of the month. Has anyone considered whether these #OKBoomer and #BoomerRemover

Aging Angry. Amanda Smith Barusch, Oxford University Press. © Oxford University Press 2024.
DOI: 10.1093/oso/9780197584644.003.0007

posts are being promoted by someone who wants to sow division in America? I think @Oldplparecool and you'll be one soon.

The first reply was dismissive: *OKBoomer*. A lot of people responded this way. But others responded to the substance of my comment. For the next hour of manic keyboarding, I felt more engaged than I had in a long time. Ideas and exclamation marks flew. *If we can't blame the boomers, who can we blame? How did we get in this mess? Blame the rich! Blame the Republicans! Blame the oil companies! Class warfare, not generational warfare!*

Two years later, when I scrolled back to find them, the most outrageous posts and some of the more vitriolic expressions were gone; some deleted by the user, others by Twitter. But the ideas are still circulating.

The Rage Contagion

The Internet can be a very angry place.[3] In 2018, researcher Rui Fan and her colleagues from Beihang University[4] reported on a study they completed with funding from the National Natural Science Foundation of China. These researchers reviewed over eleven million tweets posted by approximately 100,000 users on Weibo (a Chinese version of Twitter) over the course of six months. They found that angry tweets spread faster and further than tweets of joy, particularly when the ties between users were weak—that is, when users did not have high numbers of mutual friends, a history of reciprocal interactions, or a tendency to retweet each other's posts. They confirmed their findings through modeling on a separate set of over forty million tweets. This led them to conclude that, at least in Chinese social media, "Anger is the most contagious emotion."

There's good reason to believe that this dynamic also holds in the United States. With grants from the National Science Foundation and the Democracy Fund, William Brady, a psychology post-doc at Yale University and Professor Molly J. Crockett used machine learning software to analyze nearly thirteen million tweets from 7,331 Twitter users in the United States. They trained their system to recognize tweets expressing outrage and monitored user responses to the Brett Kavanaugh confirmation hearings (October 2018) and a United Airlines Passenger Mistreatment event (April 2017).

Brady and Crockett learned that expressions of outrage were "rewarded by the *basic design* of social media." (italics mine). Angry tweets received more likes and shares not because people enjoy the anger, but because the business model optimizes engagement with no concern for its social and emotional consequences. As they explain, "social media platforms do not merely reflect what is happening in society. Platforms create incentives that change how users react to political events over time."[5]

How does this work? In his 2020 article, "Angry by Design," Luke Munn, of New Zealand's Digital Cultures Institute, explains the design elements that foster what he calls "toxic communication" on Facebook and YouTube.[6]

In diverse venues, including congressional hearings, Facebook designers have admitted that their systems can be addictive and that they "exploit negative triggers." A mysterious algorithm determines how posts are presented to each viewer on their home page, placing some posts at the top while others require the user to scroll way down. The system privileges impulsive communication and distributes negative messages "farther and faster" than other missives. Experts agree that engagement is the key and that incendiary posts consistently have high engagement. They provoke us and we instantly react. The system does not include measures that encourage reflection or civility, such as enforced delays of a few seconds or automatic messages asking, "Are you sure?" or even the use of moderators to discourage untrue, divisive, or rude posts.

Faced with severe criticism, in 2018 Facebook expanded its modest effort to regulate content, adding approximately 10,000 workers to the "trust and safety team." According to Munn, the toll on these workers was "incredibly high," with severe performance pressure exacerbating the negative effects of reading volumes of hate speech and racist epithets.

With over two billion users per month, YouTube is aptly described as "a juggernaut of online spaces."[7] Like Facebook, YouTube uses an undisclosed algorithm to determine what videos are displayed to a particular user. Because the business model focuses on the amount of time users spend on the site, recommendations must quickly capture our attention. The site has a thumbs up/thumbs down comment system, but it prioritizes videos with comments, regardless of which way they go, who made them, or whether they are flippant, hostile, or vitriolic.

Anger attracts our attention. We are hardwired to notice and respond to it quickly. That's why anger management experts emphasize the need to pause before responding to something that makes us angry. But social media doesn't allow for that. Algorithms focus almost exclusively on engagement. That's what pays the rent. The companies that profit from offering these media experiences have no compunction to moderate the nature of the content or to slow the speed of our response. The result is a system that promotes anger among billions of humans, including growing numbers of older adults, across the globe.

Cyberspace for Rants

Anger has become so pervasive on the Internet that entire websites, known as "rant-sites" are set up to allow people to vent in a practice known as "cyberranting." People post on these sites anonymously about a person or event that has angered them.

These are not your typical Internet users. A study on the denizens of rant sites found that about a third of them believe they have anger problems, and almost half have been *told* they do. The group was combative, reporting that they experienced about one physical and more than two verbal fights each month.[8]

Ryan Martin, a psychology professor at the University of Wisconsin, found twenty such sites via Google. My own search took me to Rantrampage.com. I didn't stay there long. As Martin and his colleagues reported in 2013, the amount of hate speech and obscenity leaves a bad taste.

Martin and his team were interested in studying the effects of venting. Noting that catharsis is often used as a treatment for anger issues, they suspected venting might be a "healthy approach to anger reduction."[9] They conducted an online survey of people who use rant sites. Respondents reported that one attraction was having others comment on their rants, validating how they feel. They also reported that they read posts for curiosity, entertainment, a sense of community, and feeling better about their own lives in comparison to others. All thirty-two respondents reported feeling calm and relaxed after posting a rant.

In a second study, Martin and his team recruited ninety-one undergraduates who did not use rant sites and asked them to read rant posts for five minutes and then write a rant. They found that reading and writing rants *increased* participants' anger and decreased their happiness. They concluded that online venting may not be the most effective approach to anger management.

A Duty to Die?

Maria Jimenez-Sotomayor and her colleagues from the Instituto Nacional de Ciencias Medicas y Nutricion, published an article in 2020 based on their analysis of 18,128 tweets posted in March 2020. They found 22 percent were "intended to ridicule or offend" older adults and another 21 percent had "content implying that the life of older adults was less valuable."[10] No wonder Professor Brad Meisner, of York University, suggests that intergenerational tensions on social media are in "a state of emergency."[11]

Young people have chafed against their seniors since time immemorial. But only since the late twentieth century has ageism become a socially acceptable prejudice.[12] In the 1980s and 1990s, with funding from banks, stockbrokers, and others in the financial sector, the Concord Coalition and Americans for Generational Equity (AGE) argued that, due to the lobbying efforts of "greedy geezers," entitlements such as Social Security and Medicare would bankrupt the country leaving nothing for the young.[13] Some, like Colorado Governor Richard Lamm, went so far as to suggest that older adults have a "duty to die and get out of the way to let the other society, our kids, build a reasonable life."[14]

The pandemic worsened ageist discourse and intergenerational tensions, particularly on social media, where older adults were already portrayed as undesirable and expendable. Names for COVID-19, such as "Boomer Remover," "Senior Deleter," and "Elder Repeller," appeared in posts and tweets that emphasize a new role for the virus: cleansing the human population of older adults. The advantages of such a purge are clear to some. It might reduce the number of conservative voters, lower the tax burden associated with Social Security and Medicare, and free up jobs and housing for the young. Thus, older adults come to be seen as "surplus to requirements."

Some U.S. politicians insist that older adults are a social and economic liability. In March and April of 2020, Texas Lieutenant Governor Dan Patrick argued on Fox News that grandparents should be willing to die in order to prevent lockdowns and protect the economy for the young. He said he was willing, but no one took him up on it.[15]

Government measures taken at the height of the pandemic, ostensibly to protect older adults, may have contributed to intergenerational tensions and distancing. Canada, for example, promoted messages that discouraged contact with older adults. The World Health Organization urged those sixty years of age and older to avoid places where they might interact with people who could transmit the virus (aka everyone, everywhere). And most developed countries prioritized older adults in vaccination programs. This public health messaging homogenizes older adults, even as it fans the flame of ageist resentment.

In essence, governments conflated age with illness, despite the emerging recognition that underlying health conditions are more powerful predictors of health outcomes. They did this in part because age is much easier to measure than more complex factors such as health conditions, comorbidity, and lifestyle.

During intense COVID-19 surges, some seniors were denied care. Nursing home residents were refused treatment while politicians and the public looked the other way. In September 2021, the Delta variant raged through Idaho, filling intensive-care unit (ICU) beds beyond capacity. State public health officials asked leaders to allow hospitals to move to "crisis standards of care," which meant allocating ICU beds to those deemed most likely to survive. This likelihood is in part based on "long-term life expectancy," a measure that declines with age. The U.S. Department of Health and Human Services (HHS) Office for Civil Rights deems the use of long-term life expectancy to ration care a form of age discrimination. HHS fielded numerous complaints and sanctioned several states for use of long- rather than short-term survival as a factor in allocating care.

Although most health officials are reluctant to publicly announce their triage criteria, you can bet that older adults are among the first to be denied beds. Margaret Morganroth Gullette calls this willingness to allow seniors to die in times of crisis a "crime against humanity."[16] It certainly doesn't inspire confidence among older adults facing serious illness.

Seniors Trapped in YouTube

In 2017, South Korea's Conservative President, Park Geun-hye was officially removed from office following her impeachment. She was South Korea's first woman president and the daughter of Park Chung-hee, the politician and army general who led the country from 1961 until his assassination in 1979. Although he was an authoritarian leader, with little respect for human rights, the country's economy flourished under his administration, seeing one of the fastest drops in poverty ever recorded (from 66.9% in 1961 to 11.2% in 1979). In light of this economic growth, he enjoyed considerably popularity, especially during the 1960s.

His daughter was convicted on a string of charges related to influence peddling and abuse of power. She was fined about $17 million and sentenced to twenty-four years in jail. When she left office, the country was deeply divided. While some protested in the streets against her administration others gathered outside the courtroom in tears.[17]

Older adults, possibly remembering the economic security brought on by Park's father, generally opposed her removal. Militants among them, who came to be known as the *Taegukgi Squad,* organized aggressive street protests to seek Park's reinstatement. For a few days, they even occupied the Korean parliament.

Then came COVID-19 and the country went into a strict lockdown. The Taegukgi Squad, now known as an "Army," was not to be deterred. Ninety percent of Korea's seniors had Internet access, but few were active online. During lockdown, the right-wing militants moved their efforts onto social media platforms such as YouTube and Kakao Talk, a local version of Facebook, learning to manipulate trending hashtags and take over a space that had been a province of the young.

The backlash was swift and furious. Newspapers suggested that sweet old people had been turned into angry deluded digital soldiers. Stories with headlines like, "Elders Trapped Inside the YouTube World" claimed that older people could not distinguish fake news from true events, that they were digitally naïve and functionally illiterate. In essence, they had no business expressing their views online. Some thought they should be cut off from the Internet for their own good. Some demanded removal of their voting rights.

In April of 2020, June Oh, an interdisciplinary scholar from South Korea interrupted her PhD studies in English at Michigan State University to fly into this maelstrom. She submitted a paper on "Angry Digital Silver in the Pandemic" to the 2020 conference of the North American Network on Aging Studies

(NANAS). Luckily, the conference was held virtually, and I was able to watch her presentation. I immediately wrote to her, and we scheduled a Zoom meeting. June was appalled by the treatment of seniors in her country. Authorities asked them not to congregate, in person or digital spaces, because they were considered "virus spreaders"; a source of pollution to both virtual and physical realities. Some of the older adults in June's family participated in Taegukgi protests. This triggered hot family controversy, and the topic of the protests became taboo at the dinner table.

Meanwhile, Back in the U.S.A.

The PEW Research Center tracks Internet access by older adults in the United States, noting that they are rapidly catching up with the young. In 2000, only 14 percent of those aged sixty-five and older were online. By 2021 that figure had grown to 75 percent, though the oldest of older adults are still less likely to be found online.[18]

Social media use has also risen dramatically in the twenty-first century. Facebook led the way and young adults were the first to sign on. But seniors are catching up fast. In 2005, only 5 percent of American adults sixty-five and older reported using a social media platform. By 2021, some 50 percent of older Americans were using Facebook. By 2022, Pew reported that 73 percent of those aged fifty to sixty-four used social media sites, compared to 45 percent of those aged sixty-five and over. Even eighty- and ninety-year-olds can occasionally be found on Facebook, Twitter, and YouTube.[19]

Duration of use represents one key difference between seniors and young adults. Only 8 percent of those sixty-five and over report being "almost constantly" online, compared to 48 percent of those aged eighteen to twenty-nine years.[20] Clearly, maturity confers some advantage!

The Anger Project Online

Realizing that I was spending more time than I should on Facebook during the pandemic, I speculated that others might be doing the same. So I set up a page for The Anger Project in hope of generating discussion and recruiting people for interviews.

For my first boosted post, I used an image of a fist, and text opening with, "We want to know what makes you angry." (see Figure 7.1.) The post reached 342 people and generated a brief but interesting conversation about the media. Mary wrote, *Everybody is trying so hard to get along with each other and the media*

76 AGING ANGRY

Figure 7.1. "What makes you angry" post from The Anger Project, April 8, 2021.

doesn't help a bit. It just aggravates us. A few others, apparently young women, chimed in to agree that *enragement = engagement*.

My second post was titled, "Anger in Love," is presented in Figure 7.2.

This boosted post reached 605 people and yielded thirteen comments, all from users with feminine names. Ruthie opened the conversation: *When you throw an egg against a wall and break it, can you put it back together? So it is with words spoken in anger, you can say I'm sorry, but you cannot heal the hurt it caused initially, like it never happened.* She also posted, *Always take a few seconds to breathe before you speak in anger.* Ruthie almost seemed to be speaking to herself.

ELDERS ON SOCIAL MEDIA   77

Figure 7.2. "Anger in Love" post from The Anger Project, April 15, 2021.

Rhoda chimed in to shift the focus. *I totally agree. They say stuff to you when they are angry, but they say sorry afterwards. I believe when they say that stuff, they believe it is true, But I proved mine wrong.* No one asked who "they" were, though we might assume that Rhoda proved her lover wrong.

Minnie offered a *100% Cute* image and Marilyn wrote *Love conquers all!!!?* Adding multiple heart emojis and a panda valentine. That closing question mark indicates Marilyn may not be entirely sure about her comment. Hoping to keep things going, I added *Ah! I hope you're right. Sometimes it's hard when love and anger get together.* This triggered a flood of love images and emojis followed by Catherine's *awwww*, Irene's *ADORABLE*, and Minnie's *Ohhh how cute*.

My first post in the Anger Project revealed at least a few users aware of the role media plays in promoting anger. My second post generated advice on anger suppression and ringing endorsements for the power of love. No one mentioned that anger might signal a need for change, and no one suggested that a lover's anger might be legitimate.

Later, several of the older adults I interviewed described social media, primarily Facebook, as both a source of irritation and an outlet for their anger. Some respondents, like eighty-nine-year-old Gianna cope with their anger by venting on Facebook. Gianna says she is more active than most of her peers, using Facebook to express her "terrible" anger regarding political developments in the United States. Likewise, sixty-seven-year-old Dinah spends a good deal of time on Facebook where, as she puts it, "discussions can get a little sparky." Her partner doesn't understand why she bothers, but Dinah says, "It's because I am angry. I have to stand up! Besides, maybe it will move the needle." Seventy-three-year-old Esme went to Facebook to better understand Trump supporters. She watched pro-MAGA videos and engaged in discussions but found it only aggravated her further. Fifty-nine-year-old Kellie Ann shared a cringeworthy experience I imagine many have had. Angry at something a friend posted, she brutally clicked the unfriend button, only to regret her decision. Kellie Ann sent an apologetic note with her re-friend request.

Around the world, older adults who venture onto social media do not always find an age-friendly environment. But we do find opportunities to connect with family and friends, access services and information, and engage in public discourse from the comfort of our homes. For most, the benefits are well worth the cost. Research offers tantalizing evidence that participating on social media can reduce loneliness and depression among older adults by providing opportunities to keep in touch with distant family members and engage with those who share our interests.[21] Recent studies even suggest that it may improve mental health and enhance some cognitive functions.[22]

I wouldn't want to do it every day, but my brief foray into online intergenerational conflict was invigorating. I had a message to share and, like Dinah, imagined I might, in some small way, move the needle. Perhaps, as our numbers grow, American seniors might, like the Taegukgi Squad, appropriate social media for our own goals.

8
Lessons on Anger and Love

> Lovers' quarrels are love's renewal.
> —Terence, *The Lady of Andros*[1]

My future husband stormed out of our tiny second-floor apartment. As the door slammed behind him, my wedding plans drifted off into a void. I couldn't marry this jerk. I couldn't live with him for another minute. I paced the quiet apartment, muttering obscenities that would make a shoreman blush. How on earth had we reached such an impasse?

We lived on a tropical island and were avid scuba divers. Saltwater left my hair a crackling mess. When I took off my mask at the end of each dive, I inevitably had to pull out strands of hair that were tangled in its straps. So, after work one day, I had it cut short. It didn't even occur to me that Larry would care. But then, he came home.

"How could you?" he shouted.

It was a rhetorical question, but I didn't care.

"It wasn't hard. I just made the appointment and went in." How could a Harvard-educated man be so irrational?

I didn't know how to fight fair. I had no idea how to fight at all. My parents never fought. They just divorced.

Larry's parents quibbled on a daily basis—*in front of everyone*. But they managed to stay together. I wanted what they had. But, in order to get it, I'd have to learn how anger and love can coexist.

Homes Full of Anger

Wayne grew up in a home full of anger. His mother vented her irritations by pounding on him. "This was the 60s—70s. Mom was frustrated and didn't want to be a housewife." Her abuse continued until Wayne was about fifteen years old. "One day she was about to hit me. I just did this [he raises his arms and demonstrates how he grabbed her wrists]. I stopped her hard and said, 'I don't want to be treated like that.'" Wayne's father, also prone to unpredictable

Aging Angry. Amanda Smith Barusch, Oxford University Press. © Oxford University Press 2024.
DOI: 10.1093/oso/9780197584644.003.0008

outbursts and physical punishment, just turned to him and said, "Don't hit your mom."

Wayne expresses a grudging admiration for his dad's intervention. "He took care of both of us." He says his mother tried to contain herself after that. "Anger," he says, shaking his head, "that's complicated."

Wayne uses the phrase "bitter angry" to describe the frustrations he carried through the eighteen-year "one-way relationship" with his now-ex-wife. They never fought. They didn't even really talk. For one thing, there was no time. They had two kids—a girl and a boy. Wayne was busy establishing his construction firm. His wife worked as an X-ray technician and played pool to supplement their income. When she lost her job, she became a professional pool player. Wayne would have preferred a different strategy.

"Let's stop using credit cards," he suggested.

But his wife wasn't listening.

Looking back, he realizes she was probably unfaithful. When she told him he could be replaced, Wayne left and never went back.

At seventy-one, Wayne is tall and athletic with salt and pepper hair and a ready smile. His construction firm is well-established, and he is in a relationship with a very different kind of woman. "She's so even-keeled." His calm new wife changed him. "I listen a lot better now. Don't say much. I've learned not to respond too quickly. Not to try to fix everything.... This comes with age."

Wayne's right. Better control is part of the emotional intelligence that can come with age. His wife's calm responsiveness probably also allows the space for him to think more clearly.

These days, when he confronts anger, his own or that of a loved one, Wayne's first thought is, "Where is this going?" He considers the other person's needs and moderates his response to maintain the relationship. When anger sparks, he thinks his way through it, careful to say the right thing.

Wayne's choice to focus on relationship is common among older adults. In their study of Americans aged thirteen to ninety-nine (also mentioned in Chapter 6) Kira Birditt and Karen Fingerman report that young people are more likely to report using "exit" strategies (like yelling) when they are angry, while older adults tend to use "loyalty" strategies (like avoidance).[2]

Another study emphasizes the importance of problem-solving skills and warmth for managing late-life relationship conflicts. Leah Williams of Auburn University examined the conflict resolution strategies used by sixty-four couples in their seventies who reported moderate-to-high marital satisfaction. During two to three visits to her Auburn University research facility, couples were observed while they identified and discussed ways to solve one of the biggest problems in their relationship. Later, each member of the couple filled out a survey about their life and marital satisfaction.

The couples' methods ranged from open disagreement to flat out denial. Most (57%) showed strong problem-solving ability and considerable warmth in their discussions. But a small minority (13%) were low on both warmth and problem-solving abilities. These couples were significantly less satisfied, underscoring the importance of both traits.[3]

"There's anger and then there's love." Wayne says, explaining that in his view the two do not go together.

A few weeks after we met, I had one of those epiphanies you only get in the shower. As Wayne's words echoed in my head, I realized that he and I shared a belief that anger cancelled out love. I have since come to see this belief as a key source of tension in many marriages.

At fifty years old Tim exudes a powerfully masculine force. His rapid-fire speech, coupled with piercing blue eyes, red hair, and a square jaw remind me of a football coach. But Tim is a therapist.

Like Wayne, Tim was abused as a child. In his case, it was generational. His dad hit him, just as his grandfather had hit his dad. The abuse created a siege mentality, with Tim constantly on the lookout for threats of violence. He says he still gets scared when people are angry with him. But he doesn't show it.

By the time Tim turned fifteen he was bigger than his dad and able to put a stop to the abuse. Now it was his turn to dish it out. "In high school I was probably a bully. I was an angry kid. Football player. One kid said I was on steroids and I just beat the crap out of him. I was angry at the world, but good at sports. I was that bad guy."

Now, Tim says, "I'm a much more mellow guy." He works with domestic violence offenders, most of them successful men, teaching them "to recognize precursors and redirect their energy; avoid situations that make them angry, like fights after a long day at work. Look at where they learned anger." He also brings this attitude to his home life. "I am very patient with my kids," he says, telling me he would never hit them.

Tim describes some of his older clients as "Angry old men with internalized self-loathing and regrets." He says one of his clients "just seethes in unfairness. The whole world is against him. He's tough to be around. So isolated. Substance abuse issues. He's in the 11th hour still hoping for a change." Tim was determined not to age into that kind of man. Sadly, he died suddenly a few months after our interview.

A Panoply of Family Anger

Families can be exasperating. The Mills Brothers knew it when they wrote their 1948 hit song, "You Always Hurt the One You Love." Yet it is at home that we have a chance to learn how to hold both love and anger in our hearts at the same time.

I called my survey, "Understanding Anger," but it might as well have been called "Understanding Families." Family and friends were the number one source of anger for the people who completed the Internet survey. The only thing that came close was road rage. (These results are summarized in Table A8, Appendix 1, p. 149)

Aristotle would not have been surprised. In *Rhetoric*, he wrote that we get angrier with *philoi* (family and friends) than with relative strangers because, as Columbia University professor William V. Harris explains, we think our loved ones have obligations towards us.[4]

Joseph Keeping, a philosophy professor at York University, developed a similar argument. In his 2006 phenomenological analysis of *King Lear*, he suggests that Lear's fury with his two daughters arose because, "anger is the intuition not merely of a wrong, but . . . of a wrong which is at once a violation of expectations. Anger occurs when we conceive a wrong as a wrong that *ought not to have happened*" [p. 478, italics in the original].[5]

Each family's anger is unique, as is their ability to make constructive use of it. Still, patterns emerge. Let's look at some common themes in family anger.

The Lovers' Quarrel

The Urban Dictionary defines a lovers' quarrel as "When two lovers, sometimes of the same sex, get into a heated tiff over something petty, usually concluded with steamy intimacy."

The Greek gods can be surprisingly human. Zeus and Hera were an especially quarrelsome couple. Their whole marriage started on a bad note when Zeus ravished Hera and she married him to avoid the shame. When Zeus went around siring children with other gods and humans, Hera could hardly help being jealous. Unlike most of us, Zeus and Hera were in it for eternity, which must have added a note of desperation to their squabbles. As Harris points out, "The whole Iliad is an angry struggle between wife and husband."[6]

Among mortals, Medea and Jason's lovers' quarrel was especially brutal. As Ovid tells the story, Medea was a gifted sorceress who fell in love with Jason at first sight. Jason had heard of Medea's magic and begged her to use her skills to help him in his quest for the golden fleece. In exchange, he promised to make her his wife. With numerous magical interventions by Medea, Jason slipped away with the golden fleece and without a scratch.

Medea continued to help Jason throughout their marriage, restoring his father to youth and murdering the king who refused to cede his throne to Jason. For a good many years they lived together in Corinth, and she bore him seven children. The reasons for Jason's ultimate betrayal are lost in the fogs of mythology. All we know is that he abandoned Medea to marry a king's daughter.[7]

One can only imagine Medea's rage. In her fury, she poisoned his new bride and the bride's father for good measure. Then, she "steeped her sword in the blood of her children," murdering every single one.

Myths and legends stand the test of time because they capture complex truths. They expand our emotional lexicon, contributing words, images, and metaphors that enable us to label and describe our own experiences. They can help break the silence on difficult topics, like passion and hatred. On a somewhat moralistic level, they alert us to the dangers of anger and to a view some of us share with the ancient Greeks: that women's anger can be especially dangerous.

In modern America, lovers' quarrels seldom involve magic, but they can be just as passionate. Results of The Anger Project emphasize the centrality of family anger for many older adults, even as they illustrate its ongoing complexity.

In an especially poignant example, fifty-four-year old Tricia from rural Missouri writes in my Internet survey about an incident that made her angry. "I have been angry ever since breast cancer treatment eroded my quality of life in 2018.... My husband guilted me into cancer treatment, so I got 20 rounds of chemo, a lymphectomy [lymphadenectomy] /lumpectomy and 30 rounds of radiation. I cried a lot. I cursed a lot. I argued with everyone...." Tricia wishes she had declined treatment, which she sees as a threat to her long-term well-being. Her advice to others? "Anger might be useful in certain situations, but you should learn to take a step back and look at your situation from a neutral position before reacting."

The anger experienced by sixty-year-old Ted from Virginia feels less dramatic. He writes that he tends to, "become irritated and frustrated with my wife's mood swings." He copes by walking away to be by himself, a loyalty strategy. "Don't let anger control your actions. You will regret it afterwards." For Ted, withdrawal is as good as it gets. At the same time, the message it sends to his wife may be one of indifference or rejection.

Sixty-two-year-old Anna from Tampa writes, "Following a marital dispute we got angry. He yelled. I yelled. But *what really made me mad was he never listened to what I was saying*... then blamed the whole thing on me" [italics mine]. Anna says this happens frequently and that, "I wish I had not given my opinion on the subject. I am still hurt and sullen over it. It's easier not to talk than be yelled at for my thoughts."

The Sulk

In *The Course of Love*, a quirky meditation on mature relationships, Alain de Botton discusses the paradox of sulking.[8] In situations of intense anger, we sometimes find ourselves not unable, but unwilling to tell our loved ones why we are angry. Sulking, Botton suggests, "stems from a form of magical thinking." We believe that we shouldn't have to say why we are angry. If our partners, parents, and spouses truly love us, they will just know. They should do us "the greatest possible favor" by responding to our sulking as they would to an infant who hasn't learned to talk. That is, they should look beyond our adult selves; to engage with and forgive the disappointed, furious, inarticulate child within us.

Yet ours is not a culture that tolerates sulking. Anna almost seems to contradict herself in the advice she offers to others dealing with anger. On the one hand, she wishes she hadn't yelled at her husband. On the other, she says, "When I first got married, people said 'Don't say anything in anger you might regret.' Now I wish I hadn't been so naïve and [had] said the things that bothered me out loud and not kept it inside."

Janice, sixty, from Central Texas, also chooses silence. "Husband is Type A and often becomes vert [sic] angry and verbally abusive." When confronted with her husband's anger, Janice felt irritated as she "listened to him scream. Said nothing so it would be over faster." While reporting that her stoic patience doesn't make her feel better, Janice does not wish she had done anything differently. She sees her husband's frequent rages as an immediate threat to her well-being. I found this alarming. It hinted at Brittney Cooper's description, in *Eloquent Rage*, of a woman's occupation as living under siege.[9]

Janice's advice sounds like something she's told herself over and over, "Take several deep breaths. Figure out how to be proactive and *deal with the situation!*" But some situations can't be dealt with. After decades of marriage it would likely take something dramatic to change her husband's behavior.

Serpents' Teeth

How sharper than a serpent's tooth it is to have a thankless child! Old age brought multiple assaults to King Lear's dignity, but when both of the daughters who received his wealth disappointed his expectations he faced threats to his very life, all in the company of a fool who persistently insisted that Lear was at best, foolish; at worst, mad to have ignored the reasoned voice of his youngest daughter, Cordelia.[10]

Shakespeare's version of the legendary story opens with a resolute but misguided king, who sets out to show his courtiers how very much his daughters love him. Goneril and Regan declare their affections in magnificent, if somewhat insincere, speeches. But Cordelia will have nothing of it. She insists that any love she has for her father will have to be shared once she marries. Her father's response seems disproportionate to the offense, which has led some to suggest that he suffered from Intermittent Explosive Disorder (IED). Lear disinherits her and throws Cordelia on the mercy of her suitors without a dowry. This sets the stage for the tragedy that ends with the deaths of all three daughters.

The sacrifices we make for our children can weigh especially heavily when our kids disappoint or disrespect us. When asked what had made her especially angry lately, seventy-one-year-old Marilyn, from New Mexico, wrote, "My son who lives with me never wants to eat at a normal time." At first, it was hard to see why this would provoke such a strong response. But when she got to the question, "What did you do about it?" the answer became clear. "Nothing," she wrote. "I threw it all away." She must have felt tremendously unappreciated as she scraped the carefully prepared food into the trash. Marilyn's advice for others dealing with anger might as well have been for herself: "Life goes on. Get over it. It doesn't pay to get angry over every little thing."

Leo, a seventy-three-year-old man from Houston is one of many older adults dealing with an adult child's addiction. He writes, "I'm most [angry] with my 43 year-old son who is an alcoholic. He quits drinking, gets cleaned up, and says that he finished his LAST bottle . . . but then he starts drinking again." As Leo sees it, "My son's actions are detrimental to his long-term health." But even as he nurses his frustration, Leo explains, "I just accepted that he is going to do what he wants. Nothing I have tried in the past has had any effect. I worry what will become of him when I die." Leo's advice for others dealing with anger? "When you are angry with someone, try to reverse roles in your head in order to see the problem from the other person's perspective."

Sixty-eight-year-old Sam from New Orleans describes a scenario common to many American households. "Got in argument with my college-age son about the political climate in the country." He says this is a frequent occurrence for them. "When we didn't see eye to eye . . . I would get angry and vent . . . I later apologized." But Sam's apology didn't make him feel better. He wishes he'd paused before dumping on his son. Sam's advice for young people experiencing anger? "Always take a step back and a deep breath and realize what you are doing."

The ancient Greeks knew of the tensions that could arise between adults and their aged parents. Hesiod counted them among the evils that would come at the end of times. "Men will dishonour their aging parents . . . , they will blame them, chiding them with harsh words, hard-hearted, not knowing of the vengeance of the gods. They will not repay their aged parents the cost of their nurture."[11] Likewise, Plato reserved a special place in hell, a burning river in Hades, for those who "out of anger have done some act of violence against father or mother."

We tend to think of teenagers when we talk about anger and parents. But late life brings a whole new set of issues. The pressure of managing care for increasingly frail parents can cause long-buried fissures and family tensions to surface.

Fifty-four-year-old Karen from Milwaukee describes a fairly typical experience: "We are moving my mom in a few weeks and my sister and her family have refused to help out in any way, leaving me to plan everything." She describes them as "failing to do their fair share of a major project." Karen says her response to anger is to "keep my mouth shut so I don't say something I will regret later. . . . I vented my frustration to my husband and one of my good friends, but said nothing to my sister." She reports that the venting did make her feel better and she does not wish she had done anything differently.

Karen's situation offers a revealing glimpse into common family dynamics. When an older adult needs care, one person often assumes responsibility. At first, it feels good to be in charge. But as the tasks mount, the caregiver doesn't ask for help and resentment builds. She (it's usually a woman) doesn't speak of her anger to the people who make her mad. She tells other people. If the report gets back to the targets of her anger, they don't confront her because they aren't supposed to know. And so the tensions grow.

Seventy-year-old Bev from St. Louis writes about getting angry "when my father's caretaker was not responsible." Bev talked to a friend about the incident. She was probably quite dependent on the caretaker and may not have wanted to offend. As older adults know, deflecting is sometimes the most practical approach. Bev felt better after talking with her friend and made the decision to become more involved. Her advice to a young person dealing with anger? "Better to try and resolve the situation when calm."

Then there's the vivid description offered by fifty-one-year-old Jack, a gay man from Marion County, Indiana. He knew exactly when he got really angry. "April 3rd 2021 when my most wonderful two-faced mother called and left a smart ass voicemail on my phone." His description of his mother shows both affection and condemnation, deeply conflicting feelings that many adult children experience as they become aware of their parents' flaws.

Jack says he was enraged by his mother's voicemail and gave her the silent treatment for four days before sending her a text that said he was "very busy" and would call when he had a chance. When she didn't text him back, he wrote, "Of course you did not text me back which I'm not surprised." The text didn't make him feel any better. In retrospect, Jack wishes he had not sent it. "Should have just ignored it and moved on in life." He characterizes the incident as involving, "a person who likes to preach but that's completely opposite of what she preaches. What's good for the goose is definitely not good for the gander." I only wish he had told us what her voicemail said.

Kick the Dog Syndrome

Sometimes we displace our frustration with an external stressor onto those closest to us. We kick the dog or yell at our spouse. In some families, this displacement translates into physical violence. Several of the people I interviewed experienced abuse in their family of origin. Some, like Eddie, were still grappling with its effects. Others, like Wayne and Tim, were determined to end the generational violence that had marred their upbringing.[12]

For centuries family beatings were a normal and accepted part of family life. Even now, experts speak of the "cycle of violence" in which generation after generation of parents beat their children, often because external stresses become overwhelming. William V. Harris (author of *Restraining Rage*) notes that this pattern was also seen in Greece and Rome.

In eighty-nine-year-old Gianna's family of origin, external stressors stemmed from financial pressures and immigration. Gianna's parents brought their children to the United States from Italy when she was quite small. Her father was "very high on America." Life was so much better than it had been in Italy, but that didn't mean he wanted his daughter to embrace everything about American culture. "They brought me into this world and put me in American schools and then expected me to remain Italian."

Gianna grew up in Boston during the Depression. "Those were hard, angry times." Her father worked at the coalface of American capitalism. She describes him as "the tough guy," explaining that, in her family, "It was OK to be angry as long as you're male. Not women. We're not supposed to be angry. We're supposed to be lovely." She and her mother competed for her father's approval while he sometimes took his frustration out on them physically. Gianna's mother resorted to emotional abuse, calling Gianna "a tramp" and saying, "I pity the man who gets you."

When Gianna married a Jewish man, her devoutly Catholic parents disowned her. She and her husband moved to California. Her marriage, "wasn't good." She lost two babies and experienced what she describes as "breakdowns." When her daughter was born she suffered from postpartum depression. One day she got angry and smacked her daughter hard on the bottom. Alarms went off in her head and she went straight to a therapist. "He put his finger close to my nose and spoke very slowly in a deep voice. He said, 'Don't you ever touch a child in anger again.' I use that now when someone's being nasty or outrageous. You lower your voice and speak slowly and say, 'Stop it.' It works." Though she "suffered with anger" for most of her life, Gianna never struck a child again.

Gianna is vibrant and irrepressible. She teaches a class on memoir at the senior center, and she likes to open by asking, "Who has something they really want to do but are too embarrassed?" She urges her students to go ahead and "do it!" She describes herself as "terribly angry" about politics and copes by venting on Facebook. "I'm the most outspoken among my friends. She lives apart from her ninety-four-year-old husband, saying she feels cheated of love. "I should have left him years ago because he was a good man but not a good partner."

Reflecting on Gianna's experience helps me put my husband's anger in perspective. Given his family background, he was less reluctant than I to express anger. In later life, his outbursts are less frequent, but he recently became angry about plans for a family trip. In a classic move, he insisted that he hadn't been consulted and wasn't going to go. We would just have to cancel the reservations and forget about it.

That night I couldn't sleep. I dropped into a familiar cave, its walls lined with loneliness and fear. It felt just like the volatile early days of our marriage, except this time I had spent the preceding eighteen months studying anger.

I decided to apply Warren Farrell's advice and ask myself, not what Larry was angry about, but what made him feel vulnerable. I located some external stressor and realized that maybe, just maybe, he wasn't really, or wasn't only, angry with me. It took some persuading, but my child-self, who had been curled into a fetal ball, slowly unwound like a fern. A warm stream of affection for my perfectly imperfect husband replaced the familiar old sense of rejection and isolation and in that stream, I was able to develop and implement a healing strategy to resolve our disagreement.

Later, he and I agreed that his anger was a valuable signal that we were overextending ourselves. As Figure 8.1 illustrates, we modified our plans and went on the trip. More importantly, we agreed to see anger as an advance warning system that supports our relationship by alerting us to stress points and ruptures in the fabric of our marriage.

Figure 8.1. Amanda and Larry were glad they didn't cancel the trip.

I imagine that much of my suffering during the early years of our marriage came from a belief that anger and love don't go together. Somehow, I had imprinted on the notion that if we get angry with someone it means we don't love them. My anger often went unexpressed, but not undetected. In fact, my husband came to believe that I was angry with him at times when I was really stewing over an external stressor. In time, I learned a helpful phrase: "Yes, I'm upset. But I'm not angry with you." At the same time, my husband was inclined toward anger expression. Each time he blew his top I went through agonies, believing that our marriage was ending. Maybe the Stoics have it right. Sometimes, the false beliefs we hold about anger are more damaging than the anger itself.

Thirty-five years after we left our tropical island, Larry and I are still together. The COVID pandemic was a bad time for haircuts. I couldn't bring myself to walk into a salon and risk catching the virus. My greying hair got so long and stringy that, finally, I couldn't stand it. There was only one thing to do. On a spring day during the peak of the Delta wave, I sat on our deck with a towel draped across my shoulders. My husband stood before me with a smile on his face and a pair of scissors nestled in his hand.

"How much do you want me to take off?"

9
Aging, Angry, and Armed to the Teeth

> Me miserable! Which way shall I fly / infinite wrath or infinite despair?
>
> —John Milton, *Paradise Lost*[1]

The Las Vegas sun set at 6:30 on October 1, 2017, but heat still radiated from the concrete buildings and asphalt parking lots. Excited fans started arriving as soon as the day began to cool, bustling into the open-air concert venue carrying blankets, folding chairs, American flags, cameras, and picnics. Some danced to the country music blaring from speakers. Anticipation of music and pleasure filled the air. The air seemed electric with pre-concert bustle.

An estimated 22,000 people gathered to hear superstar Jason Aldean sing about love and heartbreak. A hush came over the crowd when he appeared on the stage. Aldean tuned his guitar and strummed the opening notes of his hit song, "When She Says Baby."

Midway through the first verse, shots echoed through the night. Stray bullets bounced off the concrete. Aldean kept singing for a few seconds before diving for cover. Gunfire came in spurts; mind-numbing blasts of destruction followed by strange quiet lulls before it started up again. This went on for ten minutes. The bullets came so fast that no one could tell where they were coming from. Lots of people dialed 911. Some thought there were multiple shooters.

Concertgoers must have felt like sitting ducks as bullets thudded around them. Someone shouted, "Turn off the lights." Someone asked, "Why are those people lying on the ground?" Some cowered. Some raced for the exits, others helped a man in a wheelchair toward shelter. Some draped their bodies over loved ones. Others lay down on top of perfect strangers. The concert grounds became an unfathomable hell. The carnage was indiscriminate. Fifty-eight dead and over five hundred wounded. It was the largest mass murder in American history. And it was committed by a sixty-four-year-old man.

No matter how much we examine, analyze, and try to understand people who commit acts of violence on this scale; no matter how we try to unpack their motives, to figure out who they are and why they did it, nothing diminishes the horror as place names become synonyms for suffering: Columbine, The Pulse,

Sandy Hook, Virginia Tech, Uvalde. Each name reminds us of lives lost. Mass murder has become a devastating hallmark of everyday life in America. It happens in other countries but is much more frequent in the United States. Victims' lives are destroyed and the rest of us can no longer even imagine that we are safe.

Then there are the damaged souls who commit these acts. We see him on the news every other week: the angry man who seized a gun and committed his own version of mayhem. Bleary-eyed sheriffs stand in front of a police station. Shoulders heavy with responsibility, they promise to get to the bottom of it. But there is no bottom. For a few days politicians and advocates battle over gun control. Someone drafts a bill to expand mental health services. It doesn't pass. By then, the American public has moved on.

The constant possibility of violence means that no place is safe. Wherever we gather, be it school, the grocery store, a club, or a shopping mall, safety is an illusion. We face the persistent and growing risk of becoming the target of some man's unbearable rage.[2] Then come the questions: What was wrong with this man? Why did he do it? What on earth can we do?

There are no simple answers. Knee jerk reactions lead us to stereotype the shooter as an anomaly, a monster. Neighbors and family members try to explain: "He was a loner." "He must have been crazy." But who are these shooters?

As we will see, some of them are aging angry.

A Very Big Year

The year 2017 was a big year for gun violence. The Gun Violence Archive (GVA) reports that the first year of Donald Trump's presidency saw more gun violence and the highest casualty count of any prior year. Based on data collected from 7,500 law enforcement agencies, the GVA lists 58,111 incidents that year, resulting in 15,728 deaths. Among these, there were 348 "mass murders" in which four or more people were killed. That's the FBI definition of a mass shooting.[3]

On September 24th of that year, sixty-four-year-old Stephen Craig Paddock drove his brand-new SUV some 83 miles from his house in Mesquite Nevada to the Mandalay Bay Resort and Casino in Las Vegas. A few days earlier he had given his girlfriend tickets to visit her family in the Philippines. This, and other actions, would lead the FBI to grudgingly admit that he "appeared to demonstrate authentic concern and responsibility for his girlfriend and certain family members while sustaining amicable relationships with previous intimate partners."[4] Stephen was no loner. He even completed his end-of-life planning.

A former accountant and realtor, Stephen was a high roller at the resort. Security footage shows him being welcomed at the VIP check-in desk. Perhaps because of his age, security considered him, "The lowest risk type individual that would come onto our property." Over the next six days, he brought in twenty-one pieces of baggage. The vice-president for security said, "He just looks like a middle-aged guy with a lot of luggage going up to his room."

Shortly before he opened fire, an alarm went off on the thirty-second floor. Someone had left the door to their room open. Security guard Jesus Campos was on the thirty-first floor when he got the call. Campos walked up the stairwell, but a metal L-bracket screwed to the doorjamb prevented him from opening the door into the thirty-second floor hallway. It struck him as strange, but not necessarily alarming. He went up to the thirty-third floor and took the elevator down.

As he walked down the hallway, Campos heard what sounded like a drill coming from one of the suites. He wondered what was going on. The sound stopped. The door to the suite swung open and a bullet pierced his leg. About the same time, a maintenance engineer named Stephen Schuck was dispatched to remove the L-bracket on the thirty-second floor. When he got off the elevator, bullets whizzed past and Campos yelled at him to take cover. Campos radioed for help, relaying the exact location of the shooter. This action, along with the distraction Campos and Schuck provided, must have saved lives.

Investigators combing through his room were appalled by the arsenal Stephen had managed to bring in. It included twenty-four assault weapons and thousands of rounds of ammunition. His planning was meticulous and he clearly intended to take his own life, which he did when the webcam he had placed in the hallway revealed a swat team heading his way.

The FBI conducted a year-long investigation into what had motivated Stephen to carry out the shooting. They assembled a multidisciplinary panel of experts who pored through thousands of pages of evidence. Here's one of their conclusions:

> Active shooters rarely have a singular motive or reason for engaging in mass homicide. More often their motives are a complex merging of developmental issues, interpersonal relationships, clinical issues, and contextual stressors. The [panel] assesses that in this regard, Paddock was no different.[5]

Stephen devoted considerable time, money, and energy to planning the attack over a one-year period. In addition to purchasing firearms and ammunition, he engaged in meticulous site selection and surveillance. In a departure from its "just the facts" style, the FBI report speculates that the preparation "was likely satisfying to Paddock as it provided a sense of direction and control despite his mental and physical decline."[6] It offers few specifics on the declines Stephen experienced, but it does observe that he was "failing to navigate common life stressors affiliated with aging."[7] With a penchant for stating the obvious, the FBI concluded that Stephen was *not* aging successfully.

The investigators did identify one unique aspect in Stephen's profile. His father was a relatively famous bank robber who spent some time on the FBI's Most Wanted list. The report suggests that Stephen might have wanted to emulate his dad by achieving a degree of notoriety.

Yeah, It Fits

In retrospect, Cecilia Nelms realizes that her ex-husband "had anger issues." He never physically hurt her but, "He had two sides. When he was in a good mood he was a great guy. When he was mad, he was mad." She says he used to "stew about perceived slights at work." Her use of "perceived" suggests she didn't take his work frustrations seriously. Even though he frequently said, "I'm just a number, who cares? I wish I were dead." she never believed him. She didn't hear the alienation and hopelessness in his voice. She divorced him, citing the inevitable "irreconcilable differences" and moved on.[8]

More than a decade later, Cecilia's ex-husband, fifty-seven-year-old Samuel James Cassidy went postal. He sprayed his house with accelerant, set a pot of explosives on the stove and left for work. A neighbor's security camera recorded him getting into his car. He wore a blue jacket and carried a bulging duffel bag, a "standard-issue rage murder accessory," according to Mark Ames, author of *Going Postal*.[9]

Sam had started off as a mechanic at the Santa Clara Valley Transit Authority (VTA), and within two years was in charge of overhead line maintenance for their substations, a job he held for over twenty years. He did stew over slights. For instance, when VTA announced a change to the vacation rules, Sam let his coworkers know he was frustrated.

A month before the shooting, in a major breach of company etiquette, Sam blew up on the VTA radio used by over one hundred employees to coordinate their work. A colleague told the press, "He sounded angry—oh yeah, you could tell, he was angry. It's kind of like being mean to a stewardess. You're mean to a stewardess, either you're off the plane or you're barred. Same thing if you say something nasty to [Operations]. They're going to report it and things are going to happen."[10]

A manager at VTA explains, "Sam had a pattern of insubordination and had gotten into verbal altercations with co-workers on at least four separate occasions. The incidents were 'elevated to management' and he faced disciplinary action." But he was good at his job. His managers defended his work and Sam was never formally disciplined. The *New York Post* reports that on the day of the shooting he was scheduled for a disciplinary hearing about his alleged use of racial slurs. A union representative denies a hearing was scheduled.

The transit authority is described in the papers as a "tight knit" agency. But in an interview, one of Sam's coworkers, Kirk Bertolet, presents the workplace culture differently. "I know some of those guys. They'll keep joking with you and they'll keep hammering you about stuff. . . [anyone] thin-skinned might not be able to handle it." COVID added another layer of stress. As one official explains, the staff "weathered months of essential work during the pandemic."[11]

Troubles also persisted in his personal life. After the divorce, Sam met Connie Wang on a website called Match. They saw each other for a while, but in 2009, he filed a restraining order accusing her of threatening to get him fired, harassing his new girlfriend, and damaging a car that was parked in his driveway. In response, she accused him of sexual assault and flying off the handle when he was intoxicated. She said, "he became a very different person" when she turned down his marriage proposal. Sam got his restraining order.[12]

On May 26, 2021, Sam parked his car and went into the first building.[13] His duffel bag held several assault weapons, over thirty magazines of ammunition, and miscellaneous explosives. His actions were deliberate. Intentional. He systematically murdered nine people. One survivor reports that Sam pointed his gun at him and paused. "I'm not going to shoot you." He said calmly, moving on. Bertolet observes, "he took his vengeance out on very specific people. . . He let others live." The Chair of the VTA Board of Directors insists, "We had no information about any tensions between Cassidy and the coworkers he shot." When Sam realized that police had entered the building, he turned his gun on himself.[14]

After the shooting, investigators learned that Sam had been detained by the Transportation Security Administration (TSA) after returning from a trip to the Philippines in 2016. He had stayed in several "sex-friendly" hotels and Homeland Security found "books about terrorism and fear and manifestos" when they searched his baggage. Sex and terrorism were sufficiently alarming to trigger an interview. The investigator notes that Sam spoke of hating his workplace during their interview. But he didn't threaten to kill anybody. After several hours, they let him go.[15]

A spokesman for the sheriff's office describes Sam as "a highly disgruntled" employee. Neighbors describe him as a "loner" who made them feel "uncomfortable." A coworker describes him as "just a little bit odd." Bertolet maintains that he had a "polite relationship" with Sam, but describes him as "an outsider, a loner who never fit in." He was, Bertolet says, "Never accepted by anybody. You look back and you go, 'yeah, it fits.'" As we know, things look different after the fact.[16]

Both Stephen and Sam clearly fit the FBI definition of active shooters: "the perpetrator of a type of mass murder marked by rapidity, scale, randomness, and often suicide."[17] In her comprehensive 2018 study of mass murderers, Criminologist Melanie Taylor argues that most like Sam, focus on targets who they feel deserve to die.[18] Stephen's motives are harder to discern. Initially, some believed he was one of a long line of angry white men who latch onto an ideology and perpetrate mayhem. It would take the FBI over a year to determine that ideology had nothing to do with his acts.

* * *

This chapter is about older adults who inexplicably cross a boundary most of us manage to avoid. It's also about the stories we tell ourselves as we carry on with our lives feeling just a little bit less safe. It's about the role of older adults in America's rising epidemic of mass destruction (see Figure 9.1).

Most of us see mass murderers via a thin layer of media coverage that advances a stereotype of young loners—gun fanatics who suffer from mental illness and are financially strapped. The reality of these devastating events only partly confirms our preconceptions. These people may be angry at "perceived" injustice; they might despair at ever being heard, but they are not who we think they are. Although the mean age of those who commit mass shootings in the United States is young (33 years),[19] each year somewhere between 20 percent and 25 percent of active shooters are fifty or older. As we have seen, the deadliest mass murder on U.S. soil was committed by a sixty-four-year-old. Shooters in their seventies and eighties, while rare, are not unheard of.[20]

In America, over 46,000 people over the age of fifty were convicted of single homicides between 1980 and 2020.[21] Laura Lundquist, the oldest murder defendant in Massachusetts history was ninety-eight when she killed her nursing home roommate. She was deemed too demented to stand trial.[22]

Regardless of how many people they kill, those who commit murder in later life contradict the stereotype as well as volumes of research indicating that we grow happier and better able to manage our emotions with age. These outliers do not conform to our expectations of later life. And it seems that late life did not conform to their expectations.

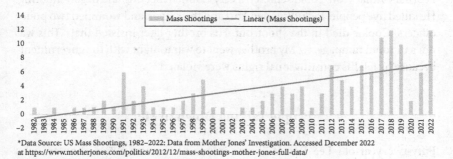

*Data Source: US Mass Shootings, 1982–2022: Data from Mother Jones' Investigation. Accessed December 2022 at https://www.motherjones.com/politics/2012/12/mass-shootings-mother-jones-full-data/

Figure 9.1. Mass Murders in America 1982–2022.

While each murderer is unique, the common denominator is anger, usually with a side order of despair and hopelessness. Let's consider a few of the older adults who have committed mass murder.

War on the Government

In the case of Charles Lee "Cookie" Thornton, a fifty-two-year-old Black man, simmering racial tensions in his community and escalating conflict with city government spilled over into an act of violence. Cookie grew up in Meacham Park, Missouri, an unincorporated community that was predominantly African American. In 1992, the predominantly white city of Kirkwood annexed his hometown. As a result, Kirkwood municipal codes were applied to Meacham Park. At first, things went alright for Cookie. He was active in community organizations and even ran unsuccessfully for city council in 1994. When a large commercial development was proposed in the late 1990s, he was one of few Meacham Park residents who supported it. Cookie thought his construction company would get the contracts.

He did get some contracts, but he'd expected more. In 1999 he filed an Equal Employment Opportunity Commission complaint alleging racial discrimination. He also filed for bankruptcy protection. Cookie started receiving citations for violations of Kirkwood municipal codes. He refused to pay them and repeatedly sued the city, appearing frequently at Council meetings to complain of persecution and discrimination. At one point the city council offered to forgive his fines if he would stop disrupting their meetings. Cookie was arrested and handcuffed at two council meetings in 2006. Later, he was arrested for assaulting Ken Yost, the city's public works director.

By 2008, Cookie owed more than $20,000 in fines to the City of Kirkwood for a range of violations including destruction of property, illegal dumping, parking construction equipment near his home, and running an unlicensed business. On February 7 that year, Cookie entered a City Council meeting and began shooting. He killed five people, including Ken Yost and the mayor, and wounded two police officers. Cookie died in the shoot-out. His brother later insisted that "This was not a random rampage.... My brother went to war tonight with the government" because he felt his constitutional rights were violated.[23]

People Talking Down to Me

Fifty-two-year-old Lee Roy Williams is one of the few active shooters who survived to provide an explanation of his behavior. Television news and newspapers in Lake Charles, Louisiana ran a picture of Lee, a big sleepy-looking man with a three-day beard and dread locks. They noted that he had a criminal history for violence and drugs. Police described him as a known crack cocaine user.

Lee lived in a mobile home south of Lake Charles with four people: twenty-eight-year-old Crystal Fruge, twenty-nine-year-old Kendrick Lavergne, nineteen-year-old Terry Lynn Banks, and twenty-six-year-old Jessica Eugene. In the early morning hours of Labor Day, 2010, he killed all of them. The murders were especially brutal. His victims' bodies had gunshot and knife wounds as well as blunt force trauma.

Lee fled the scene but, within days, police apprehended him in Baton Rouge. He was driving his blue Ford Explorer with three passengers who promptly fled the scene. After a forty-minute stand-off, he got out of the car, pretending to have a weapon. Some believe he was attempting suicide by cop. But these cops didn't bite.

Under questioning, he told police that he "snapped" when he learned that his roommates planned to evict him. "People were talking down to me like I wasn't shit."[24]

Maybe this was the first time Lee was put down by people much younger than he. Or maybe his rampage was a reaction to the cumulative effect of repeated microaggressions. Of course, given his history, it could have been the drugs. Lee pled guilty to four counts of first-degree murder and joined the growing ranks of older adults in America's prisons.

A Regular Old Neighbor

When fifty-one-year-old Michael Hance lost his job at the copy store in Copley, Ohio, he took over as caregiver for his live-in girlfriend's father, Wayne, who suffered from dementia. Wayne died in 2009, and two years later, on August 7, 2011, Michael killed six neighbors, injured his girlfriend, and murdered her brother. He was killed by police gunfire.

Michael had no criminal record and there was no evidence of arguments with his long-time girlfriend. Decades before, he was voted the "most courteous" student in his high school class. Neighbors describe him as "extremely helpful," remembering that he was always available when they were stuck in snow or their cars wouldn't start. There were tensions and arguments but at least one neighbor says, "He was just a regular old neighbor." Some of his neighbors describe him as eccentric. One remembers that he had a "faraway look on his face" while working in his yard. Another says, "He seemed to always be busy with something but never got anything done." Police found some rambling notes Michael wrote to his girlfriend and concluded that he must have had a delusional disorder.[25]

Santa's Coming

Late life was not living up to expectations for fifty-six-year-old Azizolah "Bob" Yazdanpanah from Dallas, Texas. Financial pressures were mounting, and he had recently declared bankruptcy after pleading guilty to filing a false income tax return. His house was in foreclosure and he was separated from his wife.

On December 25, 2011, dressed as Santa Claus, Bob opened Christmas presents with his family. Once all the presents were opened, he pulled out a gun and killed six people including his ex, their nineteen-year-old daughter, their fourteen-year-old son, and the family of his ex's sister. He then called 911 and said, "Help. Help. I am shooting people." He put one of the two handguns he had used in his brother-in-law's limp hand then shot himself.

A family friend told the *Daily Mail* that Bob was "upset his estranged wife was doing well on her own." Perhaps he'd hoped she would realize how much she needed him. Police attribute the violence to "marital and financial troubles."[26]

Financial vulnerability in later life can be especially challenging given that a person doesn't have time to make up funds lost to bad investments or excessive spending. Likewise, as other things slip away in later life, a long-term intimate relationship becomes even more important.

A Family Annihilator

The technical term for sixty-two-year-old Richard Wilkinson is "family annihilator." This might also be applied to Bob Yazdanpanah.

Twenty-six-year-old Jaime, her second husband, Darrell (35) and their two sons Michael (6) and Jacob (3) had lived with her father, Richard, and his wife, Linda, on and off over the years. Linda loved being a grandmother. Her employer said those kids were all she talked about.

Arguments between Richard and Jaime were frequent enough to send their boarder packing. Time and again, Richard accused her of stealing from him. A neighbor and long-time friend of the Wilkersons said that Linda often tried to intervene in the arguments. Darrell was another source of friction, and Richard had a hard time putting up with his rambunctious grandsons.

Jaime and Darrell decided to move out. They bought a used van and told their friends they were leaving. But they didn't get the chance.

On January 28, 2007, Richard shot most of his family in a bedroom of their house. Linda wasn't home at the time. When the police arrived, he went into another bedroom and shot himself.[27]

Familicide is one of the most common and increasingly frequent forms of mass killings. Dr. Elizabeth Yardley and her colleagues at Birmingham University reviewed the records of fifty-nine British family annihilators from 1980 to 2012, and developed a widely used taxonomy. Yardley suggests four types of family annihilators: the "self-righteous" perpetrator, who is out for revenge and blames his family for his own failures; the "disappointed," who views family as an extension of himself and over-reacts when they don't meet his expectations; the "anomic" who, after a financial downturn such as bankruptcy or foreclosure sees no way to recover; and the "paranoid" who sees the killing as a way of protecting his family from a threat.[28] Using Yardley's framework, Richard might be considered either disappointed or self-righteous.

Based on their review of sixty-seven studies, Dr. Linda Karlsson and her colleagues in Finland developed another taxonomy that distinguishes between the "despondent" and the "hostile" family annihilator. Based on the frequent and energetic arguments, it is probably safe to place Richard in the hostile camp.[29]

What Was Wrong with This Man?

Each of the killers in this chapter had his own unique configuration of problems. But if you passed him on the street you probably couldn't pick him out from a crowd in time to prevent serious damage. Even researchers and statisticians couldn't pick out future mass murderers among the 120.75 million adult men living in the United States in 2020.[30]

In our effort to explain *why* these tragedies happen, we blame the monster, the perpetrator. We identify with the victim and can't imagine ourselves ever being angry enough to kill. This enables us to deny the possibility that anyone could be driven that far.

We can't ask the ones who are responsible. Most mass murderers don't survive their attacks. In a desperate search for answers, we talk to people who knew them and even to those who didn't. We listen to their stories with one question in mind: "What was wrong with him?" FBI research on the precursors of active shootings sheds some light on this question.

In 2018, the FBI released a report called "A Study of the Pre-Attack Behaviors of Active Shooters in the United States between 2000 and 2013."[31] Authored by James Silver, a professor of criminology at Worcester State, Andre Simons, Supervisory Special Agent in the Behavioral Analysis Unit (BAU), and Sarah Craun also with the BAU, the report examines the "pre-attack behaviors" of 160 shooters who ranged from twelve to eighty-eight years old.

Acknowledging the sense of hopelessness the nation felt after 2017, a year when we saw an active shooting incident every twelve days and the very public deaths of hundreds of Americans, they combed through records and interviews with one goal in mind: to take a "step towards disrupting those who would seek to inflict catastrophic harm." The report sheds light on the role anger plays and reveals how active shooters are both unique and typical. It also reflects common themes in the stories we tell ourselves about those who commit this kind of violence.

No one would argue that these monsters are sane. In Stephen's case, there was some speculation after the fact that he suffered from "alexithymia," a personality trait that makes it difficult to empathize with others. Police also speculated that Michael Hance was delusional.

The FBI report indicates, however, that the frequency of mental health problems in their sample of shooters was comparable to that in the general population. About 25 percent of shooters had been diagnosed with a mental disorder. The most common diagnoses again mirror the general population: depression, bipolar disorder, and anxiety. Only three shooters had been diagnosed with a psychotic disorder.

Despair may distinguish mass shooters, the overwhelming majority of whom (90%) showed signs of suicidal ideation before the attack. Recall Sam saying, "I wish I was dead." Some 23 percent had made suicide attempts. This compares to less than 1 percent of the general population.[32]

After a mass shooting, people frequently claim that the shooter was an antisocial loner. On the contrary, 68 percent lived with at least one other person and all had significant social interactions either in-person or online.

Mass shooters also looked very much like the general U.S. population in terms of stress. They experienced multiple stressors (3.6 on average) in the year before the attacks, including: financial pressures; health concerns; conflicts with family, friends, and colleagues; mental health issues; problems with the law; and substance abuse. The top five stressors were mental health issues, financial strain, difficulties on the job, conflicts with friends and peers, and marital problems.

The FBI reports that the shooters displayed from four to five "concerning behaviors" that were observable to others. These were usually related to mental health, problematic interpersonal interactions, and "leakage" of their violent intentions. In Sam's case, his frequent comments about killing his coworkers would be considered "leakage." Over half of those with pre-attack targets had made threats, almost always in person, usually to someone other than the victim. Threats and leakage were almost never reported to authorities.

Most shooters (62%) had a history of "acting in an abusive, harassing, or oppressive way" (such as bullying or workplace intimidation) and 57 percent had "problematic interpersonal interactions." Richard Wilkinson's loud arguments with his daughter Jaime are a classic example. Also fairly common were aggressive expressions of anger. There were reports of threats and confrontations in 35 percent of cases and physical aggression in 33 percent.

After the fact, family and friends recalled some of these concerning behaviors. Spouses and partners noted them in 83 percent of the cases and coworkers in

40 percent. These behaviors seldom came to the attention of law enforcement. Instead of reporting them, the observers most often communicated directly to the active shooter (83%) or did nothing (54%). In 41 percent of cases the behavior was reported to law enforcement but did not result in intervention. Charles Lee "Cookie" Thornton, for instance, frequently came to the attention of law enforcement before he committed his attack.

The FBI researchers speculate that these behaviors go unreported out of loyalty, disbelief, or fear of the consequences. Certainly, those who observed them didn't suspect they were signals of a future mass murder. After all, these behaviors are seen among lots of people who never commit such atrocities. As the researchers note, "in retrospect certain facts may take on a heightened degree of significance that may not have been clear at the time."

Over 85 percent of the shooters had no criminal convictions.

That Nagging Sense of Unfairness

Mass shooters in America are predominantly white (63%) and overwhelmingly male (98%); the kind of men Michael Kimmel describes in his book, *Angry White Men*.[33] Based on interviews and fieldwork with a wide range of angry white men, Kimmel concludes that a common denominator is "aggrieved entitlement"; the feeling that they were unjustly deprived of something they deserved.

The FBI researchers note that 79 percent of shooters had "more than a typical feeling of resentment or passing anger." The grievance "gave a sense of purpose" to the shooter. Generally, their grievances were personal, not political or ideological. Nearly half (49%) had a "primary grievance" that could be identified, most of these related to an "adverse interpersonal or employment action." The researchers conclude that the shooter's concerns evolved into a "grossly distorted preoccupation with a sense of injustice." We might call it a "nagging sense of unfairness" coupled with a failure of hope.

Among those with an identifiable grievance, nearly half experienced a triggering or precipitating event such as a fierce argument, a breakup, or the loss of a job. Most arrived at the site of their attack with a specific target in mind. Random victims might have been killed or injured simply because they were in the wrong place at the wrong time; either that or they got between the shooter and his target.

Rage-onomics

"Going postal" has become a strange shorthand to describe mass shootings in the workplace because the first workplace massacre in the United States took place in 1986 at a U.S. post office. A few years later, Joseph Wesbecker, used an AK-47 to mow down his coworkers at Standard Gravure, killing eight and injuring twelve. Mark Ames, author of *Going Postal*, describes the attack in gruesome yet riveting detail. He observes that Wesbecker was a hard-working employee for two decades. He regularly worked overtime and volunteered for the hardest assignments, like working at "the folder." This machine exposed its handler to high concentrations of toluene, a solvent associated with nerve damage. Several employees had been excused from working the folder because it made them dizzy. When Wesbecker developed a debilitating case of bipolar disorder he asked to be excused from working the folder. The company refused. He filed a discrimination complaint, which the company stonewalled for over a year.

Standard Gravure was in the midst of an unfriendly takeover. Employees were being laid off and moved to part-time. There was a lot of stress. Eventually, Wesbecker was given the option of taking long-term disability; hardly the solution he had sought. As Ames explains, "Wesbecker sought revenge on the entire institution that mistreated, abused, injured, insulted, and eventually threw him away."[34] His attack was, in a sense, successful. The company permanently closed.

Ames argues that workplace massacres became, if not commonplace, all too common in the 1980s because the culture of corporate America changed. Employees were seen and treated as disposable commodities and managed with "an unprecedented corporate cold-bloodedness" that began with Reaganomics. In a clever turn of phrase, Ames converts the term to "rage-onomics."

Ames is one of few analysts who shifts our focus to the culture and institutions under attack in these rampages. He notes how the violence transforms our culture and the workplaces in which they occur. The rising use of "active shooter" drills in public schools is just one example of the way mass violence leaves its mark on our cities, churches, schools, and other institutions. What it hasn't done, at least so far, is change the way we approach angry people.

Not Again

In January of 2023, as this book was going to press, two older men committed mass murders in California. Both used semiautomatic weapons, and both came from immigrant communities.

Seventy-two-year-old Huu Can Tran opened fire in the Star Ballroom Dance Studio, packed with couples celebrating the Lunar New Year, killing eleven and wounding nine. Tran shot himself as police approached his car.

As usual, anger played a role in Huu's rampage. He had been a regular patron of the studio. In fact, he met his ex-wife there. Although she refused to be named, the ex-wife reported that "he could be quick to anger." Another acquaintance explained that there was a time when Huu was at the studio every night. This person described Huu as "hostile to a lot of people there." Review of his criminal record revealed a 1990 arrest for unlawful possession of a firearm. Authorities also reported that he had visited the Hemet Police Department to raise allegations of fraud, theft, and poisoning against some family members. He never returned to provide evidence.[35]

Sixty-six-year-old Chunli Zhao killed seven workers and wounded one at two mushroom farms where he had been employed. In an unusual move, Chunli drove to the sheriff's station where he was arrested without incident. Evidently, he had "workplace issues."

Indeed, a specific incident may have triggered this shooting. CBS reported that Chunli told investigators he was angry at being asked to pay $100 to repair damage to a forklift. Reuters reported that a coworker from a restaurant had secured a restraining order against Chunli after receiving assault and death threats. The article reported that "the court order is no longer in effect." The judge in the case has since imposed a gag order on media coverage.[36]

Beyond Disgruntled

Something clearly broke deep within these perpetrators, but breakage doesn't occur in a vacuum. The word, "disgruntled," comes up frequently in the lexicon of descriptors applied to those who commit mass violence. It's a strange word for the situation. The word, disgruntle, started out as "grunt." By the seventeenth century, it had become the verb, "gruntle" (to grumble, murmur, complain). The "dis" prefix adds a sense of separation or undoing as well as a hint of intensity as in, "utterly or exceedingly." These days, it means "sulky dissatisfaction or ill-humor." Or, as the Urban Dictionary suggests, "the feeling of a little stress and a little bit of anger combined."[37]

"A disgruntled worker."
"A disgruntled customer."
"A disgruntled student."

Does that sound like someone who uses an insanely powerful weapon to murder and maim a whole lot of people? What is the subtext behind this belittling word choice?

In his book about one of the young men who committed the Columbine shootings, journalist David Cullen writes:

> Eric was an injustice collector. The cops, judge and Diversion officers were merely the latest additions to a comically comprehensive enemies list, which included Tiger Woods, every girl who had rejected him, all of Western culture, and the human species.

Cullen dismisses the shooter's all-consuming rage, treating it as petty and small; even "comical." He laughs at Eric's complaints, mirroring the teachers and administrators who ignored the bullying he experienced. In dehumanizing him, Cullen turns away from the pain, anger, and hopelessness that made his violence not just possible, but inevitable.[38]

Much as we all long to turn our backs on the horror of these events, their rising frequency calls for us to question our preconceptions and stereotypes. This is particularly true in cases that involve older shooters. If nothing else, the presence of older adults, most, but not all, in their fifties and sixties, in the catalogue of mass murderers forces us to re-examine stereotypes of late life as a time of passive resignation.

The warning signs these murderers display consistently point to accumulated and unresolved anger. Some may be trying to make a statement. Some may be after revenge. Some may just want to end a life that has become unbearable.

Mass violence is a brutal reminder of the darkest aspect of anger's Janus-faced nature. Rather than moving on, we might reassess our collective relationship with anger to turn toward it and take it seriously, to listen carefully and compassionately to concerns raised by people who are "disgruntled." We might reach out to workers who find themselves drowning in hopeless rage; to family members whose frustration has become palpable. We might invite healthy dialogue about hot-button issues at both societal and personal levels. We might resolve to learn all we can from the anger of others because, particularly in a nation as heavily armed as the United States, we dismiss it at our peril.

10
Taming the Rage

> When angry, count four;
> when very angry, swear.
>
> —Mark Twain, *Pudd'nhead Wilson, A Tale*[1]

My seventy-two-year-old husband lost it in the airport. Larry and I were returning from our first trip away since the height of the COVID-19 pandemic. Our maiden voyage, as it were. We deplaned in Salt Lake City and set off on the long march to baggage claim. After four hours in N95 masks, our faces were itchy and sweaty. I knew I would have a rash when I finally took the darn thing off.

I had noticed that most people who didn't wear masks properly were white men over forty. Larry thought I was making it up. So, every time I saw a middle-aged white man with a "chin warmer" or no mask at all, I'd nudge Larry and point out the culprit. Acting out was a kind of release for me. Over time, my volume increased. "Oh look!" I'd shout, "There's another white man who doesn't know how to wear a mask."

Despite the mask mandate, there were quite a few of them in the airport that day. Larry was walking ahead of me. We were tired of travel, tired of the pandemic, and (yes) tired of wearing masks. A pot-bellied man in business attire strode into view, mask dangling from his right wrist.

"Excuse me sir. Would you please put your mask on?" Larry asked, just as we'd rehearsed on the plane. His voice echoed through the noisy terminal.

The man in question ignored Larry's request, but someone else said, "What the fuck?"

"Put on your fucking mask!" Larry shouted.

The man continued to ignore him but other people in the crowd started yelling. At us.

"It's not your problem man."

"Shut up!"

"Hey man, you need some anger management!"

I grabbed Larry's arm. He shook me off. That's when I got scared. We were heading for a confrontation. The unmasked man sped up and veered away, surreptitiously putting his mask on. Larry backed off.

Aging Angry. Amanda Smith Barusch, Oxford University Press. © Oxford University Press 2024.
DOI: 10.1093/oso/9780197584644.003.0010

A TSA officer had observed the whole thing without leaving her post. Larry and I walked over and asked her who was responsible for enforcing the airport's mask mandate.

"Not me," she assured us. She said there was a city policeman stationed outside. Of course, the mandate only applied inside the terminal.

We made our way home and took a walk to dissipate our adrenaline. The next morning, Larry called the police department and spoke with a lovely woman who patiently explained that, had the confrontation gone further, Larry was the one who would have been arrested. I briefly imagined my husband in a court-ordered anger management program.[2]

Full disclosure. Anger management is not my thing. I've seen its consequences at work. My colleague Tim, a former Marine, is direct, hostile, sarcastic, and sometimes very funny. As I came to know him better, I learned that he suffers from chronic pain that sometimes keeps him in bed all weekend. On his good days, he is funny, smart, and incredibly patient. On his worst, he'll unleash a torrent of sarcasm at anyone who asks yet another stupid question. Unfortunately, our boss came to him with yet another stupid question on one of Tim's worst days. His response led to an anger management referral. Tim was newly married and could not afford to lose his job. So, he sat through the training and came back different; chastened. His sense of humor, annihilated. His sarcasm, gone. He spoke slowly and cautiously and seemed nervous most of the time.

I've come to believe that the threat of mandatory anger management is often used as a tool for stifling dissent. I've never been "referred," but I have been told I'm "just angry" or "just jealous." I've been asked whether I'm suffering from premenstrual syndrome (PMS).

In *Civilization and its Discontents*, Sigmund Freud argues that societies have to regulate the emotional lives of their members. Cultures may differ in degree and approach, but the smooth operation of social institutions sometimes calls for prioritizing the social order over self-expression and individual emotional health.

Civilization continues, at least in part because people learn to regulate their anger and make peace with their situation. The education system requires peaceful classrooms. The political system needs polite dialogue. Sometimes, the "discontents" just need to keep their mouths shut and tolerate the status quo that is preferred by those in power.

So, it makes sense that the police would arrest my husband for making trouble, rather than the man who was peacefully ignoring the federal mask mandate. Troublemakers must be stifled, along with their troublesome emotions. It also makes sense that, in this angry era, anger management is a growing cottage industry. Anger management is designed to shackle the dangerous side of anger; a benefit that should not be underestimated.

Intermittent Explosive Disorder

A friend of mine did a brief stint in legal services when she got out of law school. When I mentioned this book, she said "You have to talk to Dan. He was the angry client whisperer. Whenever a client was super angry, we sent them to him."

We scheduled a Zoom meeting and Dan mentioned that the day before we met, a man he worked with had been ordered into anger management. Tony (as I'll call him) had come to the attention of authorities two years prior and was eventually evaluated by a psychologist who gave him the diagnosis: Intermittent Explosive Disorder (IED).[3]

Tony is a high-functioning white man, which, as Dan notes, "gives you some advantage." He has a job and his only problems with the law seem to be associated with his disorder, which manifests as verbal threats against authority figures that sometimes verge on the ridiculous. Following a police shooting, he called his local police department to say that he wanted to congratulate whoever had killed the cop. Evidently there's a video tape of Tony threatening his former lawyer. It shows a very large man yelling threats right in the lawyer's face until the attorney pulls a gun and tells him to get out of his office. He has also been incarcerated briefly for stalking a judge. As Dan observes, his behavior makes no sense but his threats "were horrific."

Intermittent Explosive Disorder (with its echoes of war in the Middle East) was "discovered" in the 1980s and initially included in the third edition of the *Diagnostic and Statistical Manual (DSM)* of the American Psychiatric Association, known fondly as "DSM-3." At the time, it was applied to rare cases of repeated impulsive aggression, either verbal or physical. Since then, the diagnostic criteria have evolved.[4]

In some ways, Tony is not a typical IED patient. Now in his forties, he is also somewhat older than a typical patient. IED usually comes on early in life, at about seventeen years of age. It is considerably more common among men than women and is often associated with substance abuse and mood disorders.[5] Tony has been able to hold down a job, although unemployment has been associated with IED. It's unclear whether he had an abusive childhood, but there is good evidence that physical abuse in childhood can predict the onset of IED.[6]

IED is a rare disorder. In 2016, Professor Kate Scott from the University of Otago, New Zealand, and Ron Kessler of Harvard University reported on a cross-national study.[7] Diagnostic household surveys were conducted in sixteen countries in conjunction with the World Mental Health Surveys initiative. Over 88,000 people participated. Their results shed light on the global distribution of IED, revealing that the United States has the highest prevalence by far. Americans yielded an IED rate of 2.7 percent compared to a global mean of 0.8 percent and a low of 0.1 percent. The country that elected Donald Trump yielded a level of pathological anger more than three times the global average.

As with most mental illnesses, people with IED generally do not seek treatment, though there is some evidence that cognitive behavioral interventions can be helpful.[8] Tony's case is still pending. If he and his family are lucky, he'll get into one of the better programs and learn to moderate his aggression.

Helping People Manage Anger

On their website, the National Anger Management Association (NAMA) describes itself as "the international professional association," offering certification trainings in twenty-six countries. They don't list the countries. There is a long code of ethics and a specialist directory that can be searched by state or country. There are no specialists listed for some countries, presumably because someone quit paying their membership dues. They offer an "Anger Management Assessment" at $39 for digital or $45 for a hard copy. Within minutes of completing the contact form, I get a reply from Dr. Rich Pfeiffer, President of NAMA, who offers to meet with me in a few days.

I envision a slick entrepreneur who thrives on our cultural appetite for anger suppression. Instead, I find a broad-faced, disarmingly friendly man with an infectious smile. The Buddhist goddess of wisdom gazes out from a poster on the wall behind him as if to say, "Surprise!"

Rich is an ordained minister and at one time planned to become a pastoral counselor. After completing a training program for counselors interested in working with people who didn't respond to the standard positive-thinking intervention developed by Norman Vincent Peale, Rich discovered a problem. "I was helping people get in touch with their anger and then I realized I knew nothing about how to help people manage their anger."

The University of Manchester had the only program he could find with a focus on anger. He got his PhD and started working in anger management. While his previous clientele had been 70 percent female, he soon found that his practice was 80 percent male. Evidently, women need help getting in touch with their anger and men need help managing theirs.

In 2003, Rich and some colleagues noticed that demand for their services was growing. "Courts became interested in having people go into programs—of course they had to pay for themselves—to help with their anger. That became the initial trigger, and we were concerned that it would become like the traffic school course videos: not very helpful. We wanted to provide practices to help people with anger that we knew worked."

"Judges don't know what's needed they just want them to be less angry . . . Sometimes courts would ask for 52 sessions or just one class, which is totally worthless. It was all over the place." Believing that anything less than eight sessions was ineffective, Rich and his colleagues tried to establish that as standard.

During each session, clients are required to describe an incident that made them angry. "Successful people come in and . . . they say, 'I could have gone into my primitive brain in a nanosecond but I chose not to. I took some deep breaths and I suspended my reaction.'"

I struggle with Rich's language, "the primitive brain" has a nineteenth-century colonial feel. The use of "primitive" and "evolved" brain is common in anger management books and programs. It obscures nuance and complexity and teaches us to conceive of ourselves as warring parts. I feel a little protective of those amygdalae that, for untold millennia, have alerted us mammals to danger. But sometimes, an angry person does need to pause.

The structured program Rich and his colleagues designed became quite successful. "People with anger like structure. . . . They don't want to go in a room and just talk about their feelings. With structure, they think, 'I can do that.'"

When I ask Rich to tell me about a successful case, he finds it hard to pick one out of the hundreds of people with whom he has worked. Then a memory clicks. After being cut off in traffic, a man got out of his car at the next red light, pulled a tire iron from the back of the stranger's truck and hit him numerous times. After serving a prison sentence, he was referred to Rich for anger management as a condition of parole.

"He was my best client ever. He said, 'I know how much I need help.'" Rich explains that this kind of motivation is "the landmark of whether someone's going to be successful or not—they understand how much they actually need it. They must get past the denial [the belief] that it's the other person . . . . Until they can get to that they can't be successful. You have to realize you're part of the dance. One person steps one way and the other steps the other way."

To succeed in anger management, Rich feels a person needs to acknowledge, not culpability, but participation in the interpersonal dynamics that make them angry. Perhaps they might go on, as Stoics advise, to avoid acting on their anger. It made me wonder whether my hostility to anger management comes from deep-seated denial. Maybe I needed to enroll in an anger management program.

Two main schools of thought inform contemporary anger management programs. The Duluth Model was developed to prevent domestic violence by neutralizing male anger. This gendered program assumes a woman victim and male perpetrator (the most common, but not the only configuration by any means). It's designed to change men's deep-seated beliefs about the privileges they enjoy.

The website for the Duluth Model claims it is the most widely used program in the world.[9] Though several studies are listed, there's no research that definitively shows the model more effective than other modalities. Clinicians I interviewed say it doesn't work. It's incredibly difficult to change someone's deep-seated beliefs, and sometimes the model's assumptions about the dynamics of domestic violence just aren't relevant.

There has been considerably more research on methods associated with the second approach to anger management: cognitive-behavioral therapy (CBT).[10] Methods that draw upon CBT aim to help people develop skills in recognizing their anger and talking themselves down, combining self-awareness and mindfulness with communication skills. CBT has proven effective in treating a wide range of psychological and social issues and clinicians generally favor this approach for a variety of clinical problems.

Questions remain as to whether anger-management programs based on CBT consistently work. In making their case for a more psychodynamic approach to violence prevention, Dr. Julian Walker (Director of Research & Development, Avon & Wiltshire Mental Health Partnership) and Jennifer Bright critiqued the CBT approach, arguing that "anger management is one of the few cognitive behavioral interventions with published studies showing no treatment benefit."[11]

Even though millions of dollars are spent and thousands of people forcibly enrolled, there is no consistent monitoring of anger management programs and little solid professional evaluation of what does and doesn't work. Nor is there a single widely accepted set of standards or best practices for the well-intentioned people who work in anger management. Most programs show utter disregard for anger's potential as a tool for change and few consider the possibility of channeling the energy of anger for productive purposes.

Stop Dictating to Us

Walker and Bright point out that some anger management programs struggle with high dropout rates. We see this in the experience of Dr. Liz Van Voorhees and her colleagues at Duke University when they set up a group anger-management program for combat veterans with diagnoses of post-traumatic stress disorder (PTSD).[12]

Theirs was the largest controlled study of its kind and the only one to include women. Veterans report that controlling their anger is one of the biggest challenges they face in adjusting to civilian life. Indeed, about 50 percent of veterans report problems controlling their anger. These problems are especially severe among those who suffer from PTSD. As Dr. Van Voorhees explained to me, the military trains people to use their anger for mastery and energy. This can be especially important in combat situations, but it can set veterans up for difficulties when they return to civilian life.

Thirty-six veterans (11 women and 25 men) were referred to the study by clinicians and assigned to either CBT or Person-Centered therapy groups that met for twelve weekly sessions of two hours each. Participants were compensated and asked not to miss more than three sessions. In a 2021 article, Van Voorhees and her colleagues report that *all* the women who were enrolled in the CBT intervention dropped out and that *all of them were all black* [italics mine].

As Van Voorhees acutely observes, their anger management program may not have been suitable for women. Based on the "survival mode" model of anger, it assumes that the angry person has "hostile attribution bias and excessive combat trauma-related physiological arousal," both of which lead to experiencing anger in "benign or ambiguous situations where it is not warranted or appropriate." Although their results suggest that both group therapy techniques reduce anger and improve anger control, the authors were forced to conclude that "it may not be appropriate to assume that anger interventions designed for male veterans will necessarily be effective for women veterans."[13]

On further examination, the composition of men in the study was "racially balanced," while all but one of the women referred to the study were black. In an unpublished manuscript, Van Voorhees and her team report that the women who dropped out all had more severe anger problems than the men.

In an unusual and highly productive move, they followed up with the women who left their study. They mailed surveys to them and held lengthy interviews to better understand what did and didn't work. The women noted the value of connecting with others who were struggling to deal with their anger. One Iraq war veteran said women need places to talk about "anger and injustice and what they deal with." She said women, "don't necessarily need fixing," just "a safe place to be heard and validated." Though much of the trauma they experienced was not combat-related, several explained that anger was a necessary part of their military life. "Women in the military need to bark, to be angry, [in order] to get where they want to go."

For some, the anger management group was just another source of irritation. Some wanted more freedom to explore ideas that weren't on the groups' agenda. One suggested that the therapists should "pay attention to what we need, as opposed to you telling us what you think we need... stop dictating to us."

One of the women raised the pernicious stereotype of the "angry black woman," warning that it can lead even well-intentioned supervisors to suppress the anger of black women. Just imagine a group of black women being told by a white male therapist that their anger is "not warranted or appropriate." No wonder they dropped out.

112 AGING ANGRY

Destroy That Monster

Rather than seeking anger management training, older adults might be more likely to turn to self-help books. With catchy imagery and clever catch phrases, these books urge readers to "let go" of anger, get "beyond anger," "uproot anger," "overcome," "destroy the monster within," "Cage your Rage," "stop losing your shit," or, more gently, "quiet the storm within."

I picked up Dr. Bernie Golden's *Overcoming Destructive Anger*.[14] It wasn't the most widely read example, but it came from a well-qualified author and was published by a trustworthy source: Johns Hopkins University Press. I also appreciated the specificity in the title and looked forward to learning more about "destructive" anger.

Like most in this genre, the book holds out the tantalizing prospect of overcoming anger and keeping it from overwhelming us. In a typical marketing move, it suggests that people might need anger management if they experience mild or intense anger several times a day, maintain a hostile attitude, or have difficulty letting go of anger. It would be hard to find someone who doesn't meet at least one of these criteria, and that's just the point. EVERYONE needs anger management so everyone should buy this book.

For Dr. Golden, there are two kinds of anger: "destructive" and "healthy." "Healthy" is a synonym for good anger; "destructive" for anger that is intense and dangerous. He posits that anger is often the result of deep suffering or injustice, but does not address or attempt to correct the conditions that cause suffering. Citing Thich Nhat Hanh, he takes the position that suffering and injustice are inevitable. As I systematically underlined each section that emphasized the importance of transcending anger, I grew more and more irritated.

Sometimes Therapy Works

When group interventions and books fail, some people turn to individual therapy. That's what Santiago did. A former student introduced me to him, saying, "He has anger issues but he's a nice guy."

Santiago introduced himself as Sargent First Class. Later, I would learn that he'd been awarded a purple heart. "I'm military. I joined the army right after 9/11 at 35 and I am retiring soon." In fact, our Zoom meeting took place right after his retirement dinner where colleagues praised his patience and calm.

Santiago's childhood home was marked by tension and physical abuse. His mother was the target of his father's rage until Santiago was fifteen or sixteen. "I had to get in front of him and make him stop. I was taller." As an adult, he lived what he called an "unhealthy lifestyle." He was an abusive drinker and the anger he experienced was "dramatic." He characterizes his fights with his first wife as "character clashes."

His time in the army was traumatic. His counselor attributes his anger issues to PTSD from five combat deployments, four in Iraq, one in Afghanistan. Even so, Santiago feels that the army saved his life by giving him ready access to mental health advisors. "You can talk to them if you're willing... get coached through something." With the army's mental health resources, he was able to restructure his relationship with anger. "I found that anger doesn't give me the results I need. That's what I found in the military. Some people [those of higher rank] might use anger to get the results they want. But I don't. I talk. Just like a normal person. I don't need to be angry to toughen them up. That's me. That's my persona. I don't use anger."

With therapy, Santiago was able to see that his relationship with anger mirrored his father's. He didn't want to talk about the things he has done that he regrets, but he wishes he had cut his losses and "backed away." He gained an appreciation for the role of triggers. "I'm looking for triggers. Problems. Pressures... Once you see a trigger your mind says I need to pause or count 10 seconds. They teach you to identify triggers and then prevent them from activating.... What comes out of your mouth right away is damaging but if you pause a little bit and think... the results are a little more calm."

Santiago is aware that he can also be a trigger and he doesn't take other people's anger personally. "When I see somebody angry at me, I realize that I was a trigger." He asks himself, "What did I say that could have been prevented?" He walks away and then comes back to talk about it. "Apology goes a long way."

Santiago sees a behavioral health counselor whenever a trigger begins to be an issue. "You just talk like you and I [are]. He'll give you options on how to do things differently. Deal with situations. Once you go several times, he's like your coach."

Sometimes he takes his work frustrations home, but his second wife knows how to manage his anger. "She figured me out a long time ago.... She gives me a time out.... I go outside, rake the lawn and come back and I'm feeling remorse. That's also me learning from my past experiences. Why be angry for 2–3 weeks? It's just a moment of anger."

Santiago sees his successful transformation as a clear win for the long-term therapy provided by the military. He also acknowledges that growing older helps. "It takes time, knowledge, experience, wisdom—the older you get the more wisdom you earn. When I was younger I didn't know how to fix my problems."

Whereas the military expects its members to channel their anger into combat, the criminal justice system is largely about "squashing the anger." Although we might expect the military to devote considerably more effort and money toward the mental health of service members than the criminal justice system does to prisoners' mental health, it is likely that both military personnel and prisoners struggle to access needed care.[15]

Kenneth, a psychologist, tells me about his work with Brad, who spent twenty years in prison for anger-related offenses. Brad was angry at the system. He was angry at the people in prison. He was angry at his probation officer. He was angry at the world and on "this perpetual loop" of fighting and getting sent back to prison. Punishment only fueled his anger. The system's approach was, as Kenneth put it, "not terribly effective with this guy." Yet, when I ask Kenneth to tell me a success story, Brad is the one who comes to mind.

"It's amazing what you can do with someone when you just listen to them and exercise some empathy. . . . I said, 'Dude, all these people want is to see you react. So you need to rise above their ignorance. You can master that.'" Eventually, Brad learned to play the game. "He would come in and brag about how he managed it."

Then a woman came into Brad's life. "She would come to therapy and wouldn't let him get away with anything." Kenneth upped the ante. He encouraged Brad to embrace "the bravado of being a man," while urging him to "upgrade to a different level of masculinity from what Dad gave you." Once Brad realized "he could be his own man," he was able to repair his relationship with his parents and commit to a positive long-term relationship.

Brad worked with Kenneth for two years on a weekly basis and they've stayed in touch for about twenty years. The last Kenneth heard, Brad was a grandfather and had achieved a measure of financial success. "Every once in a while he'll have difficulties or hit a grumpy spot" and make an appointment because *"he felt understood"*[16] [italics mine].

Time's Passage

Older adults are skilled at emotional regulation. In my survey, even the 25 percent who consider themselves angry people have relatively mild narratives about their experience with anger and regret: "I cracked the screen on my cell phone." "I just wish I hadn't sworn at him." "I should have listened more carefully." These are hardly offenses that call for professional intervention.

Ordinarily, we can rely on our own resources and the passage of time. But sometimes we need a little training or coaching to keep anger within reasonable bounds. When this happens, we should choose our helping professionals with prudence and be careful whom we trust with our anger.

Psychotherapists and anger management specialists are human. They swim in the same cultural sea as the rest of us and are immersed in its pervasive anti-age, anti-anger norms. All therapists should be aware of the role ageist stereotypes play in interactions with elders. But many aren't. Many won't even work with older adults, believing us incapable of change.

Therapists who do work with older adults may not recognize anger when they see it. Due to internalized ageism, clients may be reluctant to directly express their anger. Over a third (36%) of the older adults in my survey agreed that "When other people are angry with me I usually feel frightened." Given the carnage of our era, it's not surprising that anger's destructive potential remains foremost in people's minds.

Given that most older adults are women, clinicians working with older clients should be prepared for our unique issues. As we saw in Chapter 5, women in treatment for anger problems tend to score higher on anger scales than men, particularly on measures of intense anger. This may be because women have to be angrier than men before they seek or are referred for help with anger, possibly because of men's greater risk of committing violence.

Given a sensitive and well-informed therapist both men and women can benefit from anger management interventions, particularly when they are not coerced into participation. In time, perhaps the anger management will mature to help repair our relationships with this powerful emotion.

11
Embracing the Anger

> I was angry with my friend: / I told my wrath, my wrath did end. / I was angry with my foe: / I told it not, my wrath did grow.
> —William Blake, *A Poison Tree*[1]

In 2010, my dad was having trouble finding the bathroom at night. Then he destroyed the coffee maker and left the stove on overnight. His wife, whom I'll call Catherine, developed colitis from the stress of caregiving and couldn't bear to witness his deterioration any longer.

She found a small, assisted-living facility and took Dad for a visit, which he seemed to enjoy. She concocted an elaborate story to accomplish the move, telling Dad that their home was being tented for termite treatment, that he couldn't stay with his daytime care provider (as he had in the past) because her mother was visiting, and that Catherine was going to take the cats and stay at a friend's house.

"That's our story," she said. She asked me to stick with it.

On moving day, Dad suddenly hated the place, and Catherine found the residents less high functioning than when they had visited. She reminded Dad that he would only be there for a few days. Nonetheless, as she later explained, "He resented having no choice in the matter."

A few days later, Dad fell asleep in the facility's living room. When an aide woke him and told him he had to move to his bedroom, Dad removed his leather belt and chased her into the kitchen.

I remembered the gesture from my childhood. During a quiet moment, usually just before bedtime, Dad would slowly remove his leather belt and growl, sending us kids scurrying for cover. A game of chase would ensue with him growling and us giggling and running to escape. If caught, we were subjected to vigorous tickling until everyone collapsed into one big puppy pile on the floor. It was a great way to "get the wiggles out" of kids who resisted going to bed.

I knew Dad as a careful, quiet man who taught me to train horses. I still hear his voice from time to time when I'm in the saddle: "Let him know you're the boss" or "Don't let him see that you're afraid."

I can count on one hand the number of times he raised his voice to me. In his late eighties, he was a small wiry man. It was hard for me to imagine him threatening anyone. But the owner said Dad was "combative." He wanted Dad out and

Aging Angry. Amanda Smith Barusch, Oxford University Press. © Oxford University Press 2024.
DOI: 10.1093/oso/9780197584644.003.0011

threatened to dial 911 if Catherine didn't come get him right away. She brought him back home.

The next morning, I got an email:

> Your Dad seemed fine when I brought him home, we had a pleasant evening. But then, in the middle of the night, he became violent and threatened both me and the caregiver with anything he could find to use for a weapon. At one point he tried to strangle me. It was like he was in a trance. He has never offered me violence before. I had to call 911, and now he's in the ICU at Dominican Hospital for safety.

He also threw an Adirondack chair at her and was roving through the house looking for weapons when she called the sheriff.

Aggression is considered the most challenging of the "behavioral and psychological symptoms" (BAPS) of dementia. Estimates of its prevalence among people with dementia vary considerably. One community-based study found that 40 percent of family caregivers reported at least one severe episode of aggression.[2] Among those in residential care, estimates suggest that 4 percent to 7 percent per week, 20 percent a month, and 96 percent over a ten-year period display severe aggressive behavior.[3]

Chemical Restraint

Once labeled "combative," Dad would be on some form of chemical restraint for the remaining five years of his life. The drugs ranged from antipsychotics to sedatives. For a while, I tried to keep track of their names and doses. I looked up their side effects and begged the doctor to take him off drugs like risperidone that can cause strokes and other nasty side effects.[4] But the long-term care facilities he found himself in, three in total, either did not know how or did not care to carefully consider the anger of residents suffering from dementia. It was much easier and more cost effective to keep them sedated on antipsychotic medication or benzodiazepine, drugs known to have dangerous side effects.[5]

The Food and Drug Administration (FDA) estimates that roughly 15,000 nursing home residents die each year as the result of unnecessary use of antipsychotics.[6] Since 1987, the Nursing Home Bill of Rights has included the right to be free of chemical restraint "imposed for purposes of discipline or convenience." There is no drug authorized by the FDA for the restraint of patients, but providers skirt this by claiming, if anyone should ask, that drugs are used only to treat symptoms like aggression.[7]

Several organizations have recognized the terrible human cost of reliance on chemical restraint. In 2016, the California Advocates for Nursing Home Reform observed that "the chemical restraint of RCFE [Residential Care Facilities for the Elderly] residents knows no bounds. Unlicensed and barely trained aides give out antipsychotic drugs to residents like candy, while often little or nothing is done to respond to the underlying causes of pain, illness, despair and distress."

The stories we tell ourselves about aggression in older adults are deeply problematic. In 2021, Professor Laura Funk (University of Manitoba) and an international team of researchers studied public discourse about older adults who commit aggressive acts; not mass murderers, but run-of-the-mill aggression like homicide and physical abuse. They read 141 newspaper stories about these events and identified four ways they were framed: criminal act, childish incivility, horrific tragedy, and injustice (usually when an elderly resident attacked a staff member). They offered quotes suggesting that aggression is an inevitable consequence of dementia and that the rapid aging of Canada's population exposes ever more citizens to the threat of harm, concluding, "Existing coverage tended towards stigmatizing, fear-inducing, and biomedical framings of aggression."[8]

When the media repeatedly implies that older adults are dangerous and that aggression and dementia inevitably go together, it's easy to understand the desire to turn away from angry elders and to dismiss them as childish or criminal.

A Dose of Hope

However, as researchers consider the possible causes of aggression and identify ways to address them, there is some cause for hope.[9] Several studies have focused on nonpharmacologic interventions for reducing aggression and its precursors among older adults who suffer from dementia.

Maura Kennedy and her colleagues at Massachusetts General Hospital published an article discussing the causes and treatment of agitation among older adults in emergency rooms.[10] Among the potential causes, they list pain, fear, boredom, overstimulation, and unmet needs. They advise starting with nonpharmacologic strategies, including a caregiver who provides "a calming presence" and treatment for pain, Sensory augmentation for those with hearing or visual impairment, diversional activities (such as reading, coloring, or puzzles), soothing activities (like towel folding), fidgeting activities (card shuffling), and sensory stimulation (music, lights, videos).

In 2018, Professor Jane Fischer and Jeffrey Buchanan conducted a case study with an eighty-eight-year-old resident they called VB. "Nursing staff reported that VB slapped, pushed, scratched, cried, screamed, and swore at caregivers, usually when being undressed and changed before bed in the evening." The researchers set out to find a video or picture VB enjoyed, settling on a baby video that made her smile. They asked her caregiver to begin the changing session by putting the video on VB's television and directing her attention by saying things like, "Isn't the baby cute?" As the caregiver changed her clothes, they reminded VB about the video from time to time. The result was dramatic. Aggression was practically nil. The authors conclude that access to a "preferred stimulus" distracting dementia patients during stressful times (typically intimate care such as bathing, toileting, or changing clothes) can effectively curtail their aggression.[11]

In 2022, Dr. Tatiana Dimitriou and her colleagues in Greece reported on a randomized controlled trial in which they studied the effectiveness of nonpharmacologic interventions to reduce irritability among sixty hospitalized patients with dementia. They compared various combinations of four interventions: music therapy, a combination of aroma- and massage- therapy, validation therapy, and a psychoeducational program. They concluded that the most effective intervention combines all the modalities except validation therapy. Notably, they had no dropouts.[12]

You know that a field is maturing when people start doing "systematic reviews." So I was delighted to see one pop up on my screen. In 2019, Dr. Jennifer A. Watt (St. Michael's Hospital in Toronto) and her colleagues undertook a comparative review of pharmacologic and nonpharmacologic interventions to address dementia-associated agitation and aggression. They reviewed 163 studies involving 23,143 patients. Their conclusion: Nonpharmacologic interventions seemed to be more efficacious than pharmacologic interventions for reducing aggression and agitation in adults with dementia.[13]

American Cool

Dad's story is emblematic of how our country deals with anger and with our fear of anger. Sure, rage can be terrifying. Over a third (36%) of the older adults in my Internet survey agreed that "When other people are angry with me, I usually feel frightened." Perhaps the trauma so many of us have experienced from repeated direct and indirect exposure to violence makes us overestimate the danger. Sometimes even a mildly angry gesture can trigger this deeply ingrained fear that makes us distance ourselves from angry people. This can feel like the only way to protect ourselves.

It's natural to turn away from anger and, as we have seen, people with dementia are frequently angry. In forty years as a gerontologist, I never conducted research on dementia. I was tempted. There was a lot of grant money available.

But I just couldn't. Maybe I was scared. Anyway, I skirted the topic until Dad was diagnosed. But later, my son tested positive for the gene associated with increased risk of dementia and I could no longer avoid the topic.

After age eighty, a person's odds of getting dementia become about even—50 percent. (For those, like my son and me, who have *the gene* odds are a bit higher.) Lately, we see a growing focus on what individuals can do to avoid getting dementia; things like exercise, losing weight, doing crosswords, eating better. These are all good for you, but there's no evidence that they actually prevent dementia. My dad did all those things.

Despite the "you can do it" messaging, whether or not a person gets dementia is still largely a matter of luck and genes. To some extent the messaging distracts us from the challenge of providing high-quality care to those who pull the short straw. When we attribute dementia to lifestyle it becomes easier to blame the victim and to discount their anger and frustration.

In their 1986 book, *Anger: The Struggle for Emotional Control in America's History,* historians Carol and Peter Stearns draw upon diaries and advice literature (newspaper columns and published manuals on child-rearing, marriage, and work life) to reconstruct our collective understanding of anger from colonial America to the 1980s.[14] They trace interest in controlling, rather than expressing, anger to the middle of the eighteenth century. During the Victorian era, social norms called for channeling anger in productive directions. Workplace demands of the fully industrialized twentieth century led to an emphasis on repressing anger. This became systematized as courts and employers contracted with anger-management specialists to "fix" unruly employees and citizens.

In 1994, Peter Stearns published *American Cool: Constructing a 20th Century Emotional Style.*[15] Using advice columns and books, he contrasts the Victorian era with the twentieth century to argue that passions that were celebrated in the Victorian era had no place in the twentieth century. This applied to romantic passion as well as anger. Stearns used the phrase "American Cool" to describe our country's newfound intolerance for passion.

The Stearns were criticized for their assumption that advice literature mirrors the attitudes of the citizenry.[16] But they didn't claim that it did. They argued that purveyors of advice offer a glimpse into the public narrative about emotion; that is, the stories we tell ourselves. While they don't perfectly map onto public attitudes, they do shed light on dominant narratives of the times and, to a limited extent, on the nation's broad aspirations.

Contemporary American culture values keeping our cool. We admire people like Justice Ketanji Brown Jackson who endured the suspicions, prejudices, and downright abuse of Republican senators during her 2022 confirmation hearing. On the other hand, we tend to disapprove of those like Will Smith. The same year, he tarnished his Best Actor award by physically assaulting Chris Rock when the comedian insulted his wife.

Ours is an era of anger suppression, maybe because so many of us are so angry. But some are raising concerns about the national tendency toward anger suppression. People of color and women have tapped into generations of rage to resist those who would deny them their anger.

A Word from the Wise

Most of us don't go to a therapist when we're worried about anger. We go to friends, family, maybe a pastor or community leader. Wondering what advice the lay community has to give, I asked my participants what they would say to a younger person about anger. The question yielded nearly two hundred responses, which are summarized in Table A6 on page 148 of the Appendix. Comments ranged from "Don't get mad," offered by a fifty-six-year-old white man from Florida, to "Turn into the Hulk and kick butt," from a fifty-nine-year-old African American man also from Florida.

Lucy, a seventy-four-year-old white woman from Southern California, offered multiple strategies: "Back off. Think it through. Seek advice from a trusted and preferably uninvolved source. Get informed. Prepare a plan to approach situations with intent not to allow anger to take over. Be more powerful in control instead of out of control in anger. Continually practice doing this."

By far, the most common advice was to be careful; to not let anger get out of control; to breathe or walk away and give it time to pass. Some thirty-seven respondents suggested that we *think* about what's going on. This is interesting given that more than half the respondents agreed with the statement, "I can't think when I'm angry."

Respondents also emphasized the need to *control* anger. In our "American cool" culture, losing control of your passions can entail a serious loss of dignity or face.

Some argued for "letting go." Seventy-one-year-old Marilyn wrote, "It doesn't pay to get angry over every little thing." Others emphasized the need to choose your battles.

Those offering specific advice or recommending people channel their anger were few and far between. Fifty-two-year-old Jana, a white woman in North Carolina, wrote, "Anger can be very motivating if you learn to process it properly. Anger that is repressed will eventually make you physically ill and will never help you resolve problems or conflicts. Pay attention to what your body is telling you." This is particularly worth noting given that one statement respondents were most likely to agree with was, "*getting angry* is bad for a person's health."

Turning toward Anger

Most of us will at times experience and express anger in ways that hurt ourselves and others. Most of us will at times grapple with regret and wonder what we could have done differently. Most of the angry people we encounter are not suicidal or murderous. They're just angry.

I came across a video on Facebook about "Turning Towards Anger." It referenced a life coach named Allie Savage, so naturally I sent her a message requesting an interview. When we met via Zoom, I encountered my own ageist bias. Not only was she quite young, but she was beautiful. For a shameful instant, I wondered what this woman could possibly teach me. A lot, as it turned out. Her comments helped pull things together.

Allie and her colleague specialize in women's empowerment. After reading *Rage Becomes Her* (discussed in Chapter 5) they hit upon the idea that activism is "anger in action." They set up their own Anger Project to help women "take a stance for themselves."

Anger has become a central focus of Allie's work. She emphasizes the need for women to "turn towards their anger" both to know themselves and to operate more assertively in their everyday lives. She believes that turning toward anger takes a person out of the victim mentality. She says women are better able to locate their boundaries and articulate their needs when they tap into their rage. One of her clients posted a Facebook video about how turning toward anger helped her be more patient with her children.

Allie uses exquisite metaphors. She tells me that some of her clients don't think they are angry though they are positively "leaking" rage. She speaks of "following anger home to our core values," "building a muscle" for anger, and "harvesting a little bit of anger."

And so, the cultural change begins. Recognition dawns slowly. As we turn toward the anger of older adults, including those, like my dad, who suffer with dementia, we might be able to fix what is bothering them. They might become less angry. If we can understand that in late life accumulated traumas come home to roost, we may become more patient with seniors.

If we conceive of anger as inherently protective, we might reclaim the power of this emotion and learn to be both angry and aware. Then, perhaps, even for elders who are exploding with anger, late life can become a time of growth and maturation.

12
Changing the World

> Hope has two beautiful daughters; their names are Anger and Courage. Anger at the way things are, and Courage to see that they do not remain as they are.
>
> —attributed to St. Augustine[1]

In 1974, Carol and Steve moved to the backwoods of Oregon. They wanted to raise their four kids close to nature; away from the fuss and bother of the city. They purchased a small farm on remote acreage surrounded by national forest. They kept chickens and a donkey and grew their own food. Money was scarce, but they didn't need much.

One Spring morning in 1975 the children were fishing in Five Rivers, right by their house. "The river," Carol writes in her book, *A Bitter Fog*, "was the pulse and breath of their young lives. They knew it well."[2] A tank truck came groaning down the dirt road that passed within feet of the river, a sticky oily substance spewing out from its side, covering the children. The driver worked for the Forest Service and was assigned to spray pesticide on the roadside weeds, which would shrivel, blacken, and die. He didn't mean to spray the children, but it left them, "With smarting skin, tearing eyes, burning mouths, throats and noses."[3]

A month later helicopters sprayed the same substance over a broader area. It drifted over Carol and Steve's place as well as some dozen other homes. After that, livestock died, fishermen caught deformed fish, a fawn was born with no eyes, and public health doctors noticed an unusually high rate of miscarriages in the area.

The Forest Service was spraying Agent Orange, which contains, among other things, dioxin—one of the most toxic molecules known to man. Initially, Carol and Steve contacted government agencies, like the EPA, to no avail. Later, they would learn that the EPA had used fraudulent data to approve use of the pesticide. "It was the lies." Carol said that really got them riled up.

When the devastating effects of Agent Orange on humans came to light, the U.S. military stopped spraying it in Viet Nam. No one imagined it would ever be sprayed in the United States. After all, Rachel Carson's 1962 treatise, *A Silent Spring*, had educated the public on the environmental havoc reaped by commercial pesticides. But national forest is a "land of many uses." One of them is logging. Commercial loggers found Agent Orange a cheap and effective way to clear the undergrowth away.

Carol and her neighbors did not plan on becoming activists. Their children, their livestock, their gardens, and the wild creatures around them were suffering. They just wanted to know what was going wrong.

They met in the old Fisher Schoolhouse. Carol felt tongue-tied, but "Steve was so good at guiding a meeting. He said, " 'Look you've lived here longer than we have. What happened to you when they sprayed?' ... That opened the floodgates." Together they formed CATS "Citizens Against Toxic Sprays," and fought a decades-long battle that eventually stopped the spraying of Agent Orange in national forests. It was a huge victory.

While it's difficult to prove what causes any given case, Carol and her colleagues attribute the high rate of cancer and miscarriage in their community to the spraying. Even though she lost friends to cancer and other illnesses, Carol recalls the meetings as real high points in her life. "It was wonderful to be there meeting people on common ground. It was wonderful to feel part of something." This sense of belonging, of being part of something bigger, is one of the great rewards of activism.

At the height of the conflict between CATS and the logging industry it became clear that some people saw the leaders of CATS as a threat. Dow Chemicals, producer of the herbicides, might have been concerned about their bottom line. CATS advocates noticed that they were being followed. Hired thugs, they figured. Some received threatening phone calls. Most carried on. The cause was too important to abandon.

One night Carol and Steve's home burned to the ground. Their children died in the blaze. Firefighters said it might have been arson; an investigation was opened but never completed. Though discouraged, Carol never wanted to give up. "It just wasn't an option.... Otherwise, you're just a damn victim.... A wonderful friend of mine [Richard Kennedy], after the fire was so supportive. He put up with me being such a mess for a long time and he was driving me somewhere. I just started crying. He pulled over to the side of the road. I was so mad I wanted to punch him. He said, 'Look. You want to give up. Go ahead. That's your choice. You can just be a sad wreck forever and it won't last long because you won't.' It was so blunt that I wanted to slap him. But he was dead right. OK I'm sad but that doesn't mean I'm going to stop. That was a turning point for me."

Carol believes that de-legitimizing anger was the government's "official reaction to people out here complaining about getting poisoned. They "dismiss you." It made her feel "murderous." Just like the time helicopters came circling over her house really low. She ran out, waving a rifle at them (see Figure 12.1). "I was almost seeing red." It turned out that the FBI was chasing a bank robber and wanted to use her phone.

Figure 12.1. Carol pointing a rifle. Reproduced with permission.

Carol transcended horrendous personal suffering, never letting anger consume her and never giving in to despair. She has certainly endured more than her fair share of grief, but she is not one to dwell on her losses. "You've got to keep a sense of humor and some of those people [in CATS] were so wonderful and funny. They could see the humor in situations. It was wonderful and it keeps you from taking yourself too seriously."

Carol says she sees her activism as a tribute to her children; a legacy she can leave for them. "It's just what I do."

Her patience, joy, and research skills have certainly come in handy. She is a marvelous communicator and has learned to keep a laser focus on her work. Like most of us, she gets riled up about the news. But, as she explains, "There are a lot of upsetting things going on beyond what's going on here. I just don't think I can do anything about it. . . . Getting riled up is pointless if you can't do something to remedy it even in a small way."

Distinguishing between pointless and productive anger, she says, "You either are angry because you're helpless or you're angry and there's something you can do about it . . . . At least you're doing something about it. You're taking some kind of control over it."

Events in late life, from physical and social aging to bereavement, barrage older adults with the message that we are not in control; that we lack "agency." Like Carol, many of the other activists I met with seemed fully engaged as they took a measure of control over their own fate and that of others.

Anger Constrained?

A colleague who was active in environmental advocacy suggested I talk with Stan because he was a very effective advocate. When our Zoom call began, I admired his thick mane of white hair and coveted his tidy shelves full of perfectly aligned hardback books.

Stan worked for the Kennedy campaign in 1960 but otherwise spent his career managing engineering and production for one of America's largest boat manufacturers. When he and his wife retired, they bought forty-five acres, built their dream home, and settled in to raise cattle and enjoy life in a pastoral valley in the Intermountain West.

Shortly after they moved in, Stan and his wife were startled to learn that a group with a shell company based in Las Vegas had applied for a permit to build a 270-watt coal-fired power plant in their valley. They had no intention of living next door to a power plant. Just when he thought he was done working, "Along comes this issue that I can't ignore. As long as I'm standing up, I might as well contribute."

Stan enthusiastically detailed his advocacy efforts. He started attending county commission meetings, listening and raising uncomfortable questions. Then came a campaign of letters to newspapers and radio stations to raise awareness. Fellow activists trickled in. They called a public meeting. They filed a Government Records Access and Management Act (GRAMA) request to get material the company had withheld from the public. They formed an organization that I call "Save Our Valley" (SOV). The hearings continued. A rezoning request was approved. The Department of Air Quality issued a permit. Construction was set to begin in eighteen months.

The tide began to turn when the power company couldn't find investors. The permit was extended another eighteen months. "That upset us but that's the way it was." People dug in. Public opinion shifted. Stan ran his own candidate for county commission; a local guy who won by an overwhelming majority. SOV sent letters to major banks outlining problems with the proposed construction.

Despite growing opposition, it seemed the state was automatically approving the company's every request for an eighteen-month extension. So, SOV incorporated and hired a local lawyer to sue the state. By the time the case was heard, Tim had joined the fight. "He kept everyone from killing each other."

SOV met with four or five "big" lawyers. None of them would take the case. Stan and Tim briefly considered quitting but instead chose to represent themselves. They spent four to six months assembling documents. Shortly after submitting their materials, they learned that the case had been moved up to the state Supreme Court. "What did we unleash?" they wondered.

Once the court date was set, they started preparing their verbal presentation. They did their paperwork, rehearsed their arguments, and wrote everything down. When the day came, Stan and Tim "squeezed into ties and jackets" they hadn't worn for years. After the opposing attorneys gave their incomprehensible presentation Stan watched as Tim delivered his remarks, making eye contact with each of the judges and tailoring his argument to their responses. On December 4, 2009, the judges ruled in favor of SOV. The five-year battle was over.

Of course, Stan was hooked on activism. He's now working with a group to oppose construction of a coal-loading facility in California. "It's worth getting involved to make a community's lives better."

Stan says that his activism is not motivated by anger. In fact, he was never angry; not when the power authority misled the public, not when the County Commission disregarded his arguments and granted preliminary approval, not when he couldn't find a lawyer to take the case, not even when a judge ignored his arguments and ruled in favor of the plant's permit. Anger, Stan explains, is "counter-productive." It's important to focus on the future. I heard echoes of my father's voice telling me to "get over it."

After our interview, Stan wrote me a long e-mail expanding on his views. "There are many ways to look at anger. Some seem to relish living in anger as it may be a way to relive their frustrations." He cites Lincoln's Gettysburg Address as proof that anger has no place in public affairs. "Lincoln chose to forgo anger and direct attention to the future—that this nation, under God, shall have a new birth of freedom."

Though Stan consistently and adamantly denies that anger plays any role in his activism, he did refer me to another environmental activist, saying, "His wife says Bradley wakes up angry. It's true! If Bradley isn't angry he must be asleep."

It would take thirteen months and a hundred dollars for me to get Bradley's attention. After innumerable unanswered e-mails, I read an op-ed he wrote about an environmental issue. It was the perfect blend of sarcasm and authority. I found it informative, readable, and utterly persuasive. Besides, he really did sound angry. So, I dusted off my checkbook and sent $100 to his organization with a note reading, "I want to support your work even though you're ignoring my e-mails. Thanks so much for all you do." Within a few days, I was surprised to find an e-mail from Bradley in my inbox. He would be happy to do an interview for my book.

Bradley popped up in my Zoom frame right on time, with a floral stained-glass window behind him. He had only recently retired from the clinical practice of medicine and was tired from working on a cement project. He looked about fifty but was actually seventy-one years old.

Bradley told the wife story differently. "My wife has quipped for years that . . . the worst thing in the morning is for me to get up and not have anything to be angry about. She is certain that has never happened."

Bradley distinguishes between intellectual anger, which is experienced "on a rational plane" and emotional anger, which "can drift off into an irrational plane." While he experiences a good deal of intellectual anger, his emotional anger is reserved for inanimate objects and interpersonal relationships. He describes an accident with a ladder that broke during a house renovation project and led to a cascade of disasters. "It's my own fault for not being careful. I get angry at myself and at inanimate objects. I would absolutely take it out on an inanimate object. It's completely irrational but nonetheless anybody who claims to be rational is lying." He considers emotional anger in interpersonal relationships irrational because there's no right answer, just "value systems that reflect personal priorities, experience, and taste. [That leaves] lots of room for debate."

Bradley doesn't think anger is a "positive contributor" to his activism. "I feel an imperative to remain engaged, but I wouldn't say that frustration or anger is part of the equation. . . . If there's an injustice in the world, I feel compelled to care about if not address it. If there's idiocy in the public arena, I feel obligated to correct it . . . . I'm the one on whose shoulders it rests to post things about environmental issues so we can educate our followers."

Neither of his parents had a fiery disposition, and Bradley doesn't either. He is a well-educated man who values rationality and feels that most of the world's problems stem from irrationality. He describes his "default outlook on life" as revolving around the question, "Why are so few people trying to correct so many wrongs?"

When I ask whether, as a physician, he knows of any health differences between expressed and internalized anger, Bradley says he can only speculate.

Unexpressed anger is something a lot of counselors feel they need to nurture or harvest from people. I'm not sure that is a productive exercise. Lots of people go to counselors and get "oh you haven't dealt with this . . . and it's causing this and this . . . I'm not convinced there's smoldering anger in people. Maybe sometimes but it's not the case with most people's discontent.

There was something unsettling and vaguely stoic about Bradley's insistence on the irrationality of anger and Stan's total rejection of the emotion. I have always found deep wisdom in emotions and, though I admire their firm discipline, I found it difficult to share their certainty.

Great Old Broads and Raging Grannies

Seventy-six-year-old Mary made a career of activism. A trained scientist, she devoted decades to the preservation of public lands, working for several nonprofit environmental law organizations in the West. Most of her work involved litigation and administrative processes. Her views on anger remind me a little of Stan. "In those settings anger isn't going to get you very far . . . for me to get angry would be kind of counterproductive unless I think there's nothing else I can do. I'm always looking for what I can do."

When I ask whether she might use anger as a last resort, she says the reverse is true. Anger comes at the beginning, "right when you realize something is happening." Mary worked for three years on a collaborative agreement to protect an important stream on national forest land from cattle. As anyone who has lived in the West knows, nothing can destroy a streambed as quickly and thoroughly as the sharp hooves of grazing cattle. On a routine inspection, she found the property had been "just obliterated by cows." Mary broke into tears. "I was furious."

The permitee, a billionaire who owned the cattle and leased the grazing rights, had locked his cattle in. "They ate shrubs cows don't usually eat . . . . Such a loss . . . . It had been six years of recovery."

She made calls that night and finally got the district manager, who admitted she had allowed it. "There was nothing I could do but I could use it as an example for why things needed to be different." Mary put together a photo essay and told a lot of people what had happened. When the topic came up at a meeting, the district manager said the permitee had threatened to sue her because the federal Bureau of Land Management didn't do an archeological survey before they put in the fence to protect the stream. Mary says she might have used the word, "chickenshit" when she exploded with anger.

She tells me this story to illustrate how anger can be counterproductive. "It's one of those things that's not helpful. She [the district manager] then had an excuse to walk out of the meeting." Which is exactly what she did. As a professional and a woman of conscience, Mary looks on this as a failure. "I lost those 40 acres."

"The hardest emotion for me is just sadness . . . . When you work in the environment you're always losing. We're losing species, communities . . . . You try to delay losses. In the best circumstance you're able to restore something. Then with climate change you have the sense that any restoration is temporary. To work 30 years and not make much progress.... I'm not alone. You've got climate scientists who've been raising the evidence for climate threats for their whole career and all they have to show for it is worse conditions and resistance to change."

As we talk, Mary refines her thoughts on anger and adds to my glossary of euphemisms when she says, "I'm pretty aggressive with facts, if that counts as anger. I don't go along. I face them with facts." I ask whether she feels angry when she faces them with facts. "Probably yes. This is in front of you and you're letting this happen and it's unnecessary. Then I always go to what I think they should do." The bottom line: "You're not at the table if all you are is an angry person.... It takes being adamant and right on the facts and aggressively reasonable."

Mary acknowledges the pros and cons of anger. "When anger gets personal it can be destructive.... On the other hand, if someone is harming you, you need to be angry about that... you wish more women would get angry when they are sexually harassed. They ought to get angry right then and do something about it. Not just let it go. Then the person who is abusive goes and does that to others."

Mary is on the board of "Great Old Broads for Wilderness," an organization that emphasizes humor (illustrated by their play on the term Good Old Boys). "But you can't *just* do antics. At some point you have to settle down and get to work." The Great Old Broads have a lot of work to do but Mary emphasizes the pleasure that comes from working with others, "You have chances to make jokes, have fun planning something.... I think the angriest activists are those who try to work alone and they can't move the system at all and they can't have any power because they're just one person. They're just angry."

Mary's involvement with Great Old Broads reminds me of my first interview with one of the Raging Grannies. This activist group uses the invisibility of older women to their advantage, gaining access to corporate and government settings that might otherwise be off-limits. Sixty-nine-year-old Arlene joined up when she turned fifty, thinking, "Oooh. That's what I want to be when I grow up." The highlight of her experience was being one of five people to shut down the Tar Sands Pipeline in 2016. She and her colleagues entered the compound wearing hard hats and safety vests. "No one questioned us because we looked like workers." They cut a fence with bolt cutters and chained themselves to the pipeline shutoff valves forcing the company to shut it down. She knew she might spend a couple of years in prison but decided it was worth it.

The grannies also protested at the port commission when Shell was seeking to expand drilling. They set up a table in front of the commission headquarters and sold cookies with a big sign, "Raising money to buy back the port commission."

For Arlene, anger is fuel. "My anger is with the system itself. We sometimes target a person, but we don't hate them. It's really about the system... unless we get rid of it, we're doomed."

Of course, there are lows, too. Sometimes she feels despair over racism and patriarchy. "Despair and anger go together . . . [but] I always want to do something if I possibly can. . . . If something is wrong, I have to get off my butt and do something to change it." Mary's discussion of sadness and anger hit close to home.

Choosing Anger

My daughter lives with a chronic illness that requires regular treatment with sophisticated and expensive medication. Several times a year, her insurance company denies coverage for this medication, sometimes retroactively. The latest occasion happened as I was finishing this book.

She explains things better than I ever could in an e-mail:

I was just thinking about your book because during this last great insurance debacle there was a period where I was calling the department of labor, the state insurance commission, the health insurance company, the pharmacy, and just weeping at them and begging someone to just please help me, and then getting really sad and scared and consumed with a desire to give up.

It wasn't until I buckled down and chose anger instead of sadness (I'm pissed off they won't help me. I'm pissed off they made me feel this way. I'm pissed off they do it to everyone because they think they can get away with it.) that I picked myself up and decided I needed to make it their problem. I just decided to be too angry to accept no.

Did I yell at and swear at people over the phone? Yes. And I regret nothing, because it wasn't until I got angry that anyone paid any attention to me. They didn't hear me until I stopped making it my problem (being sad and giving up right, like a form of self-punishment. Only I would feel the despondence. They wouldn't feel anything at all.) and started making it their problem instead. And I made it clear that I was going to continue to make it their problem until they did something to help me solve it.

Sometimes the rage demon on your shoulder is there to help. Sometimes it's the path to a solution.

Striking a Light

Ultimately, I interviewed a diverse group of activists, including four who identified as men's rights activists (Joe, Eddie, Sean, and Warren), four environmental advocates (Carol, Mary, Stan, and B. M.), a justice activist from the Raging Grannies (Arlene), an education activist (Mark), and three people who worked on race issues (D. D., Ruby, and Tomas). The wonder of Zoom enabled me to travel from New York to Washington state with a few keystrokes.

Every single one of them impressed me with their dynamism, commitment, and deep engagement. They certainly don't conform to the stereotype of seniors who care only about their own comforts and petty distractions. These elders are not hostile to social change. They are making it happen. They marshal tremendous personal resources to help shape the world in which they want to live. Time and again, their activism ties back to personal experiences of injustice or, sometimes, to personal trauma.

Researchers around the globe are beginning to recognize the importance of older activists. A 2019 survey by AARP found that roughly half of American adults aged sixty-five or older volunteer with community groups and organizations, 32 percent of them on a weekly basis—more than any other age group. Their primary motivation: to make a difference.[4]

Jackie Fox (National University of Ireland) and Sarah Quinn (St. James' Hospital) conducted an in-depth study in 2012 with seven seniors who participated in a "medical care protest" that arose when the government in Ireland decided to add a means test to health insurance for older adults. They write of "the unique mindset of older adults in relation to social activism" and suggest the activism is especially good for the emotional health of older adults.

One man in his seventies put it well, "When people are in possession of a justified grievance, when they see an injustice being done to others and they don't do anything about it, then their anger turns to frustration. So, they end up cursing the darkness instead of striking a light." Another of their respondents mentioned that "all the time it's a battle against the negativity of people's feeling of hopelessness."[5]

In a similar study, Daniel Blanche-Tarragó and Mireia Fernández-Ardèvol (Universitat Oberta de Catalunya) report on in-depth interviews with fifteen members of an activist collective called the Iaioflautas ("grandmother-flutes").[6] The group emerged during Spanish protests around austerity measures in 2011. With a strong focus on civil rights and social justice, they use a variety of innovative methods to raise public awareness. Iaioflautas members occupy banks and stock exchanges to underscore financial practices that impoverish seniors. Like the Raging Grannies, they use humor and creativity to make their point. Like the Grey Panthers, they share a commitment to intergenerational solidarity.

In his 2012 study of grassroots organizing in America, Jeffrey Stout argues that anger provides essential fuel to activists: "Someone who professes love of justice, but is not angered by its violation, is not likely to stay with the struggle for justice through thick and thin, to display the passion that will motivate others to join in, or to have enough courage to stand up to the powers that be."[7]

Anger may be an essential motivator for activists, but is it relevant to older adults in this field? A 2023 study by Jasimine Lorenzini and Jan Rosset at the University of Geneva suggests it may be. They studied the emotions that motivated climate protestors in eleven cities around the world. Their results suggest that those over sixty years of age were *more* likely to experience anger about climate change and less likely to report feeling fear than those under thirty-five years old.[8] Their findings are echoed in a recent book by sociologist Gary Alan Fine, of Northwestern University.

Fine's 2023 book, *Fair Share,* offers the findings of his ethnographic study of older activists.[9] Dr. Fine spent three years (from 2015 to 2017) with an organization called Chicago Seniors Together (CST), participating in their protests and interviewing professional staff and dues-paying members. I had a chance to talk with Dr. Fine as this book went to press.

When I asked about anger, Dr. Fine said he didn't see much anger or rage expressed at CST. Although there was certainly some "scripted anger," the organization's gatherings were more often characterized by joy, humor, and something Fine terms, "pleasure in resistance." This might be because, as we have seen, expressing anger is risky for older adults who are, as a result, likely to be dismissed, ridiculed, or labeled demented. Fear, the more socially acceptable emotion, was more often used in the organization's rhetoric.

Although anger certainly plays a role in late-life activism, its effects are as complex as the social problems themselves. Activists must be judicious in their expression of thus stigmatized emotion, even as they must access its energy to accomplish their goals.

Late-life activists pursue diverse change agendas, but many see themselves resisting the pervasive ageism that contributes to social aging. As one of the Fox and Quinn respondents put it, they are pushing back against "a negative and damaging discourse . . . about older adults." In terms that sound quite familiar, Iaioflautas aims to "counter the culturally devalued identity of older adults and retirees." Iaioflautas member, sixty-two-year-old Biel, describes how activism brings dignity to later life:

> It is not only that they are useful, but that they are needed.
> And that gives you a personal value in your own life that
> the system intended to make you lose. It brings back your dignity.
> You are no longer a being that is used and thrown away.[10]

I wish the #OKBoomer types on Twitter could meet these inspiring individuals. They might persuade the cynics that not all older adults are self-consumed and indifferent to the future. It might even turn them on to the vibrant possibilities of later life.

Conclusion

The Eye of the Heart

> Come not between the dragon and his wrath.
> —Shakespeare, *King Lear*[1]

When I was a child, school was my sanctuary from the chaos of family dysfunction. It brought just the right balance of predictability and challenge. And I loved it. More than anything, I wanted to be a teacher—like my mother, my aunts, my grandmother.

I was lucky. Born after birth control pills were invented and growing up in a rare moment of increased investment in public education, I had the chance to complete my PhD at the tender age of thirty and found my first tenured position the same year.

Life in the classroom wasn't always easy. For the first few years, my students were older than me and it took a while to win their respect. But I came to cherish my job. I had a shelf full of awards and, more important to me, a drawer full of notes from students on what my teaching meant to them. Walking up the stairs to the building where I taught, I sometimes whispered, "I can't believe I get to work here."

For decades, I flourished. Then my hair turned grey. Crow's feet and brow wrinkles made their appearance. One day, a few years before the new dean arrived, I found myself trying to generate discussion about an assigned reading for one of my favorite all-day elective workshops. I'd become pretty good at leading discussions as my students and I grappled with the complexities before us. I would throw out a question and usually a few students volunteered answers. If not, I could tolerate long silences while students pondered their options. No response was ever wrong. I praised their comments even when they strayed from what I was after.

But this day was different. I had reminded the students before we met that the readings were "REQUIRED." The agenda showed that we would be discussing them during the hour after lunch so I imagined they might use the break to glance over the material. But when I threw out my first question no one raised their hand. No one even met my eye. My practiced techniques yielded nothing. Finally, a woman in the back row stood up and exclaimed, "Look! I don't have time to read all this crap!"

Aging Angry. Amanda Smith Barusch, Oxford University Press. © Oxford University Press 2024.
DOI: 10.1093/oso/9780197584644.003.0013

In the loaded silence that followed, I looked down. My hands were shaking. My whole body quivered. I wasn't sure what made me so angry but knew I couldn't go on with the class. I sat down, took a breath, and eeked out four words: "That's it. We're done." As I gathered my notes and books, a few students came forward to ask whether class was really over. The rest tiptoed out of the room.

I had blown it, lost my cool, failed to accomplish the task at hand. My first impulse was to talk to our dean, a man with great empathy whom I trusted completely. I walked to his office (The door was always open.) and said, "I think I just made a big mistake." We sat down and I told him what happened. He reassured me and, as my heartrate returned to normal, we moved quickly toward collaborative problem-solving, exploring whether my student's outburst might be a signal that something needed to change.

The following week, I spoke with my students individually. Each saw the incident differently. Some were embarrassed by their classmate's outburst. Most agreed there was too much reading in the program. A few told me they were worried about me. That was unnerving but these conversations were tremendously valuable. Afterwards, I resolved to consider the situation from the students' perspective. Their time was precious, and I realized that they needed to know why I thought the readings were worth their while. In the coming weeks I made it a habit to introduce the readings before I expected the students to engage with them. I told them why I assigned each one; sharing my enthusiasm for the insights, stories, or frameworks it had to offer. This would become an opportunity to let my students know, in very specific terms, why each reading was important *to them*.

I can't remember much more about that semester. For a while we all walked on eggshells, but we carried on. They did their reading. I did my grading. And now, years later, I am grateful to the student who was brave enough to express her frustration, to the dean for his support, and to myself for turning toward my student's anger and taking it seriously.

Speaking with colleagues about the incident, I learned that I was not the only senior professor to experience difficulties in the classroom. Most felt it was happening more often. Some said student attitudes toward professors had changed. Others thought students were particularly antagonistic toward those of us with grey hair. These colleagues shared their reactions, saying, "I am more peeved now than ever!" and "I never expected to be this angry once I got old."

No one expects to be angry when they get old. When I asked my graduate students what they thought it would feel like to be old, they told me it should feel "calm," "wise," "content," "maybe a little sad." Their views reflected what they had been taught.

Social work students, like nearly all in the helping professions, study Erik Erikson's stages of social development. Each stage is characterized by a conflict between two ego states, as well as a virtue that is expected to emerge as a result. The final two stages address later life.

In Erikson's seventh stage, which some place at ages forty to seventy-five, adults struggle between generativity and stagnation. Those who are successful develop the ego strength he called "care." Erikson's eighth stage extends for the rest of the lifespan. Here, the conflict is between integrity and despair. Its resolution should lead to wisdom, enabling an elder "to look back on their life and accept death without fear."

Is that what aging is all about? Learning to accept death?

Erikson's theory and my students' expectations reflect widely held norms that view later life as a quiet time of reflection. A time to let go of earthly concerns; a time to quit and grow gently wise; a time to prepare for death; certainly not a time to get angry and change the world. Perhaps this expectation is what led one early reviewer of my book to ask for proof that "older people are feeling some kind of rage, rather than . . . depression, isolation, and withdrawal."

The proof is all around us. I saw it in my shaking hands that day. We see it when families struggle with intergenerational conflict. We see it in South Korea, where the Taegukgi Squads take to the streets and the Internet to protest political developments. In Spain, where the Iaioflautas occupy banks and stock exchanges to protest systemic inequities. In Ireland, where seniors protest cuts in national health coverage. In Canada and the Pacific Northwest, where the Raging Grannies stand up against environmental degradation with humor and creativity.

In 1977, economic theorist E. F. Schumacher wrote a deep meditation on how to be fully human in the material world. In his brief essay, *A Guide for the Perplexed*, he argues for the importance of emotions, saying that "The Eye of the Heart, which produces insight, is vastly superior to the power of thought, which produces opinions."[2] His thoughts echo the fourteenth-century Persian poet, Rumi, who coined the term and argued that the eye of the heart was "seventy-fold more seeing than the 'sensible eyes' of the intellect." When anger helps clarify our core values, it truly does serve as "the eye of the heart."

I have come to see anger as essential. It reveals those things, as Winston Churchill said, "up with which I will not put." By signaling the presence of a wrong, it clarifies our values and calls on us to take charge of our lives and our social worlds. My anger in the classroom that day signaled how deeply I valued student engagement. Older adults are angry; and angry people deserve attention, compassion, and respect. We all deserve to be taken seriously. Anger happens. We can't just turn it off. And when we declare someone's anger illegitimate, we declare the angry person "less than." Historically, anger suppression has been a means of oppressing the powerless, particularly people of color and women. It may also be a way of enforcing norms of behavior for older adults.

Anger is not simply an emotion. It is a highly evolved biological process and a deeply personal experience. Rather than judging, stifling, or fearing our anger, we should turn toward it and listen carefully. We should notice what it does to our bodies. And, once we have taken the vital pause to allow those signals to ease, we can put our cerebral cortex in the driver's seat and interrogate our anger, asking what is wrong and deciding what action is or is not called for in this socio-cultural context.

We might need to reassure a loved one by saying, "Yes, I am angry. But I'm not mad at you." Or, "I love you *and* I'm angry with you." We might need to listen more carefully to a student. Like the man in Figure C.1, we might need to march for our grandchildren. We might need to go outside and chop some wood.

Old age need not be a time of poignant withdrawal. Some of us must still rage against the dying of the light. One of the great gifts of age is the freedom to address our anger and harness its power to accomplish change. Late life can be a time to reclaim our thoughtful present anger for the benefit of ourselves and those around us.

Figure C.1. We might need to march for our grandchildren. Photo by Roya Ann Miller on Unsplash.

Postscript

Since I wrote this book there have been developments. Major players have changed jobs at the university in moves reminiscent of musical chairs. Some have left altogether. Larry and I have celebrated the birth of our first grandchild, which radically shifts our center of gravity. Recollections of the events that triggered my retirement no longer raise my blood pressure. After fueling three years of research and writing, my anger has run its course leaving me free to look forward, not to the end of the story, but toward its next exciting chapter.

APPENDIX 1

The Anger Project

Research is a marvelous window into the human experience. It can discipline our ramblings and disabuse us of faulty expectations. For some strange reason, when I set out to ask other people about their experiences, I expected them to be similar to mine. I shake when I'm very angry. I find it embarrassing and a little puzzling. I was surprised to learn how few people experienced shaking as an anger signal. On the other hand, I have not (yet) experienced a decline in the intensity or frequency of anger in my later years, so I was surprised by how many of my respondents in their fifties and sixties had.

I was taught to keep my mouth shut when angry. For decades, I thought this experience was unique to me. Through the research I conducted for this book, I learned that women have been given this same message for thousands of years. This connected to my longtime interest in social justice and, as a result, I came to see anger suppression as a tool for the oppression of vulnerable and marginalized people.

The bibliography that follows this section provides a list of sources I have used to better understand anger. Here, I will outline my threefold attempt to learn how other older adults experience anger. This effort involved: (1) setting up a Facebook page, (2) conducting interviews, and (3) administering an Internet survey to a nationally representative sample of older adults.

Ethical Approval

I called the study, *Anger in Later Life* and described it to the University of Utah Institutional Review Board (IRB), saying:

> The proposed work will serve as the basis of a book tentatively titled, "Aging Angry." In it, I examine how older adults experience anger and what they do about (or with) it. I plan to begin with an Internet survey designed to provide respondents an opportunity to describe an important or memorable experience they have had with anger in the past five years. This experience might relate to: a national issue, family life, the workplace, or another topic. Respondents will draft a brief narrative describing the experience then respond to a series of questions designed to expand on the inciting incident(s), physiological responses, appraisals, subsequent behaviors, and retrospective analysis and evaluation.

I planned to adapt the "critical incident technique. Here's how I explained it:

> There is considerable evidence that older adults report experiencing anger less frequently than younger adults. Among the negative emotions, older adults are more likely to report experiencing sadness. Indeed, there is a general predilection in late life to report higher life satisfaction than young adults. This led Laura Carstenson and her colleagues at Stanford to introduce the concept of "socio-emotional selectivity"

(Fung et al, 2001); They argue that, in essence, older adults manage their social and emotional lives more effectively than young adults.

There is another fairly well-established stream of work examining the link between emotions and physical health. Klabbers (2012), for instance, identified a correlation between mortality and cognitive hostility in middle-aged and older adults. Like his study, most of this work is correlational.

To my knowledge, no work in the area of late-life emotions has examined how older adults experience and react to anger. The method I'm proposing bears some resemblance to a study reported by Lucas Hamilton and Eric Allard in 2019. They asked sixty-one young and fifty-seven old volunteers to describe negative life events and categorize them as angry or sad and report on the intensity (on a 6-point scale). They found more similarities than differences between young and older adults and concluded that recall is relatively stable over the lifespan. Of course, they did not address the possibility that their sample may not provide sufficient power to detect age differences.

Like these researchers, I propose to ask older adults to recall events—in this case, events that made them angry. I propose to examine several factors: the nature and appraisal of the inciting event, the remembered physiological response, subsequent behaviors, and the extent to which later analysis emphasizes regret versus lessons learned. I will then focus on experiences that evoke what I'm calling "transformative anger." That is, anger that results in a (positive) change in the individual or their social context. I plan to explore this aspect of anger through in-depth interviews with selected participants from the Internet survey as well as high-profile activists of my acquaintance.

I promptly received notice that the IRB considered my project "exempt" from full review because it posed minimal risk to human beings.

The Facebook Page

Realizing that I spent more time than I should on Facebook during the pandemic, I speculated that others might be doing the same. So I set up a page for The Anger Project and posted comments in hope of generating interesting discussions and recruiting people to complete interviews. I used images from Unsplash, a website that asks only that you acknowledge the source of your photos.

This approach is new for me, and I'm not even sure I'd call it research. I was able to generate and curate a few interesting discussions (perhaps moving the needle a bit) and I identified other projects liked to mine and found several have ongoing discussions about anger on Facebook. Boosting cost $20 per post but it made a huge difference. Ordinarily my posts reached less than a dozen people.

For the first boosted post, found on page 76, I used an image of a fist, with text opening with, "We want to know what makes you angry." This post reached 342 people and generated a brief but interesting conversation about the media. First, "Mary" wrote, "Everybody is trying so hard to get along with each other and the media doesn't help a bit. It just aggravates us." A few others (apparently young women) chimed in to agree that in the media "enragement = engagement."

The second boosted post, found on page 77 was titled, "Anger in Love." It featured a picture of two puffins fighting over a nest and the text read, "Can anger and love go together?

Does some small part of you believe your loved one doesn't love you when they're mad at you? How does this affect your intimate relationships? Join the conversation here!" This boosted post reached 605 and yielded thirteen comments, all of them from people with feminine names, such as Ruthie and Minnie.

The conversation opened with Ruthie's comment: *When you throw an egg against a wall and break it, can you put it back together? So it is with words spoken in anger, you can say I'm sorry, but you cannot heal the hurt it caused initially, like it never happened.* She seemed to be sharing advice she herself found useful. Then Ruthie posted again, *Always take a few seconds to breathe before you speak in anger.* She almost seemed to be speaking to herself, but Rhoda chimed in and shifted the focus. *I totally agree. They say stuff to you when they are angry, but the say sorry afterwards. I believe when they say that stuff, they believe it true, But I proved mine wrong.* No one asked who "they" were, though we might assume that Rhoda proved her lover wrong. Minnie offered a "100% Cute" image and Marilyn wrote, *Love conquers all!!!?* adding multiple heart emojis and a panda valentine image. That closing question mark adds a degree of interest. Marilyn may not be entirely sure about her comment. Hoping to keep things going, I added *Ah! I hope you're right. Sometimes it's hard when love and anger get together.* This triggered a flood of love images and emojis followed by Catherine's *awwww,* Irene's *ADORABLE*, and Minnie's *Ohhh how cute.* So much for serious conversation.

Eventually, I discovered another page called "The Anger Project: Wisdom & Lessons for the EMPATH," curated by Allie Savage and Natalika Lankenvich. I quickly applied to join this private group, where life coach Allie offered a word of wisdom as well as a video conversation with one of her clients on "turning towards anger."

"The Depression Project," founded by Danny and Matthew Baker, hosted a discussion on, "What is depression anger like?" Pretty awful, according to their 572 comments.

Both of these sites were established by people who offer therapy and/or other services. So in some ways, Facebook is just an elaborate advertisement. Conversations in the public sphere have a superficiality to them, but they do reveal something about mass attitudes. For instance, my first post revealed how at least a few FB users were aware of the role media plays in promoting anger. My second post on love and anger generated advice on anger suppression and ringing endorsements for the power of love. No one saw anger as a signal of the need for change and no one even suggested that a lover's anger might be legitimate.

The Interviews

There were some advantages to doing interviews during the pandemic. Foremost was the widespread adoption of Zoom technology. I only ran into two people who preferred to be interviewed by phone. The rest gave at least a glimpse into the geography of their lives through the Zoom window.

Initially, I completed five pilot interviews to refine my questions. Then, I conducted two kinds of interviews. The first, "respondent interviews," involved asking older adults to tell me about their experiences of anger. Ultimately, I did thirty-two interviews. Then I conducted twelve "expert interviews" with people whose published articles or books were of interest.

Recruiting for these interviews began with my professional network. Colleagues recommended people who might be interested (and interesting) then I used a snowball method to expand my reach. A few times, as with Carol (Activism chapter), I learned about someone through the media and contacted them directly. I found a treasure trove of men's rights activists through the Anger Project Facebook page. The first such activist that I interviewed volunteered through posts on that page. After our interview, he contacted one man to seek permission for me to contact him. That man did the same.

The interview sample had a mean age of sixty-five and a range from fifty to eighty-nine years of age. It was predominantly (76%) Caucasian, with whites being proportionate to the U. S. population (76%). Table A1 provides details on each interview respondent.

The dynamics of these interviews were considerably more fraught than simple life-history interviews. Asking about anger opens people up to some of their worst experiences. Initially, some respondents, like Connie, were wary. "That's not in my nature," she said, when I asked about a time she had been "really angry." By the end of the interview I think she realized that I wasn't going to judge her for getting angry. She told me how she "blew" the day before when speaking with her daughter-in-law. Sometimes people never did really open up and "let it all hang out." But when they did, the conversation suddenly became lively. We laughed and cried and communed over the absurdity, the power, and the wisdom of human emotions.

The Internet Survey

I used SurveyMonkey to host the Internet Survey. Following a small pilot test of the instrument, I added a link to my e-mail signature (which yielded about a half-dozen responses) and used boosted posts on Facebook to recruit people into the survey. "If you are 50 years old or over, we want to hear from you!" This method yielded thirty-five completed surveysfifty-eight s over a period of several weeks, including three who did not meet inclusion criteria for the study.

As the effectiveness of my Facebook posts dwindled, I realized it could take a year to collect a reasonable sample using that method. I decided to try crowdsourcing, which Patrick Mullen (from William and Mary) and colleagues from other universities defined as "the use of global workers to complete a task, obtain information, or gain insight" (p. 221). Essentially, I would use the Internet to outsource work to a crowd of willing individuals. Several platforms offer crowdsourcing on a fee-basis: Amazon's Mechanical Turk (MTurk), Qualtrics Panel, and SurveyMonkey Audience.

Mullen and colleagues (2021) described several advantages to this method. Most important for me was that crowdsourcing offers a more diverse sample than can be obtained through other methods. These methods are also time-efficient and relatively inexpensive.

I used the "SurveyMonkey Audience" collector, in large part because my survey was already posted on their platform. Mullen and colleagues also reported that the incentive system used by Amazon (which was considerably less expensive) tended to result in careless responses.

Andrew Jones and colleagues (2022) suggest that about 12 percent of respondents in a crowdsourced context are "careless responders." Researchers have devised a range of strategies, including attention checks, repetition of similar questions, and deleting respondents who finish the survey with implausible speed to deal with this problem.

Given the importance of essay questions in my survey, I didn't want to take a chance on useless replies. The essays did provide a great way to identify careless responders. In my case, for instance, one respondent wrote, "this survey is shit" in response to every essay

Table A1 Pseudonyms, Demographics & Themes for Interview Respondents (n = 32)

Pseudonym	Age (Mean = 65 yrs)	Gender (66% women)	Race/Ethnicity (76% Caucasian)	Themes
Arlene	69	Woman	Caucasian	Raging Grannies Activist
Bradley	71	Man	Caucasian	Environmental Activist
Carlie	56	Woman	Caucasian	Exercise it out, rape survivor
Carol	81	Woman	Caucasian	Environmental Activist, humor
Connie	71	Woman	Caucasian	Suppressed anger, Resistance
Dinah	67	Woman	Caucasian	Israeli immigrant, Enjoys anger
Donald	57	Man	Caucasian	Humor, Regrets FB unfriend
Esme	73	Woman	Caucasian	Dutch Immigrant, "extreme disillusionment"
Fiona	68	Woman	African American	Discussions on race & anger
Georgia	71	Woman	Caucasian	Abusive father, activist– Advice for men/women
Gianna	89	Woman	Latinx/Hispanic	Immigrated as child (Italy), family disowned her
Joe	61	Man	Caucasian	Men's rights
Karen	64	Woman	Caucasian	Retired in anger, pushed out
Kay	76	Woman	Asian	Conflict resolution, education activist
Kellie Ann	59	Woman	Caucasian	Diplomat, conflict w/ spouse, addiction
Paul	67	Man	Caucasian	Workplace discrimination@ age
Mark	50	Man	Caucasian	Workplace discrimination@ sexual orientation
Mary	76	Woman	Caucasian	Environmental activist, there's a place for anger
Norma	65	Woman	Caucasian	Marital tension
Ron	56	Man	Caucasian	Workplace anger, forced out works
Ruby	87	Woman	African American	Advocates for herself & family,
Rachel	60	Asian	Asian	Anger management specialist
Sandra	56	Woman	Caucasian	Angrier than ever, can't hide it
Santiago	55	Man	Latino/Hispanic	Military Officer

(continued)

Table A1 Continued

Pseudonym	Age (Mean = 65 yrs)	Gender (66% women)	Race/Ethnicity (76% Caucasian)	Themes
Sean	51	Man	Caucasian	Men's rights, False Accusations
Shauna	64	Woman	Caucasian	Relationship with anger
Stan	82	Man	Caucasian	Activist, not angry
Tim	50	Man	Caucasian	Angry young man, abusive father, works with DV
Tomas	59	Man	Latinx/Hispanic	Culture & anger, immigrant from Uruguay
Valerie	59	Woman	Caucasian	Community and BLM activist
Wayne	71	Woman	Caucasian	Peacemaker, abusive Dad, Marital tension
Wendy	55	Woman	Asian	Retired, ruminating @ anger

question. A few others gave responses that clearly indicated they didn't understand the question. It was easy to delete these, as well as anyone who completed the survey in less than five minutes. I wasn't sure how to deal with the person who wrote, "Neanderthal" when asked to identify their race. But when I checked their essays, the responses seemed thorough and well-considered. The same held for another who identified their race as "human." Though it does mess up my race stats, I guess it's alright for them to have a little fun.

Mullen and colleagues argue that researchers have an ethical obligation to provide reasonable compensations because some people are making their living as paid respondents. SurveyMonkey offers an easy system for determining the cost of various sampling limitations. So, for instance, I restricted my sample to people fifty years of age and over. This raised the cost from $2.50 per person to $5.00. Completion data for my survey indicated an average completion time of twenty minutes. I estimated that if 20 percent of the cost went to the platform it still would leave $12 per hour, so my respondents received more than the federal minimum wage of $7.25 per hour. In addition to the $297.40 fee to host the survey, I paid $754.25 to SurveyMonkey Audience for a sample of 150 respondents.

There were some constraints. SurveyMonkey's design guidelines, for instance, limit the number of questions that can be asked to fifty. So I had to give up a few questions and convert some of my essay questions into multiple-choice items. I had planned to recruit people into interviews from the Internet survey, but their system would not permit me to collect personal information such as e-mails. At one point, the survey was put on hold because too many people were starting and not completing. After some back and forth e-mails with staff, I was able to get it reinstated without (as I had feared) having to amend the instrument.

APPENDIX 1   145

Table A2 Internet Sample (n = 239) Demographics

Gender:	# (%)		# (%)	2020 Total U. S. Population*	2020 U. S. pop. 65+ **
Women	137 (55%)				
Men	107 (43%)				
Trans	2 (.8%)	Race/Ethnicity	21% non-white	24% non-white	24% non-white
Prefer not to say	2 (.8%)	White/Caucasian	196 (82.3%)	76.3%	76%
		Hispanic/Latinx	9 (3.7%)	18.5%	9%
		Asian	9 (3.7%)	5.9%%	5%
		Black/African American	11 (4.6%)	13.4%	9%
		Multiracial/ethnic	3 (1.2%)	2.8%	.8%
		Native American or Alaska Native	1 (.4%)	1.3%	.6%
		Other	9 (3.7%)	0.2%	NA
				Self-Reported Health:	
				Poor	5 (2%)
Age: Mean= 62; range= 50–89				Fair	59 (23%)
50–59 years	104 (44%)			Good	105 (41%)
60–69 years	83 (35%)			Very Good	67 (26%)
70–79 years	42 (18%)			Excellent	19 (7%)
80–89 years	7 (3%)				

*Source: https://www.census.gov/quickfacts/fact/table/US/PST045221
** Source: 2020 Profile of Older Americans, May 2021

Within a few days, my sampling was complete, and I had a total of 211 additional respondents. SurveyMonkey Audience included sixty-one extras in case I needed to exclude some. Two were clearly problematic. One wrote, "survey is shit" in most of the comment boxes, and the other obviously did not understand the questions. Other respondents either didn't meet the age criteria or didn't provide complete data. I ended up with 207 usable responses from SurveyMonkey Audience. With those recruited via Facebook, the sample totalled 239. Their demographic features are summaried in Table A2.

Ultimately, I think the most valuable part of the instrument was the "Incident" section. This was also where people were most likely to quit on the survey. Those who completed it provided fascinating information about the types of experiences that made them angry, as well as their responses to these experiences. The closing "advice" question also provided an interesting glimpse into what people thought should be done about/with anger.

Results

Most of the results are presented in the text of this book. For open-ended questions, a colleague and I generated thematic codes and then we coded the responses separately. We met to check our reliability and sort out any disagreements. I used descriptive, bivariate, and correlational techniques to capture patterns in the data. To maintain readability, I decided to move tables to this appendix. The sample sizes in the tables vary because some people had missing data. Tables A3 through A8 offer summaries of other results discussed in this book.

References

Fung, H. H., L. L. Carstensen, and F. R. Lang. 2001. "Age-Related Patterns in Social Networks among European Americans and African Americans: Implications for Socioemotional Selectivity across the Life Span." *The International Journal of Aging and Human Development* 52 (3): 185–206. doi:10.2190/1ABL-9BE5-M0X2-LR9V.

Jones, Andrew, J. Earnest, M. Adam, R. Clarke, J. Yates, and C. Pennington. 2022. "Careless Responding in Crowdsourced Alcohol Research: A Systematic Review and Meta-Analysis of Practices and Prevalence." *Experimental and Clinical Psychopharmacology* Advance online publication. https://doi.org/10.1037/pha0000546.

Hamilton, Lucas, and Eric Allard. 2019. "Age Differences in Reappraisal of Negative Autobiographical Memories." *Experimental Aging Research* 47(2): 1–18.

Klabbers, Gonnie, H. Bosma, M. van den Akker, G. I. J. M. Kempen, and J. Th. M. van Eijk. 2013. "Cognitive Hostility Predicts All-Cause Mortality Irrespective of Behavioural Risk at Late Middle and Older Age." *European Journal of Public Health* 23(4): 701–705. https://doi.org/10.1093/eurpub/cks060

Mullen, Patrick R., F. Fox, J. Goshorn, and L. K. Warraich. 2020. "Crowdsourcing for online samples in counseling research." *Journal of Counseling & Development* 99: 221–226.

Table A3 How Has Your Experience of Anger Changed with Age?
(n = 162)

Code	Description	Example	Number (Percent)
Expression's Different	Person expresses anger (verbally, physically, or otherwise) differently	I express my feelings more.	24 (15%)
Control	Mentions "control" of anger or its expression	I am much more in control of my emotions now.	17 (10%)
Less Anger	Person experiences anger either less often or less intensely than when younger	I was much angrier when younger.	17 (10%)
Cognitive: Awareness, Thoughts during or about anger, or understanding of anger has changed.	Person has come to understand or think about anger differently; or describes being better able to think while angry	I have learned to process my feelings before acting on them and identify my triggers and focusing inward rather than outward for resolving conflicts.	12 (7%)
Mellow/Calm/Laid Back	Person describes themselves as more "mellow" "calm" or "laid back" now	I am more mellow now.	11 (7%)
I Changed	Person locates a change within themselves but not mellow.	I am less volatile now or I matured.	11 (7%)
Takes more to make angry	Person says it takes more to make them angry	Slower to anger.	7 (4%)
More Anger (or more intense)	Person experiences anger either more often or more intensely than when younger	I'm angrier than in my younger years.	7 (4%)
Better	Person says things are "better" now	Can handle it better now.	5 (3%)
Worse	Person says things are "worse" now	Worse, menopause hasn't helped!!!! It has gotten worse because of poor life choices over my adult life.	4 (2%)
Takes less to make angry	Person says it takes less to make them angry	Lose temper quicker	3 (2%)
Circumstances changed	Circumstances associated with aging have changed anger experiences	My kids are all grown up now. No more anger at teenagers!	2 (1%)
Legitimate	Person acknowledges a right to be angry now	I am allowed to be angry now.	1 (.6%)
NA	Didn't really answer the question	Aging happens; cognitive decline occurs	

148   APPENDIX 1

Table A4 What Do You Feel in Your Body When You Get Angry?

Answers from 213 older adults
(Total exceeds 100% because some gave more than one response.)

Code	Description	Example(s)	Number (Percent)
Emotional	Describes emotional rather than physical experience	*Anxiety, frustrated*	37 (17%)
Tense	Tightness, tension	*A tight feeling in my chest & arms*	36 (17%)
Cardiac	Blood pressure, heart rate	*Blood pressure rise. My heart rate rises*	36 (17%)
General discomfort	Upset, bad, pain	*Not good, body pains, sick, stress*	28 (13%)
Nothing	Not non-response—says, "nothing"	*Nothing*	13 (6%)
Action	Describes an action or desire to do something	*Urge to lash out. Want to run away*	12 (6%)
Heat	Mentions heat, hot, fire, flush, sweating	*I feel my blood boiling.*	11 (5%)
Face/head	Headache, face, light-headed (Not when face is red or hot—that's heat)	*Headache*	9 (4%)
Thoughts	Mind racing, specific thoughts, can't think	*Racing thoughts, Can't think before I speak*	9 (4%)
Energy	Rush, energy, adrenaline	*Adrenaline rush*	8 (4%)
Digestive	Nausea, stomach referenced	*I usually get nauseous, can't eat, Sick stomach.*	6 (3%)
Voice/Throat	saying something, cursing or related to throat	*Lump in the throat*	6 (3%)
Shaking	Experiences shaking		3 (1%)
Cry	Uses word cry		2 (.9%)
Non-Response	Doesn't respond to question	*Contempt*	6 (3%)

Table A5 Reflecting On What You Did during the Incident that Made You "Really Angry"

	Did it make you feel better?		Looking back, do you wish you had done anything differently?	
	No	Yes	No	Yes
Female	52 (47%)	58 (53%)	55 (51%)	52 (49%)
Male	40 (54%)	34 (46%)	54 (73%)	20 (27%)
Total	92 (50%)	92 (50%)	109 (60%)	72 (40%)

Table A6 What Advice Would You Give to Someone Younger about Anger? (n = 197)

Themes	Examples	n (%)
Be **Careful**/Think about it/Think about others	Think before you speak or react	37 (19%)
Suppress/**Control** it/	Keep it under control	25 (13%)
Let go	Life goes on, get over it. It doesn't pay to get angry over every little thing or to let that anger grow and hang on.	25 (13%)
Descriptive Warnings about Anger	It doesn't solve anything and can be bad for your health in the long run.	23 (12%)
Smile, be nice, be calm, be happy	Try to be calm	18 (9%)
Breathe	Take a deep breath and back the truck up	18 (9%)
Solve the problem	Find the source and address the problem	14 (7%)
Wait for anger to go away (count, pause, know it will pass)	Take your time, things will pass and get better.	11 (5.5%)
Do Speak, seek help	When I first got married people said don't say anything in anger you might regret. Now I wish I hadn't been so naive and [had] said the things that bothered me out loud and not kept it inside.	10 (5%)
Withdraw from situation	Walk away and cool off before reacting	10 (5%)
Avoid triggers, Don't get angry	Not sure other than control what you can and move away things you can't that make you lose control aka angry.	7 (3.5%)
Specific **Advice** on how to cope	Anger can be very motivating if you learn to process it properly. Anger that is repressed will eventually make you physically ill and will never help you resolve problems or conflicts. Pay attention to what your body is telling you.	6 (3%)
Channel it / Use it	Try to channel your anger in a productive way. Give yourself a day before you respond to someone who angers you.	5 (2.5%)
Don't Speak, don't act, don't hurt others	It's better to bite your tongue than say something you will regret later	5 (2.5%)
Choose your battles	Don't blow up at bank tellers, it doesn't help. Pick your battles.	4 (2%)
Don't let it Control You/ **Don't trust** it	Do not trust your emotions, especially anger and jealousy.	4 (2%)
Forgive, be grateful	I would tell them to not let it affect them to the point where they cannot forgive others.	3 (1.5%)
Vent; Get it out!	Express it ! Don't hold it in.	3 (.5%)

APPENDIX 1

Table A7 Do You Consider Yourself an Angry Person?

Race	No	Yes	Total
People of Color	23 / 56%	18 / 44%	41 / 100%
Whites	152 / 80%	39 / 20%	191 / 100%
	175 / 75%	57 / 25%	232 / 100%

Chi Sq: p = .003(2 sided); Chi Sq = 10.044 df=1

Gender			
Male	66 (69% of men)	30 (31% of men)	96
Female	106 (80% of women)	26 (20% of women)	132
Total	172	56	228

Chi Sq: p = .045(2 sided); Chi Sq = 4.004 df=1

Age	Mean = 63 years	Mean = 59 years

(T Test: p=.004 Equal Variances assumed t=2.880 df=229)

Table A8 Type of Incident that Made Respondents Angry (n = 209)

	Number/Percent	Illustrative Quote
Family Issue	73 (35%)	My husband drinking to [sic]much and he gets ill I don't like it when he drinks and acts that way
Car/Traffic/Driving	25 (12%)	I was cut off in traffic. I displayed my anger with a visual middle finger.
Politics/Events	23 (11%)	I am angry at the Biden administration for too many policies to mention here including the southern border and his foreign policies.
Work Issue	16 (8%)	My computer still doesn't work.my boss know and does crap dilio about it. but wants to hold me accountable for production. I want to hit her across with my computer and say here's your crappy production!!!!
Friends/Neighbors	16 (8%)	The neighbor left a diaper on the sidewalk.
COVID-19	8 (4%)	COVID protocols were not followed in the manner we were told they would be followed.
Customer Service	9 (4%)	On the phone trying to get issues resolved about bill. Very frustrated
Other	36 (17%)	My credit card was stolen.

APPENDIX 2

The Interview Protocol

General Greetings

Consent Form

- Purpose of the study is to better understand anger and its consequences. Material will be used in a book.
- Interview is not recorded. I will take notes. Respondent will receive a summary of our conversation and may provide corrections or expansions.
- If direct quotes are used, I will disguise respondents' name and location.
- Please don't feel you have to answer all of my questions. If you'd rather skip one we'll just move on. You may stop the interview at any time.
- Minimal risk, but if you find the questions make you uncomfortable please let me know.
- Any questions? Alright to go on?

Questions (Ideas and Experiences of Anger)
Birth Year: _____
Zip Code: _____
Now—to survey the landscape. Looking back on the past month. Can you tell me how many times you've been angry? Do you consider yourself an angry person?
Looking back to a time you can remember when you were most (or very angry). Can you tell me about it?

- What made you angry? What happened?
- What did your body feel like?
- What did you do?
- Any regrets?
- How did you learn about anger? (Parents? Teachers? Other?)
- Is your experience of anger different now than in the past? (i.e., when you were
- in high school, 20s, 30s, etc.)
- Can you control your anger?
- Have you ever done something you regretted when you were angry?
- Why do you think people get angry? (Does it serve a purpose? Evolutionary? Social? Personal? Desire to control or blow off steam?)
- In your experience, can anger be productive?
- Do you think anger is bad for your health/well-being? (Is there a difference between anger at self and anger at others?)
- Does it frighten you when other people are angry with you?
- Have you ever held a grudge?
- How do other people respond to your anger? Do they tell you you're scary?
- What advice would you give to a young person about anger?

APPENDIX 3
Internet Survey Instrument

Understanding Anger

The Anger Project studies how people experience and cope with anger. We are interested in the vast range of human experiences and we definitely want to hear from you!

The survey is designed to take about 15 minutes.

It is being conducted by Amanda Barusch, Professor Emeritus from the University of Utah. If you have any questions or concerns please contact her at amanda.barusch@socwk.utah.edu.

The "Prev" and "Next" buttons at the bottom of each page enable you to move forward and backward through the survey.

By clicking "Next" below you consent to participate. Let's get started!

Understanding Anger

*1. Do you consider yourself an angry person?
- ○ Yes
- ○ No

Understanding Anger

* 2. Now, we need some information about you.

First, what is your gender?

- ○ Female
- ○ Male
- ○ Trans
- ○ Other
- ○ Prefer not to say

* 3. What year were you born?

[   ]

APPENDIX 3

* 4. How is your health?
    - ○ Poor
    - ○ Fair
    - ○ Good
    - ○ Very Good
    - ○ Excellent

* 5. What is your race or ethnicity?
    - ○ Asian
    - ○ Black or African American
    - ○ Hispanic or Latino
    - ○ Middle Eastern or North African
    - ○ Multiracial or Multiethnic
    - ○ Native American or Alaska Native
    - ○ Native Hawaiian or other Pacific Islander
    - ○ White
    - ○ Another race or ethnicity, please describe below

Self-describe below:

[   ]

* 6. What zip code do you live in?

[   ]

Understanding Anger

* 7. Our experiences of anger can range from irritation to rage. Please use the scale below to indicate how often you have experienced each type of anger in the past month.

	Never	Once or Twice	Three to Five Times	More than Five Times
Irritated or Frustrated	○	○	○	○
Somewhat angry	○	○	○	○
Angry	○	○	○	○
Very Angry	○	○	○	○
Enraged	○	○	○	○

APPENDIX 3   155

Understanding Anger

* 8. Now, let's explore some of your beliefs and experiences. Please indicate the extent you agree or disagree with each of the following statements:

	Strongly Disagree	Disagree	Unsure	Agree	Strongly Agree
In my experience, anger is usually productive.	○	○	○	○	○
When other people are angry with me I usually feel frightened.	○	○	○	○	○
In my experience, anger is usually destructive.	○	○	○	○	○
There is no difference between men and women when it comes to anger.	○	○	○	○	○
When I'm angry I do things I regret later.	○	○	○	○	○
The person I'm most often mad at is myself.	○	○	○	○	○

Understanding Anger

* 9. The following questions ask you to focus on a single incident that made you angry recently. If there have been several, please choose the time you were MOST angry and describe it in the following sections.

First of all, please briefly describe the incident. Tell us about the people involved, what happened, and how you felt about it.

[   ]

* 10. When did this incident take place?

○ Within the last month
○ Within the last year
○ More than a year ago

156 APPENDIX 3

* 11. How angry were you? (Please choose ONE option.)
   - ◯ I was irritated or frustrated.
   - ◯ I was angry, but not VERY angry.
   - ◯ I was VERY angry.
   - ◯ I was enraged.
   - ◯ Other (please specify)

   [   ]

Understanding Anger

* 12. What did you do during this incident?

   [   ]

* 13. Did it make you feel better?
   - ◯ Yes
   - ◯ No

* 14. When you look back on this experience do you wish you had done anything differently?
   - ◯ Yes
   - ◯ No

Understanding Anger

15. Please use this space to expand on what you wish you had done and why.

   [   ]

APPENDIX 3   157

Understanding Anger

* 16. Please choose the option below that best describes this incident.

- ○ It involved a threat to my immediate well-being
- ○ It involved a threat to my long-term well-being
- ○ A person treated me unfairly
- ○ A person treated someone else unfairly.
- ○ Someone or something made me unable to accomplish my goal.
- ○ Someone was inconsiderate to me.
- ○ A person was inconsiderate to someone else (not me).
- ○ Someone misunderstood what I was saying or doing.
- ○ Other (please specify)

* 17. How often has this kind of incident happened to you?

- ○ Never before. This was the first time.
- ○ It's happened before a few (3-6) times.
- ○ It happens frequently.
- ○ It happens all the time.
- ○ Other (please specify)

Understanding Anger

* 18. What do you feel in your body when you get angry?

Understanding Anger

*19. Let's return to your beliefs and experiences. Please indicate the extent you agree or disagree with each of the following statements:

	Strongly Disagree	Disagree	Unsure	Agree	Strongly Agree
I have never experienced rage.	○	○	○	○	○
Anger motivates me to make things better.	○	○	○	○	○
I feel powerful when I'm angry.	○	○	○	○	○
When I'm very angry my body shakes uncontrollably	○	○	○	○	○
I get angry over things I can't control.	○	○	○	○	○
When angry, women are more dangerous than men.	○	○	○	○	○

Understanding Anger

*20. This section focuses on your response to anger.

Please choose items that complete this sentence: **When I get angry I usually:**

- ☐ Say something I'll regret later
- ☐ Do something like slam a door
- ☐ Get into an argument
- ☐ Make snide or sarcastic remarks
- ☐ Express myself clearly and maturely
- ☐ Tell someone how I feel
- ☐ Lose my temper
- ☐ Pout or sulk
- ☐ Hold a grudge
- ☐ Keep my feelings in
- ☐ Withdraw from the situation
- ☐ Yell at someone.
- ☐ Criticize myself afterwards.
- ☐ Try to defuse the situation
- ☐ Find it hard to think rationally

☐

Other (please specify)

APPENDIX 3   159

Understanding Anger

* 21. This is the last section about your beliefs and experiences. Please indicate the extent you agree or disagree with each of the following statements:

	Strongly Disagree	Disagree	Unsure	Agree	Strongly Agree
When other people are angry with me I usually get angry.	○	○	○	○	○
Getting angry is bad for a person's health.	○	○	○	○	○
I find anger invigorating.	○	○	○	○	○
Women are more likely than men to suppress their anger.	○	○	○	○	○
I generally get most angry at the people I love.	○	○	○	○	○

Understanding Anger

* 22. Here are some things that can make people angry. Would you please indicate the extent to which this is the case for you?

	Doesn't make me angry at all	Makes me a little angry	Unsure	Makes me angry	Makes me very angry
Workplace problems	○	○	○	○	○
Family Problems	○	○	○	○	○
Discrimination	○	○	○	○	○
Social Injustice	○	○	○	○	○
The COVID pandemic	○	○	○	○	○

Understanding Anger

23. Have you ever been discriminated against?

○ Yes
○ No

* 24. Please indicate the type of discrimination you experienced.

- ☐ Gender
- ☐ Race
- ☐ Age
- ☐ Gender identity
- ☐ Sexual
- ☐ orientation
- ☐ Physical disability

Other (please specify)

Understanding Anger

* 25. Has your experience of anger changed since you were younger?

○ Yes
○ No

Understanding Anger

26. If yes, how has it changed?

Understanding Anger

* 27. Finally, what advice would you give to someone younger about anger?

Notes

Preface: Who's Angry Now?

1. Excerpt from "Do Not Go Gentle Into That Good Night" by Dylan Thomas, from *The Poems of Dylan Thomas*, copyright ©1952 by Dylan Thomas. Reprinted by permission of New Directions Publishing Corp and The Dylan Thomas Trust.
2. See: https://www.eeoc.gov/newsroom/eeoc-releases-fiscal-year-2019-enforcement-and-litigation-data, https://www.zippia.com/advice/age-discrimination-statistics/, and https://www.eeoc.gov/reports/state-age-discrimination-and-older-workers-us-50-years-after-age-discrimination-employment#_ftn147
3. Rebecca Perron. *The Value of Experience: AARP Multicultural Work and Jobs Study*. Washington, DC: AARP Research, July 2018. https://doi.org/10.26419/res.00177.000
4. See: David Cutler and David Wise (Eds.). 2009. *Health at Older Ages: The Causes and Consequences of Declining Disability*. Chicago: University of Chicago Press.

Chapter 1

1. *The Land of Heart's Desire*, 1894.
2. See: Max Rose, Esteban Ortiz-Ospina, and Hannah Ritchie. (2019). Life Expectancy. Our World in Data. https://ourworldindata.org/life-expectancy.
3. This distinction was introduced by renowned gerontologist Bernice Neugarten. See: Bernice L. Neugarten. 1974. "Age Groups in American Society and the Rise of the Young Old." *The Annals of the American Academy of Political and Social Science* 415: 187–198. Lately, those over eighty or eighty-five have been termed the "oldest old." See also: Robert Binstock. 1985. "The Oldest-Old: A Fresh Perspective or Compassionate Ageism Revisited?" *Millbank Memorial Fund Quarterly, Health and Society* 63(2): 420–451.
4. Martha C. Nussbaum. 2016. *Anger and Forgiveness: Resentment, Generosity, Justice*. New York: Oxford University Press, 95..
5. I checked by completing searches using "Academic Search Ultimate" (a major database for scholarly journals). The first used the keywords "Youth and young* adults" and "anger" the second, "elderly and old* adults" and "anger." Of a total of 116 studies that came up, 82 percent focused on youth or young adults. Only 18 percent had "elderly or old* adult" in their titles.
6. James J. Gross, Laura L. Carstensen, Jeanne Tsai, Carina Gotestam Skorpen, Angie Y.C. Hsu, J. J. Gross, L. L. Carstensen, et al. 1997. "Emotion and Aging: Experience,

Expression, and Control." *Psychology & Aging* 12(4): 590–599. doi:10.1037/0882-7974.12.4.590.
7. Please see the appendix for greater detail on the Anger Project's methodology.
8. Robert W. Firestone. 2014. "The Simple Truth About Anger: Suppressing Angry Feelings Inevitably Has Destructive Consequences." *Psychology Today*. (October 28). Accessed September 2022 from https://www.psychologytoday.com/us/blog/the-human-experience/201410/the-simple-truth-about-anger.
9. Keith Oatley and Philip N. Johnson-Laird. 1987. "Towards a Cognitive Theory of Emotions." *Cognition and Emotion* 1, no. 1: 29–50.
10. Robert Binstock. 2010. "From Compassionate Ageism to Intergenerational Conflict." *The Gerontologist* 50(5):574–585.
11. D. W. Sue. 2010. "Microaggressions, Marginality, and Oppression: An Introduction." In D.W. Sue (Ed). *Microaggressions and Marginality: Manifestation, Dynamics, and Impact*. Hoboken, NJ: John Wiley & Sons. (Quote on p. 3.)
12. See: C. Friedlaender. 2018. "On Microaggressions: Cumulative Harm and Individual Responsibility. *Hypatia* 33(1): 5–21 or M. Williams. 2020. "Psychology Cannot Afford to Ignore the Many Harms Caused by Microaggressions." *Perspectives on Psychological Science* 15(1): 38–43. Striking to me is that a March, 24, 2020 title search on "microaggression" and "elderly or aged or older or elder or geriatric" in Academic Search Ultimate yielded NO results.
13. M. M. Gullette. 2017. *Ending Ageism or How Not to Shoot Old People*. New Brunswick, NJ: Rutgers University Press. Gerontologists and feminists emphasize the disadvantages of invisibility. On the other hand, in her 2020 book, *How to Disappear*, Akiko Busch spells out the advantages of "the inconspicuous life."
14. J. Fox. 2020. "Coronavirus Deaths by Age: How It's Like (and Not Like) Other Diseases. Bloomberg Opinion, May 7, 2020. https://www.bloomberg.com/opinion/articles/2020-05-07/comparing-coronavirus-deaths-by-age-with-flu-driving-fatalities
15. M. Stevis-Gridneff, M. Apuzzo, and M. Prnczuk. 2020. "When COVID-19 Hit, Many Elderly Were Left to Die." *New York Times*, August 8, 2020. https://www.nytimes.com/2020/08/08/world/europe/coronavirus-nursing-homes-elderly.html.
16. Social Science Research Council, June 11, 2006. Understanding Katrina. https://items.ssrc.org/category/understanding-katrina/; Bill Blythway. 2007. "The Evacuation of Older People: The Case of Hurricane Katrina." Social Science Research Council. March 15, 2007. https://items.ssrc.org/understanding-katrina/the-evacuation-of-older-people-the-case-of-hurricane-katrina/; V. Adams. 2011. "Aging Disaster: Mortality, Vulnerability, and Long-Term Recovery among Katrina Survivors." *Medical Anthropology* 30(3): 237–270. https://www.ncbi.nlm.nih.gov/pmc/articles/PMC3098037/
17. R. Fry.2019). "Baby Boomers Are Staying in the Labor Force at Rates Not Seen in Generations for People Their Age." *Pew Research Center*. (July 24, 2019). Accessed March 12, 2020 at: https://www.pewresearch.org/fact-tank/2019/07/24/baby-boomers-us-labor-force/.
18. R. W. Johnson and P. Gosselin. 2018. "How Secure Is Employment at Older Ages?" The Urban Institute. Retrieved March 13, 2020 from: https://www.urban.org/research/publication/how-secure-employment-older-ages/view/full_report

19. P. Gosselin. 2018. "If You're Over 50, Chances Are the Decision to Leave a Job Won't Be Yours." ProPublica. Retrieved March 13, 2020 from: https://www.propublica.org/article/older-workers-united-states-pushed-out-of-work-forced-retirement
20. P. Span. 2018. "He Called Older Employees 'Dead Wood.' Two Sued for Age Discrimination." *New York Times* (July 6). Retrieved March 13, 2020 from: https://www.nytimes.com/2018/07/06/health/age-discrimination-ohio-state.html
21. Alicia Munnelland April Wu. 2013. "Do Older Workers Squeeze Out Younger Workers?" SIEPR Discussion Paper No. 13-011, Stanford Institute for Economic Policy Research. Accessed September 2022 at file:///Users/amandabarusch/Downloads/Do.older_.workers.squeeze.out_.younger.workers_2.pdf
22. S. L. Brown and I.-F. Lin. 2012. "The Gray Divorce Revolution: Rising Divorce among Middle-Aged and Older Adults, 1990–2010." *Journals of Gerontology Series B: Psychological Sciences and Social Sciences* 67(6): 731–741, doi:10.1093/geronb/gbs089.
23. L. R. Phillips. 1983. "Abuse and Neglect of the Frail Elderly at Home: An Exploration of Theoretical Relationships. *Journal of Advanced Nursing* 8(5): 379–392.
24. J. Lee, A. Wachholtz, and K. Choi. 2014. "A Review of the Korean Cultural Syndrome Hwa-Byung: Suggestions for Theory and Intervention." *Journal of Asia Pacific Counseling* 4(1): 45–64. (quote on p. 55)
25. See: A. S. Barusch. 2021. "Cougars and Crones: Maverick Archetypes for Older Women. In A. Teodorescu. (Ed.). *Shaping Ageing Social Transformations and Enduring Meanings.* London: Routledge Press, where I explore the role of mavericks in expanding social norms for older women.
26. M. Kuhn. 1991. *No Stone Unturned: The Life and Times of Maggie Kuhn.* New York: Ballantine Books, 129.
27. Judith Matloff. 1999. "Kazakstan's Elderly Go Activist: Irina Savostina Leads Pensioners' Drive to Keep Key Issues in Focus, and Keep Heat on President Nazarbayev." *Christian Science Monitor* (January 29). Accessed September 2022 at https://www.csmonitor.com/1999/0129/p8s1.html
28. SBS News. 2019. "This 97-year-old Activist has some advice for Extinction Rebellion. . (October 23). Accessed August 2023 at https://www.sbs.com.au/news/the-feed/article/this-97-year-old-veteran-activist-has-some-advice-for-extinction-rebellion/wglw7s2ns/
29. Emily Carr. 2009. *Hundreds and Thousands: The Journals of Emily Carr.* Vancouver, Canada: Douglas & McIntyre Publishers, 351.

Chapter 2

1. George Bainton. 1890. *The Art of Authorship.*
2. Jori Hofstra. 2021. "Beside Oneself with Rage: The Doubled Self as Metaphor in a Narrative of Brain Injury with Emotional Dysregulation." *Journal of Medical Humanities 42*: 131–146 (quote on p. 133).

3. "catharsis, n." OED Online. September 2022. Oxford University Press. https://www-oed-com.ezproxy.lib.utah.edu/view/Entry/28926?redirectedFrom=catharsis (accessed September 24, 2022).
4. See: Saussure, Ferdinand de (original 1916; reprint 1998) *Course in General Linguistics*. Open Course Classics.
5. Zacharias Kotzé. 2005. "Humoral Theory as Motivation for Anger Metaphors in the Hebrew Bible." *Southern African Linguistics and Applied Language Studies* 23(2): 205–209.
6. Zoltán Kövecses. 2010. "Cross-Cultural Experience of Anger: A Psycholinguistic Analysis." In *International Handbook of Anger*. Potegal, M., Stemmler, G., and Spielberger, C. (Eds). New York: Springer Science+Business Media. 157–174.
7. Donald Howard. 1956. "United States Marine Corps Slang." *American Speech* 31(3): 188–194.
8. Grammarphobia. 2016. *Pissy Language* (August 29). Accessed September 2022 at https://www.grammarphobia.com/blog/2016/08/pissed-off.html.
9. Another popular, and more crude, idiom has the "shit hitting the fan."
10. Carolyn O'Meara and Asifa Majid. 2020. "Anger Stinks in Seri: Olfactory Metaphor in a Lesser-Described Language." *Cognitive Linguistics*. (https://www.degruyter.com/document/doi/10.1515/cog-2017-0100/html).
11. Hofstra, "Beside Oneself with Rage."
12. Kövecses, "Cross-Cultural Experience of Anger," p. 163.
13. Judy Woon Yee Ho. 2009. "The Language of Anger in Chinese and English Narratives." *International Journal of Bilingualism* 13(4): 481–500.
14. Y.H. Zhang and K. Rose. 1999. *Who Can Ride the Dragon? An Exploration of the Cultural Roots of Traditional Chinese Medicine*. Brookline, MA: Paradigm, 202–203.
15. Paul Heelas. 1984. "Indigenous Representations of Emotions: The Case of the Chewong." *Journal of the Anthropological Society of Oxford XIV*: 87–103.
16. James Patrick Craig. 2018. *Modern Irish Grammar. (Classic Reprint)* London, England: Forgotten Books. .
17. Grace Gredys Harris. 1978. *Casting Out Anger: Religion among the Taita of Kenya*. Cambridge MA: Cambridge University Press.

Chapter 3

1. Søren Kierkegaard, *Journalen* JJ:167. 1843. *Søren Kierkegaards Skrifter*, Søren Kierkegaard Research Center, Copenhagen, 1997–, volume 18, page 306. (https://homepage.math.uiowa.edu/~jorgen/kierkegaardquotesource.html)
2. See L. Tornstam. 1989. "Gero-Transcendence: A Reformulation of the Disengagement Theory." *Aging (Milano)*. *1*(Sep 1): 55–63. doi: 10.1007/BF03323876. PMID: 2488301.
3. G. Sadler. 2018. "One Sentence Summary on Aristotle and Anger." Accessed via: *https://medium.com/@Gregory_Sadler/one-sentence*-summary-on-aristotle-and-anger-c9f5b57aa37e.

4. Aristotle (350 BCE). *Nicomachean Ethics*. Translated by W. D. Ross. Book VII, Part 6. Accessed September 2022 at http://classics.mit.edu/Aristotle/nicomachaen.7.vii.html
5. Aristotle (384 BCE). *Rhetoric*. Translated by W. Rhys Roberts. Book 1, Part 11. Accessed September 2022 at http://bocc.ubi.pt/pag/Aristotle-rhetoric.html.
6. See: Stoic writings on anger, such as Cicero's *Tusculan Disputations* and Seneca's *De Ira*.
7. Project Gutenberg (nd). *Cicero's Tusculan Disputations by Marcus Tullius Cicero*. 3, 22. Accessed September 2022 at https://www.gutenberg.org/files/14988/14988-h/14988-h.htm.
8. Ibid., 3, 11.
9. J. Fitch. 2008. *Seneca*. New York: Oxford University Press.
10. Seneca *De Ira*. Translated by Aubrey Stewart. Independently published in 2017. Book 5.
11. Ibid., Book 7.
12. PEW Research Center. 2014. *Religious Landscape Study*. Frequency of Reading Scripture. Accessed September 2022 at https://www.pewresearch.org/religion/religious-landscape-study/frequency-of-reading-scripture/
13. J. Edwards. 1959. *The Selected Works of Jonathan Edwards*, vol. 2, Sermon 7. London: Banner of Truth, 183–199.
14. John R.W. Stott and Alister McGrath. 2021. *The Cross of Christ*. IVP: Stott Centennial Edition, 173.
15. Encyclopedia Britannica (nd). Lactantius, Christian Apologist. Accessed September 2022 at https://www.britannica.com/biography/Lactantius.
16. Lactantius. *De Ira Dei* (A treatise on the anger of God). Chapter 6. Accessed September 2022 at http://www.documentacatholicaomnia.eu/03d/0240-0320,_Lactantius,_De_Ira_Dei_[Schaff],_EN.pdf.
17. Ibid., Chapter 16.
18. C. H. Dodd. 1959. *The Epistle of Paul to the Romans* (2nd ed.). London and Glasgow: Collins, 50.
19. Encyclopedia Britannica (nd). Sir Thomas Aquinas, Italian Christian Theologian and Philosopher. Accessed September 2022 at https://www.britannica.com/biography/Saint-Thomas-Aquinas.
20. W. J. Martin. 2016. "Thomas Aquinas on Wrath or Anger." *Anglican Way Magazine*. Accessed June 2022 at https://anglicanway.org/2016/02/15/thomas-aquinas-on-wrath-or-anger/

Chapter 4

1. William James (1893) *Psychology*, New York: Henry Holt and Company, p. 380.
2. Speaking biologically rather than metaphorically, there is no "seat of anger" in the brain, just as there is no specific location for musical or mathematical talent, love, or creativity. Rather than structures, anger is located in physical processes.

3. See Kaoru Nashiro, Mishiko Sakaki, and Mara Mather. 2012. "Age Differences in Brain Activity During Emotion Processing: Reflections of Age-Related Decline or Increased Emotion Regulation." *Gerontology* 58(2): 156–163. doi: 10.1159/000328465
4. Michael McCloskey, Luan Phan, Mike Angstadt, Karla Fettich, Sarah Keedy, and Emil Coccaro. 2016. "Amygdala Hyperactivation to Angry Faces in Intermittent Explosive Disorder." *Journal of Psychiatric Research* 79: 34–41.
5. Joseph LeDoux. 2012. "Rethinking the Emotional Brain." *Neuron* 73(4): 653–676. doi: 10.1016/j.neuron.2012.02.004 (Accessed at: https://www.ncbi.nlm.nih.gov/pmc/articles/PMC3625946/_)
6. Unfortunately, no one has bothered to research some of the questions that keep me up at night: Why do those women feel anger in their throats? Could it be the result of hundreds of years of cultural conditioning that tells them not to express their anger? What about the ones who deny feeling anything physical when they're angry? Are they out of touch with their bodies? Or is their wiring different?
7. JAMA. 1896. "The Physiologic Effects of the Indulgence in Anger." *Journal of the American Medical Association* 26: 781–782. (reprinted in *JAMA 100 Years Ago*) doi:10.1001/jama.1996.03530380016012 (quote on p. 781).
8. Gina Cherelus. 2022. "How Anger Affects the Body." *The New York Times*, December 17. Accessed December 2022 at https://www.nytimes.com/2022/12/17/style/anger-body-health-effects.html#:~:text=In%20a%20sense%2C%20anger%20can,fight%2Dor%2Dflight%20response.
9. For meta-analytic reviews in support of this finding see: Jennifer Schum, L. Randall Jorgensen, Paul Verhaeghen, Marie Sauro, and Ryan Thibodeau. 2003. "Trait Anger, Anger Expression, and Ambulatory Blood Pressure: A Meta-Analytic Review." *Journal of Behavioral Medicine* 26(5): 395–415. Also: J. Suls, C. K. Wan, and P. T. Costa. 1995. "Relationship of Trait Anger to Resting Blood Pressure: A Meta-Analysis." *Health Psychology* 14: 444–456.
10. Jameson K. Hirsch, Jon R. Webb, and Elizabeth L. Jeglic. Mental Health. 2012. "Forgiveness as a Moderator of the Association between Anger Expression and Suicidal Behaviour." *Religion & Culture* 15(3): 279–300.
11. Gonnie Klabbers, H. Bosma, M. Vanden Akker, GIJM Kempen, and JThM van Eijk. 2012. "Cognitive Hostility Predicts All-Cause Mortality Irrespective of Behavioural Risk at Late Middle and Older Age." *European Journal of Public Health*, 23(4), 701–705. (quote on p. 290).
12. Carol Magai, Michael-David Kerns, Michael Gillespie, and Bu Huang. 2003. "Anger Experience and Anger Inhibition in Sub-Populations of African American and European American Older Adults and Relation to Circulatory Disease." *Journal of Health Psychology* 8(4):413–432. (quote on p. 414).
13. See:J. Dimsdale, C. Pierce, D. Schoenfeld, A. Brown, R. Zisman, and R. Graham.1986. "Suppressed Anger and Blood Pressure: Effects of Race, Sex, Social Class, and Age." *Psychosomatic Medicine* 48:430–436.
14. See: C. L. Broman and E. H. Johnson. 1988. "Anger Expression and Life Stress among Blacks: Their Role in Physical Health." *Journal National Medical Association* 80: 1329–1334. Also: E. H. Johnson and B. Broman. 1987. "The Relationship of

Anger Expression to Health Problems among Black Americans in a National Survey." *Journal of Behavioral Medicine 10*: 103–116.

15. See also: Sandra Thomas. 2002. "Age Differences in Anger Frequency, Intensity, and Expression." *Journal of the American Psychiatric Nurses Association 8*(2): 44–50.

    Karina Davidson, Michael MacGregor, Judith Stuhr, Kim Dixon, and David MacLean. 2000. "Constructive Anger Verbal Behavior Predicts Blood Pressure in a Population-Based Sample." *Health Psychology 19*(1): 55–64.

    Karina Davidson and Elizabeth Mostofsky. 2010. "Anger Expression and Risk of Coronary Heart Disease: Evidence from the Nova Scotia Health Survey." *American Heart Journal 159*(2): 199–206.

    P. M. Eng, G. Fitzmaurice, L. D, Kubzansky, E. B. Rimm, and I. Kawachi. 2003. "Anger Expression and Risk of Stroke and Coronary Heart Disease among Male Health Professionals." *Psychosomatic Medicine 65*: 100–110. http://dx.doi.org/10.1097/01.PSY.0000040949.22044.C6

16. G. Keinan, H. Ben-Zur, M. Zilka, and R. S. Carel. 1992. "Anger In or Out, Which Is Healthier? An Attempt to Reconcile Inconsistent Findings." *Psychology and Health 7*: 83–98.

17. Jiyoung Park, Abdiel Flores, Kirstin Aschbacher, and Wendy Berry Mendes. 2018. "When Anger Expression Might Be Beneficial for African Americans: The Moderating Role of Chronic Discrimination." *Cultural Diversity and Ethnic Minority Psychology 24*(3): 303. (quote on p. 314).

18. Some of these include: Kimberly A. Rapoza, Denise T. Wilson, Wendy A. Widmann, Michelle A. Riley, Thomas W. Robertson, Elizabeth Maiello, Nikisha Villot, Dana J. Manzella, and Alberto L. Ortiz-Garcia. 2014. "The Relationship between Adult Health and Childhood Maltreatment, as Moderated by Anger and Ethnic Background." *Child Abuse & Neglect 38*(3): 445–456.

    Jiyoung Park, Abdiel Flores, Kirstin Aschbacher, and Wendy Berry Mendes. 2018. "When Anger Expression Might Be Beneficial for African Americans: The Moderating Role of Chronic Discrimination." *Cultural Diversity & Ethnic Minority Psychology, 24*(3), 303–318.

    Nancy Dorr, Jos F. Brosschot, John J. Sollers III, and Julian F. Thayer. 2007. "Damned If You Do, Damned If You Don't: The Differential Effect of Expression and Inhibition of Anger on Cardiovascular Recovery in Black and White Males." *International Journal of Psychophysiology 66*(2): 125–134.

19. Jennifer Morozink Boylan and Carol D. Ryff. 2015. "High Anger Expression Exacerbates the Relationship between Age and Metabolic Syndrome." *Journals of Gerontology Series B: Psychological Sciences and Social Sciences 70* (1): 77–82.

    Jennifer Morozink Boylan, Tené T. Lewis, Christopher L. Coe, and Carol D. Ryff. 2015. "Educational Status, Anger, and Inflammation in the MIDUS National Sample: Does Race Matter?" *Annals of Behavioral Medicine 49*(4): 570–578.

20. Anissa I. Vines, Thu Thi Xuan Nguyen, Myduc Ta, Denise Esserman, and Donna D. Baird. 2011. "Self-Reported Daily Stress, Squelching of Anger and the Management of Daily Stress and the Prevalence Of Uterine Leiomyomata: The Ultrasound Screening Study." *Stress and Health 27*(3): e188–e194.

Chapter 5

1. William Shakespeare. 1564–1616. *King Lear*. Oxford: Clarendon Press, 1877, Act II, Scene 4.
2. Ovid, 43 BC–AD 17 or AD 18. *Ovid's Metamorphoses*. Dallas, TX: Spring Publications, 1989. Book 4.
3. Hesiod. *Theogony* 281; Pseudo-Apollodorus, *Bibliotheke* Book II, part iv, nos. 1–3. "The Library: Books 1–3.9." Translated by J. G. Frazer (Loeb Classical Library). Harvard University Press, 1921 (reprint), 155–161.
4. Ari Mermelstein. 2021. *Power and Emotion in Ancient Judaism: Community and Identity in Formation*. Cambridge, MA: Cambridge University Press, 71.
5. Ari Mermelstein. 2019. "Conceptions of Masculinity in the Scrolls and the Gendered Emotion of Anger." *Dead Sea Discoveries* 26: 314–338.
6. See: Carl Jung. 1935. "The Relations between the Ego and the Unconscious." In *Two Essays on Analytical Psychology*. Also: Martin Schmidt. (n.d.). *Individuation and the Self*. Society of Analytic Psychology. Accessed September 2022 at https://www.thesap.org.uk/articles-on-jungian-psychology-2/about-analysis-and-therapy/individuation/
7. Judith Butler. 2004. *Undoing Gender*. New York: Routledge.
8. Betty Friedan and Brigid O'Farrell. 1997. *Beyond Gender: The New Politics of Work and Family*. Washington, DC: Woodrow Wilson Center Press.
9. May Sarton. 1973. *Journal of a Solitude*. New York: Norton Books.
10. Miriam R. Dexter. 2010. "The Ferocious and the Erotic." *Journal of Feminist Studies in Religion* 26(1): 25–41 (quote on p. 26).
11. Helene Cixous. 1976. "The Laugh of the Medusa." *Signs: Journal of Women in Culture and Society* 1(4): 875–893. Translated by Keith and Paula Cohen (quote on p. 885).
12. Magdalena Budziszewska and Karolina Hansen. 2020. "Anger Detracts from Beauty": Gender Differences in Adolescents' Narratives about Anger. *Journal of Adolescent Research* 35(5): 635–664.
13. Jilly B. Kay. 2019. "Anger, Media, and Feminism: The Gender Politics of Mediated Rage." *Feminist Media Studies*, 19(4): 591–615 (quote on p. 591).
14. Ezra Klein. 2018. "The Ford-Kavanaugh Sexual Assault Hearing Explained." (Sept. 27, 2018). https://www.vox.com/explainers/2018/9/27/17909782/brett-kavanaugh-christine-ford-supreme-court-senate-sexual-assault-testimony)
15. Benjamin Weiser, Lola Fadulu, and Kate Christobek. 2023. "Trump Is Found Liable for Sex Abuse in Civil Trial." *New York Times*, May 10, 2023. Accessed May 2023 at https://www.nytimes.com/live/2023/05/09/nyregion/trump-carroll-rape-trial-verdict.
16. Michael Kimmel. 2013; 2017. *Angry White Men: American Masculinity at the End of An Era*. New York: Bold Type Books.
17. Hollida Wakefield and Ralph Underwager. 1990. "Personality Characteristics of Parents Making False Accusations of Sexual Abuse in Custody Disputes." *IPT Journal* 2(3). Available online: http://www.ipt-forensics.com/journal/issues90.htm. (May 23, 2021)
18. David Lisak, Lori Gardinier, Sarah Nicksa, and Ashley Cote. 2010. "False Allegations of Sexual Assault: An Analysis of Ten Years of Reported Cases." *Violence Against Women* 16(12): 1318–1334 (quote on p. 1319).

19. Elizabeth Cozzolino. 2018. "Who Goes to Jail for Child Support Debt?" Populations Research Center, The University of Texas at Austin. Accessed December, 2022 at chrome-extension://efaidnbmnnnibpcajpcglclefindmkaj/https://repositories.lib.utexas.edu/bitstream/handle/2152/65192/prc-brief-3-6-cozzolino-child-support.pdf.
20. Farrell explained to me that women don't fall in love with men who complain. They fall in love with "alphas." So, men want to be "alphas" and it seems contradictory for a man to say, "I'm an alpha male, I want rights." So he doesn't like use of the phrase, "Men's Rights." Instead preferring "Men's Issues."
21. Jerry Deffenbacher, Eugene Oetting, Gregory Thwaites, Rebekah Lynch, Deborah Baker, Robert Stark, Stacy Thacker, and Lora Eiswerth-Cox. 1996. "State-Trait Anger Theory and the Utility of the Trait Anger Scale." *Journal of Counseling Psychology* 43(2): 131–148 (quote on p. 146).
22. Todd Kashdan, Fallon Goodman, Travis Mallard, and Travis DeWall. 2016. "What Triggers Anger in Everyday Life? Links to the Intensity, Control, and Regulation of These Emotions and Personality Traits." *Journal of Personality* 84(6): 737–749.
23. Todd Kashdan. 2015. *The Power of Negative Emotion: How Anger, Guilt, and Self-Doubt Are Essential to Success and Fulfillment*. Grantham, UK: Grantham Book Services (GBS).
24. Robin Simon and Kathryn Lively. 2010. "Sex, Anger and Depression. *Social Forces*, 88(4), 1543–1568.
25. Kira Birditt and Karen Fingerman. 2003. "Age and Gender Differences in Adults' Descriptions of Emotional Reactions to Interpersonal Problems." *Journal of Gerontology: Psychological Sciences* 58B(4): P237–P245 (quote on p. P239).
26. I use the word with caution. It seems both inaccurate and inconsistent with this book's central argument to label anger "negative."
27. See: Isaac Burt. 2014. "Identifying Gender Differences in Male and Female Anger Among an Adolescent Population." *Professional Counselor* 4(5): 531-540. .

    Lindsay V. Healey, Vanessa Holmes, Susan Curry, Michael C. Seto, and Adekunle G. Ahmed. 2019. "Self-Reported Dysfunctional Anger in Men and Women at a Psychiatric Outpatient Clinic." *Journal of Rational-Emotive & Cognitive-Behavior Therapy* 37(4): 395–410.
28. Audrey Lord. 1981. "The Uses of Anger." *Women's Studies Quarterly* 9(3): 7–10. Accessed September 2022 at https://academicworks.cuny.edu/cgi/viewcontent.cgi?article=1654&context=wsq (quote on p. 9)
29. Ursula Le Guin. 2017. "About Anger." In *No Time to Spare*. New York: Harper Perennial, 136–141.
30. Martha Nussbaum. 2016. *Anger and Forgiveness: Resentment, Generosity, Justice*. New York and London: Oxford University Press, 249–250 .

Chapter 6

1. *The Divine Comedy of Dante Alighieri*. Translated by Henry Wadsworth Longfellow. 1867. London: Routledge, canto XII, lines 95–96.

2. A note on my positionality: Growing up near the Mexican border, I had a close look at the emergence of Chicano identity. By the time I was ten years old, the La Raza movement was going strong. Its leaders reclaimed the word "Chicano" and my friends proudly embraced this new identity. Cesar Chavez and Dolores Huerta cofounded the United Farm Workers. Their initial victories included improved conditions for migrant workers, the election of Chicanos to serve in public office, and the hiring of Chicano teachers in our schools. The success of the grape boycott in support of farm workers enabled us to enjoy a brief moment of confidence before our hopes were dashed by the murders of Martin Luther King and Malcom X.
3. Carter A. Wilson. 2015. *Racism: From Slavery to Advanced Capitalism*. Newbury Park, CA: Sage Publications.
4. Kimberlé Williams Crenshaw. 2021. "Emancipation and the Supreme Court." Lecture for MasterClass: Black History, Black Freedom, & Black Love: Lessons from influential black voices.
5. Blackpast.org (n.d.). "Racial Violence in the United States since 1526." Accessed September 2002 at https://www.blackpast.org/special-features/racial-violence-united-states-1660/.
6. National Geographic (n.d.). "The Bloody History of Anti-Asian Violence in the West." Accessed September 2022 at https://www.nationalgeographic.com/history/article/the-bloody-history-of-anti-asian-violence-in-the-west.
7. Martin Luther King .1968. *The Other America*. Speech delivered March 14, 1968, Grosse Pointe High School. Accessed September 2002 at https://www.gphistorical.org/mlk/mlkspeech/#:~:text=And%20I%20must%20say%20tonight,justice%20have%20not%20been%20met.
8. The Guardian. 2020. "At Least 25 Americans were Killed During Protests and Political Unrest During 2020." Accessed September 2022 at https://www.theguardian.com/world/2020/oct/31/americans-killed-protests-political-unrest-acled
9. Beckett, Lois (2020). "At least 25 Americans were killed during protests and political unrest in 2020. *The Guardian*, October 31. Accessed September 2023 at https://www.theguardian.com/world/2020/oct/31/americans-killed-protests-political-unrest-acled.
10. Claudia Rankine. 2014. *Citizen: An American Lyric*. Minneapolis, MN: Graywolf Press, 7).
11. CDC: Table 15. Life expectancy at birth, at age 65, and at age 75, by sex, race, and Hispanic origin: United States, selected years 1900–2016. https://www.cdc.gov/nchs/pressroom/nchs_press_releases/2021/202107.htm
12. Roni Caryn Rabin. 2022. "U.S. Life Expectancy Falls Again in 'Historic' Set Back." *New York Times*, August 31, 2022. Accessed Sept. 3, 2022 at https://www.nytimes.com/2022/08/31/health/life-expectancy-covid-pandemic.html.
13. M.D. Wong, M. F. Shapiro, W. J. Boscardin, S. L. Ettner. 2002. "Contribution of Major Diseases to Disparities in Mortality." *New England Journal of Medicine 347*: 1585–1592. https://www.nejm.org/doi/full/10.1056/NEJMsa012979
14. Frank Edwards, H. Lee, and M. Esposito. 2019. "Risk of Being Killed by Police Use of Force in the United States by Age, Race-Ethnicity, and Sex." *Proceedings of the National Academy of Sciences of the United States of America*. Accessed: https://www.pnas.org/content/116/34/16793.)

15. Audre Lorde. 1984. *Sister Outsider: Essays and Speeches*. Freedom, CA: Crossing Press.
16. Michelle Boyd. 2008. *Jim Crow Nostalgia: Reconstructing Race in Bronzeville*. Minneapolis: University of Minnesota Press, XII (Introduction).
17. Cornell West explores the paradox of "Black Love" for America in his lecture titled, "Black Love: A Love Like No Other." Delivered for MasterClass: Black History, Black Freedom, & Black Love: Lessons from influential black voices.

Chapter 7

1. William Wordsworth (1798) The Tables Turned, in William Wordsworth and Samuel Taylor Coleridge (eds), *Lyrical Ballads*. Printed by T.N. Longman & O. Rees for J. & A. Arch, London. Accessed Sepbember, 2023 at https://archive.org/stream/lyricalballadswi00word/lyricalballadswi00word_djvu.txt.
2. Matthew Impelli. 2022. "Mike Tyson Post about Punching People in the Face Resurfaces." *Newsweek*. April 21, 2022. Retrieved September 2022 from https://www.newsweek.com/mike-tyson-post-punching-people-resurfaces-1699875.
3. That's just one of many criticisms aimed at social media. Indeed, complaining about public media is a well-established tradition. I don't know what happened when printing presses came on the scene, but I'm pretty sure someone complained that all this reading was bad for the nation. Radio supplanted newspapers as a source of entertainment and news in the 1930s and some criticized its use as a propaganda tool and the oversized influence of talk radio. In his 1929 critique, media commentator Jack Woodford described radio programs as "brainless diversions that erode listeners' ability to think, inquire, and judge." Likewise, critics (and researchers) would later argue that watching television inured children to violence and disrupted their language acquisition and educational achievement.

    The 1970s brought Richard Nixon to the White House, with Spiro Agnew as his considerably less-popular vice president. After the Watergate scandal but before he disappeared into the bowels of history, Spiro Agenda described the media as "nattering nabobs of negativism." He wasn't pleased with their coverage of his administration's scandal. Since then, the media has become much more global and, some might say, more negative than ever. Nonetheless, droves of old folks are logging in.
4. Rui Fan, Ke Xu, and Jichange Zhao. 2018. "Higher Contagion and Weaker Ties Mean Anger Spreads Faster Than Joy in Social Media." arXiv:1608.03656. Accessed September, 2023 via Cornell University Computer Science – Social & Information Networks. (https://arxiv.org/abs/1608.03656,).
5. William J. Brady and M. J. Crockett. 2019. "How Effective Is Online Outrage?" *Trends in Cognitive Science* 23(2): 79–80. https://doi.org/10.1016/j.tics.2018.11.004.
6. Luke Munn. 2020. "Angry by Design: Toxic Communication and Technical Architectures." *Humanities and Social Sciences Communications* 7(53). doi.org/10.1057/s41599-020-00550-7 (quote is from p. 5).

7. Ibid., p. 5.
8. B. O. Olatunji, J. M. Lohr, B. J. Bushman. 2007. "The Pseudo-Psychology of Venting in the Treatment of Anger: Implications and Alternatives for Mental Health Practice." In T. A. Cavell and K. T. Malcolm (Eds.) *Anger, Aggression and Interventions for Interpersonal Violence*. Mahwah, NJ: Lawrence Erlbaum Associates Publishers, 119–141.
9. R. C. Martin, Kelsey Ryan Coyier, Leah M. VanSistine, and Kelly L. Schroeder. 2013. "Anger on the Internet: The Perceived Value of Rant-Sites." *Cyberpsychology, Behavior and Social networking*, 16(2), 119–122.
    (quote on p. 119).
10. Maria Jimenez-Sotomayor, C. Gomez-Moreno, and E. Soto-Perez-de-Celis. 2020. "Coronavirus, Ageism, and Twitter: An Evaluation of Tweets about Older Adults and COVID-19." *Journal of the American Geriatrics Society* 68: 1661–1665 (quote on p. 1661).
11. Brad A. Meisner. 2021. "Are you OK, Boomer? Intensification of Ageism and Intergenerational Tensions on Social Media Amid COVID-19." *Leisure Sciences: An Interdisciplinary Journal* 43: 1–2, 56–61. doi: 10.1080/01490400.2020.1773983 (quote on p. 56).
12. See: Robert Binstock. 2010. "From Compassionate Ageism to Intergenerational Conflict." *The Gerontologist* 50(5): 574–585.
13. See: Jill Quadagno. 1996. "Social Security and the Myth of the Entitlement 'Crisis.'" *The Gerontologist* 36(3): 391–399.
14. Associated Press. 1984. "Gov. Lamm Asserts Elderly, If Very Ill, Have 'Duty to Die.'" *New York Times* (March 29, 1984), Accessed March, 2020 at: https://www.nytimes.com/1984/03/29/us/gov-lamm-asserts-elderly-if-very-ill-have-duty-to-die.html
15. Jamie Knodel. 2020. "Texas Lt. Governor Dan Patrick Suggests He, Other Seniors Willing to Die to Get Economy Going Again." *NBC News*. March 24. Accessed September 2022 at https://www.nbcnews.com/news/us-news/texas-lt-gov-dan-patrick-suggests-he-other-seniors-willing-n1167341.
16. Flory, Susan Flory. (n.d.). "Ageism and the Virus: Some Triage Guidelines "Like Eruptions of Pus in the Body Politique." Accessed September 2022 at https://www.susanflory.com/margaret-morganroth-gullette-2/)
17. BBC news: https://www.bbc.com/news/world-asia-43666134??
18. Pew Research Center. 2021. "7% of Americans Don't Use the Internet. Who Are They?" Accessed April 6, 2022 at https://www.pewresearch.org/fact-tank/2021/04/02/7-of-americans-dont-use-the-internet-who-are-they/
19. Pew Research Center. 2022. "Share of Those 65 and Older Who Are Tech Users Has Grown in the Past Decade" (by Michelle Faverio). https://www.pewresearch.org/fact-tank/2022/01/13/share-of-those-65-and-older-who-are-tech-users-has-grown-in-the-past-decade/
20. Ibid.
21. See, for instance: Kaitlin Lewin, Dar Meshi, Amy M. Schuster, and Sheila R. Cotton. 2023. "Active and Passive Social Media Use Are Differentially Related to Depressive Symptoms in Older Adults." *Aging & Mental Health* 27(1):: 176–183.

Kunyi Zhang, Kyungmin Kim, Nina M. Silverstein, Qian Song, and Jeffrey Burr. 2021. "Social Media Communication and Loneliness among Older Adults." *Gerontologist* 61(6): 888–896.
22. See, for instance: Amanda Hunsaker and Eszter Hargittai. 2018. "A Review of Internet Use among Older Adults." *New Media & Society* 20(10), 3937–3954.
Kelly Quin. 2018. "Cognitive Effects of Social Media: A Case of Older Adults." *Social Media & Society*, 4(3). https://doi.org/10.1177/2056305118787203
Jinyan Xu and Quinqian Zhang. 2023. "The Relationship between Internet Use and Mental Health of the Elderly: Analysis of the Differences between Urban and Rural." *PLoS ONE* 18(1): e0280318. https://doi.org/10.1371/journal.pone.0280318

Chapter 8

1. *The Lady of Andros* in *Terence: Volume 1*. Translated by John Sargeaunt. 1912. Loeb Classical Library. London: William Heinemann; New York: Macmillan line 555..
2. Kira Birditt and Karen Fingerman. 2003. "Age and Gender Differences in Adults' Descriptions of Emotional Reactions to Interpersonal Problems." *Journal of Gerontology: Psychological Sciences* 58B(4): P237– P245.
3. Leah Megan Williams. 2014. *Conflict Behaviors and Marital Satisfaction in Older Adulthood: A Typology*. Master's Thesis at Auburn University.
4. William V. Harris. 2002. *Restraining Rage: The Ideology of Anger Control in Classical Antiquity*. Cambridge, MA: Harvard University Press (quote on p. 272)).
5. Joseph Keeping. 2006. "'Strike Flat the Thick Rotundity o' the World:' A Phenomenology of Anger in Shakespeare's *King Lear*." *Philosophy Today* 50(5): 477–485.
6. William V. Harris. 2002. *Restraining Rage: The Ideology of Anger Control in Classical Antiquity*. Cambridge, MA: Harvard University Press (quote on p. 287).
7. Ovid. *Metamorphosis (A New Verse Translation)*. Translated by David Raeburn. Penguin Classics. Book 4.
8. Alain de Botton. 2017 reprint. *The Course of Love: A Novel*. Simon & Schuster.
9. Brittney Cooper. 2018. *Eloquent Rage: A Black Feminist Discovers her Superpower*. New York: St. Martin's Press.
10. David Bevington (Ed). 1988. *The Complete Works of William Shakespeare. Vol V. King Lear*. New York: Bantam Books.
11. Cited in Harris, *Restraining Rage*, 288.
12. When we think of domestic violence we generally assume its victims are women and children. Usually that is the case. But a surprising number of men (the Centers for Disease Control and Prevention [CDC] estimate 1 in 10, compared to 1 in 4 women) experience intimate partner violence during their lifetimes. The CDC defines Intimate Partner Violence to include: "physical violence, sexual violence, stalking, psychological aggression, and control of reproductive or sexual health by a current or former intimate partner."

Chapter 9

1. John Milton (1667) *Paradise Lost*, reprinted in 2021, New York: Penguin Classics Illustrated Edition, Book 4, lines 73–74.
2. There is a clear consensus among researchers that the number and lethality of mass shootings has been rising in the United States since the mid-1960s. My computation, based on the Mother Jones database indicates the average number of victims per shooting more than doubled from 11.8 in the five-year period from 1985 through 1989 to 27.87 for 2015 through 2019.
3. Gun Violence Archive (n.d.) *Past Summary Ledgers*. Accessed September 2022 at https://www.gunviolencearchive.org/past-tolls.
4. Federal Bureau of Investigation. 2018. *Key Findings of the Behavioral Analysis Unit's Las Vegas Review Panel (LVRP)*. Washington, DC: U.S. Department of Justice. (Accessed 3/4/22 at: https://www.hsdl.org/?abstract&did=820782) (quote on p. 3).
5. Ibid. (quote on p. 1).
6. Ibid. (quote on p. 2).
7. Ibid. (quote on p. 2).
8. David Debolt, Ethan Baron, Robert Salonga, and Aldo Doledo. 2021. "San Jose VTA Shooter Had Dark Past, Including Allegations of Violent, Aggressive Behavior." *The Mercury News*. Accessed December 2022 at https://www.mercurynews.com/2021/05/26/heavy-police-presence-at-home-of-vta-employee-which-caught-fire-wednesday-morning/
9. Mark Ames. 2005. *Going Postal: Rage Murder and Rebellion From Reagan's Workplaces to Clinton's Columbine and Beyond*. Brooklyn, NY: Soft Skull Press.
10. David Debolt, Fiona Kelliher, Robert Salonga and Maggie Angst. 2021. "VTA Shooter Blew Up on Radio Dispatch, Complained about Pay, Vacation Coworkers Say." *Daily Democrat*. May 29, 2021. Accessed December 2022 at https://www.dailydemocrat.com/2021/05/29/vta-shooter-blew-up-on-radio-dispatch-complained-about-pay-vacation-coworker-say/
11. Chea Terence, Stefanie Dazio, and Jocelyn Gecker. 2021. "Survivor: California Shooter was "Outsider" in Workplace." AP News. Accessed December 2022 at https://apnews.com/article/california-shootings-022a10f1ce378c68c9425d5501551323
12. Tom Vacar and Evan Sernoffsky. 2021. "What We Know about the VTA Light Rail Gunman Sam Cassidy." KTVU News. Accessed December 2022 at https://www.ktvu.com/news/what-we-know-about-the-vta-light-rail-gunman-sam-cassidy
13. The year 2021 was another record breaker, with the Gun Violence Archive reporting 691 mass shootings. See Gun Violence Archive, *Past Summary Ledgers*.
14. Ibid.
15. Rachael Levy. 2021. "San Jose Shooter was Previously Questioned by Law Enforcement Over Hatred of Workplace." *Wall Street Journal*. May 27, 2021. Accessed December 2022 at https://www.wsj.com/articles/san-jose-shooter-was-previously-questioned-by-law-enforcement-over-hatred-of-workplace-11622142384
16. Vacar and Sernoffsky, "What We Know about the VTA."
17. U.S. Department of Homeland Security (n.d.). "Active Shooter: How to Respond." Accessed December 2022 at https://www.dhs.gov.

18. Melanie Taylor. 2018. "A Comprehensive Study of Mass Murder Precipitants and Motivations of Offenders." *International Journal of Offender Therapy and Comparative Criminology* 62(2): 427–449.
19. Rockefeller Institute of Government (n.d.). Mass Shooting Fact Sheet. Mass shootings in the United States: 1966–2020. Accessed September 2022 at https://rockinst.org/gun-violence/mass-shooting-factsheet/.
20. National Institute of Justice. 2022. "Public Mass Shootings: Database Amasses Details of a Half Century of US Mass Shootings with Firearms, Generating Psychosocial Histories." Accessed March 5, 2022 at: https://nij.ojp.gov/topics/articles/public-mass-shootings-database-amasses-details-half-century-us-mass-shootings#mass-shooting-demographics. Federal Bureau of Investigation. 2021a. *Active Shooter Incidents in the United States in 2020*. Washington, DC: U.S. Department of Justice. Accessed March 4, 2022 at: https://www.fbi.gov/file-repository/active-shooter-incidents-in-the-us-2020-070121.pdf/view).
21. Data from FBI Supplementary Homicide Reports online, Filtered by Age of Offender 50+. Accessed September 2022 at https://www.ojjdp.gov/ojstatbb/ezashr/asp/off_display.asp
22. John Luciew. 2014. "Woman, Age 102, Won't Stand Trial in Strangling Death of Nursing Home Roommate: Justice?" Accessed September 2022 at https://www.pennlive.com/midstate/2014/06/woman_age_102_wont_stand_trial.html
23. Mike Nizza and Carla Baranauckas. 2008. "Mourning in Missouri as Shooter's Motives Emerge." *New York Times*, February 8, 2008.
24. KPLC News. 2010. "Judge Says Evidence Adequate, Williams Held On No Bond." Accessed September 2022 at https://www.kplctv.com/story/13244528/2010/09/Thursday/preliminary-hearing-being-held-for-quadruple-murder-suspect/.
25. Murderpedia (n.d.) Accessed September 2022 at https://murderpedia.org/male.H/h/hance-michael.htm
26. Dallas Morning News. (December 24, 2012). "Documents Bring Glimpse of Troubled Life of Grapevine Mass Shooter." Accessed September 2022 at https://www.dallasnews.com/news/crime/2012/12/25/documents-bring-glimpse-of-troubled-life-of-grapevine-mass-shooter/
27. Source: Washington County Genealogical Society Obituary for Darrel Jason Lee published in Omaha World-Herald. January 31, 2007. http://www.newashcogs.org/obituary.asp?item=12551
28. Elizabeth Yardley, David Wilson, and Adam Lynes. 2013. "A Taxonomy of Male British Family Annihilators, 1980–2012." *The Howard Journal of Criminal Justice* 53(2): 117–140.
29. Linda Karlsson, J. Antfolk, H. Putkonen, S. Amon, J. Guerreiro, V. de Vogel, S. Flynn, and G. Weizmann-Henelius. 2021. "Familicide: A Systematic Literature Review." *Trauma, Violence, & Abuse* 22(1): 83–98.
30. Statistica (n.d.) Population Data. Accessed September 2022 at https://www.statista.com/statistics/241488/population-of-the-us-by-sex-and-age/.
31. J. Silver, A. Simons, and S. Craun. 2018. *A Study of the Pre-Attack Behaviors of Active Shooters in the United States Between 2000–2013*. Federal Bureau of Investigation, U.S. Department of Justice, Washington, D.C. 20535.

32. American Foundation for Suicide Prevention (n.d.) Suicide Statistics. Accessed December 2022 at https://afsp.org/suicide-statistics/
33. Michael Kimmel. 2013. *Angry White Men: American Masculinity at the End of an Era*. New York: Bold Type Books.
34. Ames, *Going Postal*, 21.
35. Nouran Salahieh, Jeffrey Winter, Casey Tolan, Ralph Ellis, and Scott Glover. 2023. "What We Know about the Suspect in the Monterey Park Massacre." January 26, 2023. CNN. Retrieved February 13, 2023 from https://www.cnn.com/2023/01/23/us/huu-can-tran-monterey-park-shooting-what-we-know/index.html.
36. CBS Redwood City. 2023. "Half Moon Bay Shooting Suspect Chunli Zhao Sobs in Court during Hearing on Media Access." February 10, 2023. CBS Bay Area. Accessed February 13, 2023 at https://www.cbsnews.com/sanfrancisco/news/half-moon-bay-shooting-suspect-chunli-zhao-breaks-down-in-court/; Alexandra Ulmer and Tim Reid. 2023. "California Reels from Back-to-Back Shootings that Killed 18." Reuters. January 24, 2023. Accessed February 13, 2023 at https://www.reuters.com/world/us/california-staggered-by-deadly-back-to-back-mass-shootings-2023-01-24/
37. Urban Dictionary Entry, "Disgruntled" (n.d.). Accessed September 2022 at https://www.urbandictionary.com/define.php?term=disgruntled
38. Dave Cullen. 2009. *Columbine*. New York: Twelve (Hachette Book Group) (quote on p. 61).

Chapter 10

1. Mark Twain. 1894. *Pudd'nhead Wilson, A Tale*. Later published as *The Tragedy of Pudd'nhead Wilson, and the Comedy of Those Extraordinary Twins*. Serialized in The Century Magazine and later released as a novel available on Wikimedia Commons.
2. It truly was an incongruous image. Larry is the most law-abiding person I know. He has had one parking ticket in his life and we still tease him about it.
3. In some ways, U.S. media culture fetishizes IED. Audiences are drawn to rage like moths to a flame. Action movies normalize explosive expression of anger as the revenge paradigm portrays righteous anger again and again. The story doesn't advance if the lead character manages their anger. What if the Terminator paused to consider and turned away from the fight?
4. Prior to 1980, the *DSM* included an anger-related disorder known as "passive-aggressive personality, aggressive type." The attributes of IED have been refined in successive editions of the *DSM*. The current, the fifth, edition, includes IED as an Axis I clinical disorder.
5. Kate Scott, C.W. Lim, I. Hwang, T. Adamowski, A.O. Al-Hamzawi, E. Bromet, B.Bunting, M.P. Ferrand, S. Florescu, O. Gureje, H. Hinkov, C. Hu, E.G. Karam, S. Lee, J. Posada-Villa, D.J. Stein, H. Tahimor, M.C. Viana, M. Xavier & R. Kessler. 2016. "The Cross-National Epidemiology of DSM-IV Intermittent Explosive Disorder." *Psychological Medicine* 46: 3161–3172.

6. See: Angela Nickerson, I. Aderka, R. Bryant, and S. Hoffmann. 2012. "The Relationship between Childhood Exposure to Trauma and Intermittent Explosive Disorder." *Psychiatry Research 197*: 128–134.

   Also: Jennifer Fanning, J. Meyerhoff, R. Lee, and E. Coccaro. 2014. "History of Childhood Maltreatment in Intermittent Explosive Disorder and Suicidal Behavior." *Journal of Psychiatric Research 56*: 10–17.
7. Scott, et al., "Cross-National Epidemiology."
8. See, for instance: M. S. McCloskey, K. L. Noblett, J. L. Deffenbacher, J. K. Gollan, and E. F. Coccaro. 2008. "Cognitive-Behavioral Therapy for Intermittent Explosive Disorder: A Pilot Randomized Clinical Trial." *Journal of Consulting and Clinical Psychology 76*(5): 876–886. https://doi.org/10.1037/0022-006X.76.5.876.

   Also: Michael McCloskey, Yunice Chen, Thomas Olino, and Emil Coccaro. 2022. "Cognitive-Behavioral versus Supportive Psychotherapy for Intermittent Explosive Disorder: A Randomized Controlled Trial." *Behavior Therapy 53*(6): 1133–1166. doi 10.1016/j.beth.2022.05.001.
9. See: https://www.theduluthmodel.org/what-is-the-duluth-model/research-duluth-model-domestic-violence/ for studies that support the program as well as response to criticism. The "Reply to Dutton and Corvo" is particularly interesting. Unfortunately, as of this writing, the effectiveness of this popular intervention has not been established through a randomized controlled study.
10. See, for instance: Kevin Henwood, Shihning Chou, and Kevin Browne. 2015. "A Systematic Review and Meta-Analysis on the Effectiveness of CBT Informed Anger Management." *Aggression & Violent Behavior 25*: 280–292.
11. Julian Walker and Jennifer Bright. 2009. "Cognitive Therapy for Violence: Reaching the Parts that Anger Management Doesn't Reach." *Journal of Forensic Psychiatry and Psychology 20*(2): 174–201. doi: 10.1080/14789940701656832 (quote on p. 176).
12. Elizabeth E. Van Voorhees, Kirsten Dillon, Sarah Wilson, Paul Dennis, Lydia Neal, Alyssa Medenblik, Patrick Calhoun, Eric Dedert, Kelly Caron, Nivedita Chaudhry, Jeffrey White, Eric Elbogen, and Jean Beckham. 2021. "A Comparison of Group Anger Management Treatments for Combat Veterans with PTSD: Results from a Quasi-Experimental Trial." *Journal of Interpersonal Violence 36*(19–20): NP10276–NP10300. doi: 10.1177/0886260519873335.
13. Ibid., 1029.
14. Bernard Golden. 2016. *Overcoming Destructive Anger: Strategies that Work*. Baltimore: Johns Hopkins University Press.
15. Both systems have been criticized for the failure to provide mental health care. See: Lisa Colpe, J. Naifeh, P. Aliaga, N. Sampson, S. Heeringa, M. Stein, and R. Ursano. 2015. "Mental Health Treatment among Soldiers with Current Mental Disorders in the Army Study to Assess Risk and Resilience in Service Members (Army STARRS)." *Military Medicine 180*(10): 1041–1051. Accessed September 2022 at https://academic.oup.com/milmed/article/180/10/1041/4160597

    Also: KiDeuk Kim, M. Becker-Cohen, and M. Serakos. 2015. "The Processing and Treatment of Mentally Ill Persons in the Criminal Justice System: A Scan of Practice and Background Analysis." *Report by the Urban Institute*. Accessed September 2022 at https://www.basicknowledge101.com/pdf/The-Processing-and-Treatment-of-Mentally-Ill-Persons-in-the-Criminal-Justice-System.pdf

16. The therapeutic alliance is widely seen as a key element in the effectiveness of psychological interventions. See, for instance: Lisa Dixon, Y. Holoshitz, and I. Nossel. 2016. "Treatment Engagement of Individuals Experiencing Mental Illness: Review and Update." *World Psychiatry 15*(1): 13–20. Accessed September 2022 at https://onlinelibrary.wiley.com/doi/10.1002/wps.20306

    Also: Emily Hamovitch, M. Choy-Brown, and V. Stanhope. 2018. "Person-Centered Care and the Therapeutic Alliance." *Community Mental Health Journal 54*: 951–958. Accessed September 2022 at https://link.springer.com/article/10.1007/s10597-018-0295-z

Chapter 11

1. William Blake, A Poison Tree, In *Songs of Innocence and of Experience*. London: R. Brimley Johnson, 1901, lines 1–4.
2. Maria Crespo and Violeta Fenandez-Lansac. 2014. "Factors Associated with Anger and Anger Expression in Caregivers of Elderly Relatives." *Aging & Mental Health 18*(4): 454–462. http://dx.doi.org/10.1080/13607863.2013.856857
3. The 4 to 7 percent comes from: Terri Roberton and Michael Daffern. 2020. "Improving the Assessment of Risk for Imminent Aggression in Older Adults in Residential Facilities." *Aggression and Violent Behavior 51*: 1–9 (who reviewed CDC data for a quarter in 2018).

    The 20 percent comes from: Laura Funk, Rachel Herron, Dale Spencer, and Starr Thomas. 2021. "Aggression and Older Adults: News Media Coverage across Care Settings and Relationships." *Canadian Journal on Aging 40*(3): 500–511. doi:10.1017/S0714980820000197

    The 96 percent comes from: Janet Keene, Tony Hope, Christopher Fairburn, Ronbin Jacoby, Kathy Gedling, and Christopher Ware. 1999. "Natural History of Aggressive Behaviour in Dementia." *International Journal of Geriatric Psychiatry 14*(7): 541–548.
4. See, for instance, Tsu Wan-Ting, Amin Esmaily-Fard, Chih-Cheng Lai, Darshan Zala, Sie-Huei Lee, Shy-Shin Chang, Chien-Chang Lee. 2017. "Antipsychotics and the Risk of a Cardiovascular Accident: A Systematic Review and Meta-Analysis of Observational Studies." *Journal of the American Medical Directors Association 18*(8): 692–699. doi: 10.1016/j.jamda.2017.02.020.
5. This is an abbreviated version of Dad's story. For a more detailed account, please see: A.S. Barusch. 2018. "A Place for Dad." In S. Chivers and U. Kriebernegg (Eds.), *Care Home Stories: Aging, Disability, and Long-Term Residential Care*. Bielefeld, Germany: Verlag Transcript, pp. 53–74.
6. Nursing Home Abuse Guide (n.d.) Chemical Restrains on Elderly. https://nursinghomeabuseguide.com/abuse-injuries/elderly-restraints/chemical/

7. Julie A. Braun and Lawrence A. Frolik. 2000. "Legal Aspects of Chemical Restraint Use in Nursing Homes," *Marquette Elder's Advisor 2*(2): Article 5. Available at: http://scholarship.law.marquette.edu/elders/vol2/iss2/5
8. Laura Funk, Rachel Herron, Dale Spencer, and Starr Thomas. 2021. "Aggression and Older Adults: News Media Coverage across Care Settings and Relationships." *Canadian Journal on Aging 40*(3): 500–511. doi:10.1017/S0714980820000197 (quote on p. 500).
9. And also cause for concern. Consistent with my usual practice, I initially used three main search terms: older adults, anger, and dementia (in their various forms). To my surprise, the results were paltry. Nothing of interest, really. After a couple of days spent trying various databases and search engines I had a breakthrough when I replaced "anger" and its derivatives with "aggression." With this new term I hit the mother lode and found a lot of interesting material. I guess when it comes to dementia we aren't as much worried about the internal emotion experience as by its external manifestations.
10. Maura Kennedy, Jennifer Koehl, Christina Shenvi, Allyson Greenberg, Olivia Zurek, Michael LaMantia, and Alexander Lo. 2020. "The Agitated Older Adult in the Emergency Department: A Narrative Review of Common Causes and Management Strategies." *Journal of the American College of Emergency Physicians – OPEN 1*: 812–823.
11. Jane Fischer and Jeffrey Buchanan. 2018. "Presentation of Preferred Stimuli as an Intervention for Aggression in a Person with Dementia." *Behavior Analysis: Research and Practice 18*(1): 33–40.
12. Tatiana Dimitriou, John Papatriantafyllou, Anastasia Konsta, Dimitrios Kazis, Loukas Athanasiadis, Panagiotis Ioannidis, Efrosini Koutsouraki, Thomas Tegos, and Magda Tsolaki. "Assess of Combinations of Non-Pharmacological Interventions for the Reduction of Irritability in Patients with Dementia and their Caregivers: A Crossover RCT." 2022. *Brain Sciences 12*: 691.
13. Jennifer Watt, Zahra Goodarzi, Areti Veronidi, Vera Nincic, Paul Khan, Marco Ghassemi, Yuan Thompson, Andrea Tricco, and Sharon Strauss. 2019. "Comparative Efficacy of Interventions for Aggressive and Agitated Behaviors in Dementia: A Systematic Review and Network Meta-Analysis." *Annals of Internal Medicine 171*: 633–642 (quote on p. 633).
14. Carol Stearns and Peter Stearns. 1986. *Anger: The Struggle for Emotional Control in America's History*. University of Chicago Press.
15. Peter Stearns. 1994. *American Cool: Constructing a Twentieth-Century Emotional Style*. New York University Press.
16. see Carl Degler's 1986 review in *Science*. https://www.science.org/doi/10.1126/science.234.4782.1447 - Carl Degler review of Stearns' book.

Chapter 12

1. This popular attribution may be apocryphal. See: Francis Xavier. Hope and her daughters. *First Things*. 2021. Accessed May 2023 at https://www.firstthings.com/article/2021/03/hope-and-her-daughters.

2. C. Van Strum. 2021. *A Bitter Fog: Herbicides & Human Rights* (3rd ed.). New York: Jericho Hill Publishing (quote from p. 18).
3. Ibid., 19.
4. AARP. 2019. *Giving Back: Attitudes and Behaviors Across the Lifespan.* doi: https://doi.org/10.26419/res.00265.001
5. Jackie Fox and Sarah Quinn. 2012. "The Meaning of Social Activism to Older Adults in Ireland." *Journal of Occupational Science* 19(4): 358–370 (quotes from p. 365).
6. D. Blanche-Tarragó and M. Fernández-Ardèvol. "The Iaioflautas Movement in Catalonia: A Seniors' Networked Social Movement." Paper session presented at the 5th ECREA European Communication Conference, Lisbon, Portugal, November 2014 (quote from p. 7).

Ibid., 7.

7. Jeffrey Stout. 2021. *Blessed Are the Organized: Grassroots Democracy in America.* Princeton University Press, 64 (cited by Fine, 2023).
8. Jasmine Lorenzini and Jan Rosset. 2023. "Emotions and Climate Strike Participation among Young and Old Demonstrators." *Social Movement Studies* March: 1–17.
9. Gary Alan Fine. 2023. *Fair Share: Senior Activism, Tiny Publics and the Culture of Resistance.* University of Chicago Press.
10. Jackie Fox & Quinn, Sarah (2012). The meaning of social activism to older adults in Ireland. *Journal of Occupational Science* 19(4): 358–370 (quote on p. 365).

Chapter 13

1. William Shakespeare. *King Lear.* Oxford: Clarendon Press, 1877, Act I, Scene 1.
2. Ernst F. Schumacher. 1977. *A Guide for the Perplexed.* New York: Harper & Row, 57.

Bibliography

(Cited references may be found in chapter endnotes.)

Age Differences

Aktürk, Tuba, Ümmühan İşoğlu-Alkaç, Lütfü Hanoğlu, and Bahar Güntekin. "Age Related Differences in the Recognition of Facial Expression: Evidence from EEG Event-Related Brain Oscillations." *International Journal of Psychophysiology* 147 (2020): 244–256.

Amorim, Maria, Andrey Anikin, Augusto J. Mendes, César F. Lima, Sonja A. Kotz, and Ana P. Pinheiro. "Changes in Vocal Emotion Recognition across the Life Span." *Emotion* 21, no. 2 (2021): 315.

Bannerman, Rachel L., Paula Regener, and Arash Sahraie. "Binocular Rivalry: A Window into Emotional Processing in Aging." *Psychology and Aging* 26, no. 2 (2011): 372.

Berger, Natalie, Anne Richards, and Eddy J. Davelaar. "Differential Effects of Angry Faces on Working Memory Updating in Younger and Older Adults." *Psychology and Aging* 33, no. 4 (2018): 667.

Brown, Robyn Lewis. "The Influence of Stressor Exposure and Psychosocial Resources on the Age–Anger Relationship: A Longitudinal Analysis." *Journal of Aging and Health* 28, no. 8 (2016): 1465–1487.

Bucher, Alica, Andreas Voss, Julia Spaniol, Amelie Hische, and Nicola Sauer. "Age Differences in Emotion Perception in a Multiple Target Setting: An Eye-Tracking Study." *Emotion* 20, no. 8 (2020): 1423.

Charles, Susan Turk, and Laura L. Carstensen. "Unpleasant Situations Elicit Different Emotional Responses in Younger and Older Adults." *Psychology and Aging* 23, no. 3 (2008): 495.

Charles, Susan T., Jacqueline Mogle, Kate A. Leger, and David M. Almeida. "Age and the Factor Structure of Emotional Experience in Adulthood." *Journals of Gerontology: Series B* 74, no. 3 (2019): 419–429.

Duffy, Deirdre Niamh. "Time to Look In/At Anger: Considerations on the Position and Policing of Young People's Anger." *Journal of Youth Studies* 20, no. 1 (2017): 1–15.

Ebner, Natalie C., and Marcia K. Johnson. "Age-Group Differences in Interference from Young and Older Emotional Faces." *Cognition and Emotion* 24, no. 7 (2010): 1095–1116.

Etxeberria, Igone, Itziar Etxebarria, Elena Urdaneta, and Jose Javier Yanguas. "Age Differences among Older Adults in the Use of Emotion Regulation Strategies. What Happens among over 85s and Centenarians?" *Aging & Mental Health* 20, no. 9 (2016): 974–980.

Freudenberg, Maxi, Daniel N. Albohn, Robert E. Kleck, Reginald B. Adams Jr, and Ursula Hess. "Emotional Stereotypes on Trial: Implicit Emotion Associations for Young and Old Adults." *Emotion* 20, no. 7 (2020): 1244.

Fung, Helene H. L., and Jin You. "Age Differences in the Likelihood of Destructive Anger Responses under Different Relationship Contexts: A Comparison of Mainland and Hong Kong Chinese." *Psychology and Aging* 26, no. 3 (2011): 605.

Gunning-Dixon, Faith M., Ruben C. Gur, Alexis C. Perkins, Lee Schroeder, Travis Turner, Bruce I. Turetsky, Robin M. Chan, J. W. Loughead, D. C. Alsop, J. Maldjian, and R. E. Gur. "Age-Related Differences in Brain Activation during Emotional Face Processing." *Neurobiology of Aging* 24, no. 2 (2003): 285–295.

Kunzmann, Ute, and Stefanie Thomas. "Multidirectional Age Differences in Anger and Sadness." *Psychology and Aging* 29, no. 1 (2014): 16.

Kunzmann, Ute, Margund Rohr, Cornelia Wieck, Cathleen Kappes, and Carsten Wrosch. "Speaking about Feelings: Further Evidence for Multidirectional Age Differences in Anger and Sadness." *Psychology and Aging* 32, no. 1 (2017): 93.

MacCormack, Jennifer K., Teague R. Henry, Brian M. Davis, Suzanne Oosterwijk, and Kristen A. Lindquist. "Aging Bodies, Aging Emotions: Interoceptive Differences in Emotion Representations and Self-Reports across Adulthood." *Emotion* 21, no. 2 (2021): 227.

Mienaltowski, Andrew, Paul M. Corballis, Fredda Blanchard-Fields, Nathan A. Parks, and Matthew R. Hilimire. "Anger Management: Age Differences in Emotional Modulation of Visual Processing." *Psychology and Aging* 26, no. 1 (2011): 224.

Murphy, Jennifer, Edward Millgate, Hayley Geary, Caroline Catmur, and Geoffrey Bird. "No Effect of Age on Emotion Recognition after Accounting for Cognitive Factors and Depression." *Quarterly Journal of Experimental Psychology* 72, no. 11 (2019): 2690–2704.

Navon–Eyal, Meital, and Orit Taubman–Ben-Ari. "Can Emotion Regulation Explain the Association between Age and Driving Styles?" *Transportation Research Part F: Traffic Psychology and Behaviour* 74 (2020): 439–445.

Nikitin, Jana, and Alexandra M. Freund. "Adult Age Differences in Frequency Estimations of Happy and Angry Faces." *International Journal of Behavioral Development* 39, no. 3 (2015): 266–274.

Orgeta, Vasiliki, and Louise H. Phillips. "Effects of Age and Emotional Intensity on the Recognition of Facial Emotion." *Experimental Aging Research* 34, no. 1 (2007): 63–79.

Phillips, Louise Helen, Julie D. Henry, Judith A. Hosie, and Alan B. Milne. "Age, Anger Regulation and Well-Being." *Aging and Mental Health* 10, no. 3 (2006): 250–256.

Richter, David, Cathrin Dietzel, and Ute Kunzmann. "Age Differences in Emotion Recognition: The Task Matters." *Journals of Gerontology Series B: Psychological Sciences and Social Sciences* 66, no. 1 (2011): 48–55.

Trnka, Radek, Josef Mana, and Martin Kuska. "Age-Related Differences in Valence and Arousal of Emotion Concepts." *Ageing & Society* 42 (2022): 1991–2007.

Anger and Physical Health

Anton, Stephen D., and Peter M. Miller. "Do Negative Emotions Predict Alcohol Consumption, Saturated Fat Intake, and Physical Activity in Older Adults?" *Behavior Modification* 29, no. 4 (2005): 677–688.

Boylan, Jennifer Morozink, and Carol D. Ryff. "Varieties of Anger and the Inverse Link between Education and Inflammation: Toward an Integrative Framework." *Psychosomatic Medicine* 75, no. 6 (2013): 566.

Casagrande, Maria, Francesca Favieri, Angela Guarino, Enrico Di Pace, Viviana Langher, Giuseppe Germanò, and Giuseppe Forte. "The Night Effect of Anger: Relationship with Nocturnal Blood Pressure Dipping." *International Journal of Environmental Research and Public Health* 17, no. 8 (2020): 2705.

Eckerie, William, Amol Koldhekar, Matthew Muldoon, Jesse Stewart, and Tom Kamarck. "Independent Associations between Trait-Anger, Depressive Symptoms and Preclinical Artheroscleaotic Progression." *Annals of Behavioral Medicine* 57, no. 5 (2023): 409–417.

Hosseini, Seyed Hamzeh, Vahid Mokhberi, Reza Ali Mohammadpour, Mahsa Mehrabianfard, and Nasrin Bali Lashak. "Anger Expression and Suppression among Patients with Essential Hypertension." *International Journal of Psychiatry in Clinical Practice* 15, no. 3 (2011): 214–218.

Kidwell, Katherine M., Tori R. Van Dyk, Kassie D. Guenther, and Timothy D. Nelson. "Anger and Children's Health: Differentiating Role of Inward versus Outward Expressed Anger on Sleep, Medical Service Utilization, and Mental Health." *Children's Health Care* 45, no. 3 (2016): 342–358.

Memedovic, Sonja, Jessica R. Grisham, Thomas F. Denson, and Michelle L. Moulds. "The Effects of Trait Reappraisal and Suppression on Anger and Blood Pressure in Response to Provocation." *Journal of Research in Personality* 44, no. 4 (2010): 540–543.

Staicu, Mihaela-Luminița, and Mihaela Cuțov. "Anger and Health Risk Behaviors." *Journal of Medicine and Life* 3, no. 4 (2010): 372.

Shallcross, Amanda J., Brett Q. Ford, Victoria A. Floerke, and Iris B. Mauss. "Getting Better with Age: The Relationship between Age, Acceptance, and Negative Affect." *Journal of Personality and Social Psychology* 104, no. 4 (2013): 734.

Spencer, Justine M. Y., Allison B. Sekuler, Patrick J. Bennett, Martin A. Giese, and Karin S. Pilz. "Effects of Aging on Identifying Emotions Conveyed by Point-Light Walkers." *Psychology and Aging* 31, no. 1 (2016): 126.

Streubel, Berit, and Ute Kunzmann. "Age Differences in Emotional Reactions: Arousal and Age-Relevance Count." *Psychology and Aging* 26, no. 4 (2011): 966.

West, Jeffrey T., Sheena M. Horning, Kelli J. Klebe, Shannon M. Foster, R. Elisabeth Cornwell, David Perrett, D. Michael Burt, and Hasker P. Davis. "Age Effects on Emotion Recognition in Facial Displays: From 20 to 89 Years of Age." *Experimental Aging Research* 38, no. 2 (2012): 146–168.

Wrosch, Carsten, Meaghan A. Barlow, and Ute Kunzmann. "Age-Related Changes in Older Adults' Anger and Sadness: The Role of Perceived Control." *Psychology and Aging* 33, no. 2 (2018): 350.

Yeung, Dannii Yuen-Lan, and Helene H. Fung. "Age Differences in Coping and Emotional Responses toward SARS: A Longitudinal Study of Hong Kong Chinese." *Aging and Mental Health* 11, no. 5 (2007): 579–587.

Zhao, Min-Fang, Hubert D. Zimmer, Xunbing Shen, Wenfeng Chen, and Xiaolan Fu. "Exploring the Cognitive Processes Causing the Age-Related Categorization Deficit in the Recognition of Facial Expressions." *Experimental Aging Research* 42, no. 4 (2016): 348–364.

Zimprich, Daniel, and Anna Mascherek. "Measurement Invariance and Age-Related Differences of Trait Anger Across the Adult Lifespan." *Personality and Individual Differences* 52, no. 3 (2012): 334–339.

Anger Expression

Caska, Catherine M., Bethany E. Hendrickson, Michelle H. Wong, Sadia Ali, Thomas Neylan, and Mary A. Whooley. "Anger Expression and Sleep Quality in Patients with Coronary Heart Disease: Findings from the Heart and Soul Study." *Psychosomatic Medicine* 71, no. 3 (2009): 280.

Dautovich, Natalie D., Sarah Ghose, and Dana Schreiber. "Sleep Quality and Anger Expression: An Examination of Psychosocial Mechanisms Across the Adult Lifespan." *Aggression and Violent Behavior* 57 (2021): 101505. doi: 10.1016/j.avb.2020.101505.

Gouin, Jean-Philippe, Janice K. Kiecolt-Glaser, William B. Malarkey, and Ronald Glaser. "The Influence of Anger Expression on Wound Healing." *Brain, Behavior, and Immunity* 22, no. 5 (2008): 699–708.

Guenther, Kassie D., Tori R. Van Dyk, Katherine M. Kidwell, and Timothy D. Nelson. "The Moderating Role of Dysfunctional Parent-Child Relationships on the Association Between Outward Anger Expression and Physical Health in Youth From Low-Income Families." *Journal of Pediatric Health Care* 30, no. 4 (2016): 366–373.

Russell, Michael A., Timothy W. Smith, and Joshua M. Smyth. "Anger Expression, Momentary Anger, and Symptom Severity in Patients with Chronic Disease." *Annals of Behavioral Medicine* 50, no. 2 (2016): 259–271.

Tuck, Natalie L., Kathryn S. Adams, and Nathan S. Consedine. "Does the Ability to Express Different Emotions Predict Different Indices of Physical Health? A Skill-Based Study of Physical Symptoms and Heart Rate Variability." *British Journal of Health Psychology* 22, no. 3 (2017): 502–523.

Anger Interventions (Anger Management)

Bailey, Cassandra A., Betsy E. Galicia, Kalin Z. Salinas, Melissa Briones, Sheila Hugo, Kristin Hunter, and Amanda C. Venta. "Racial/Ethnic and Gender Disparities in Anger Management Therapy as a Probation Condition." *Law and Human Behavior* 44, no. 1 (2020): 88.

Shepherd, Gary, and Matthew Cant. "Difficult to Change? The Differences between Successful and Not-So-Successful Participation in Anger Management Groups." *Counselling and Psychotherapy Research* 20, no. 2 (2020): 214–223.

Anger Regulation

Phillips, Louise Helen, Julie D. Henry, Judith A. Hosie, and Alan B. Milne. "Age, Anger Regulation and Well-Being." *Aging and Mental Health* 10, no. 3 (2006): 250–256.

Mefford, Linda, Sandra P. Thomas, Bonnie Callen, and Maureen Groer. "Religiousness/Spirituality and Anger Management in Community-Dwelling Older Persons." *Issues in Mental Health Nursing* 35, no. 4 (2014): 283–291.

Anger Suppression

Anderson, David E., E. Jeffrey Metter, Hidetaka Hougaku, and Samer S. Najjar. "Suppressed Anger Is Associated with Increased Carotid Arterial Stiffness in Older Adults." *American Journal of Hypertension* 19, no. 11 (2006): 1129–1134.

Burns, John W., Phillip J. Quartana, Wesley Gilliam, Justin Matsuura, Carla Nappi, and Brandy Wolfe. "Suppression of Anger and Subsequent Pain Intensity and Behavior among Chronic Low Back Pain Patients: The Role of Symptom-Specific Physiological Reactivity." *Journal of Behavioral Medicine* 35, no. 1 (2012): 103–114.

Cundiff, Jenny M., J. Richard Jennings, and Karen A. Matthews. "Social Stratification and Risk for Cardiovascular Disease: Examination of Emotional Suppression as a Pathway to Risk." *Personality and Social Psychology Bulletin* 45, no. 8 (2019): 1202–1215.

Langner, Carrie A., Elissa S. Epel, Karen A. Matthews, Judith T. Moskowitz, and Nancy E. Adler. "Social Hierarchy and Depression: The Role of Emotion Suppression." *Journal of Psychology* 146, no. 4 (2012): 417–436.

Li, Lingyan, Yanjie Yang, Jincai He, Jinyao Yi, Yuping Wang, Jinqiang Zhang, and Xiongzhao Zhu. "Emotional Suppression and Depressive Symptoms in Women Newly Diagnosed with Early Breast Cancer." *BMC Women's Health* 15, no. 1 (2015): 1–8.

Penedo, Frank J., Jason R. Dahn, Dave Kinsinger, Michael H. Antoni, Ivan Molton, Jeffrey S. Gonzalez, Mary Anne Fletcher, Bernard Roos, Charles S. Carver, and Neil Schneiderman. "Anger Suppression Mediates the Relationship between Optimism and Natural Killer Cell Cytotoxicity in Men Treated for Localized Prostate Cancer." *Journal of Psychosomatic Research* 60, no. 4 (2006): 423–427.

Poole, Joseph C., Harold Snieder, Harry C. Davis, and Frank A. Treiber. "Anger Suppression and Adiposity Modulate Association between ADRB2 Haplotype and Cardiovascular Stress Reactivity." *Psychosomatic Medicine* 68, no. 2 (2006): 207–212.

Quartana, Phillip J., K. Lira Yoon, and John W. Burns. "Anger Suppression, Ironic Processes and Pain." *Journal of Behavioral Medicine* 30, no. 6 (2007): 455–469.

Quartana, Phillip J., and John W. Burns. "Painful Consequences of Anger Suppression." *Emotion* 7, no. 2 (2007): 400.

Quartana, Phillip J., Sara Bounds, K. Lira Yoon, Burel R. Goodin, and John W. Burns. "Anger Suppression Predicts Pain, Emotional, and Cardiovascular Responses to the Cold Pressor." *Annals of Behavioral Medicine* 39, no. 3 (2010): 211–221.

Rice, Simon M., David Kealy, John S. Ogrodniczuk, Zac E. Seidler, Linda Denehy, and John L. Oliffe. "The Cost of Bottling It Up: Emotion Suppression as a Mediator in the Relationship between Anger and Depression among Men with Prostate Cancer." *Cancer Management and Research* 12 (2020): 1039.

Ruffman, Ted, Michelle Ng, and Thomas Jenkin. "Older Adults Respond Quickly to Angry Faces Despite Labeling Difficulty." *Journals of Gerontology: Series B* 64, no. 2 (2009): 171–179.

Rutter, Lauren A., David Dodell-Feder, Ipsit V. Vahia, Brent P. Forester, Kerry J. Ressler, Jeremy B. Wilmer, and Laura Germine. "Emotion Sensitivity across the Lifespan: Mapping Clinical Risk Periods to Sensitivity to Facial Emotion Intensity." *Journal of Experimental Psychology: General* 148, no. 11 (2019): 1993.

Ryan, Melissa, Janice Murray, and Ted Ruffman. "Aging and the Perception of Emotion: Processing Vocal Expressions Alone and with Faces." *Experimental Aging Research* 36, no. 1 (2009): 1–22.

Angry Bodies

Dorr, Nancy, Jos F. Brosschot, John J. Sollers III, and Julian F. Thayer. "Damned If You Do, Damned If You Don't: The Differential Effect of Expression and Inhibition of Anger on Cardiovascular Recovery in Black and White Males." *International Journal of Psychophysiology* 66, no. 2 (2007): 125–134.

Allen, John J. B., and John P. Kline. "Frontal EEG Asymmetry, Emotion, and Psychopathology: The First, and the Next 25 Years." *Biological Psychology* 67, no. 1–2 (2004): 1–5.

Glynn, Laura M., Nicholas Christenfeld, and William Gerin. "The Role of Rumination in Recovery from Reactivity: Cardiovascular Consequences of Emotional States." *Psychosomatic Medicine* 64, no. 5 (2002): 714–726.

Harmon-Jones, Eddie. "Trait Anger Predicts Relative Left Frontal Cortical Activation to Anger-Inducing Stimuli." *International Journal of Psychophysiology* 66, no. 2 (2007): 154–160.

Jorgensen, Randall S., and Monika E. Kolodziej. "Suppressed Anger, Evaluative Threat, and Cardiovascular Reactivity: A Tripartite Profile Approach." *International Journal of Psychophysiology* 66, no. 2 (2007): 102–108.

LeDoux, Joseph E. "Emotion Circuits in the Brain." *Annual Review of Neuroscience* 23, no. 1 (2000): 155–184.

LeDoux, Joseph. "Rethinking the Emotional Brain." *Neuron* 73, no. 4 (2012): 653–676.

Mauss, Iris B., Crystal L. Cook, Jennifer YJ Cheng, and James J. Gross. "Individual Differences in Cognitive Reappraisal: Experiential and Physiological Responses to an Anger Provocation." *International Journal of Psychophysiology* 66, no. 2 (2007): 116–124.

Vrana, Scott R. "Psychophysiology of Anger: Introduction to the Special Issue." *International Journal of Psychophysiology: Official Journal of the International Organization of Psychophysiology* 66, no. 2 (2007): 93–94.

Stemmler, Gerhard, Tatjana Aue, and Jan Wacker. "Anger and Fear: Separable Effects of Emotion and Motivational Direction on Somatovisceral Responses." *International Journal of Psychophysiology* 66, no. 2 (2007): 141–153.

Biblical Anger

Grant, Deena. "Human Anger in Biblical Literature." *Revue Biblique* 118, no. 3 *(1946-)* (2011): 339–361.

Kruger, Paul A. "Emotions in the Hebrew Bible: A Few Observations on Prospects and Challenges." *Old Testament Essays* 28, no. 2 (2015): 395–420.

Michael, Matthew. "Anger Management and Biblical Characters: A Study of "Angry Exchange" among Characters of Hebrew Narrative." *Old Testament Essays* 28, no. 2 (2015): 451–480.

Schlimm, Matthew R. "Emotion, Embodiment, and Ethics: Engaging Anger in Genesis." in Tamar Kamionkowski and Wonil Kim (Eds), *Bodies, Embodiment, and Theology of the Hebrew Bible*. pp. 146–58. New York: T&T Clark, 2010.

Segal, Eliezer. "Human Anger and Divine Intervention in Esther." *Prooftexts: A Journal of Jewish Literary History* 9, no. 3 (1989): 247–256.

Van Wolde, Ellen. "Sentiments as Culturally Constructed Emotions: Anger and Love in the Hebrew Bible." *Biblical Interpretation* 16, no. 1 (2008): 1–24.

Constructive Anger

Halperin, Eran, Alexandra G. Russell, Carol S. Dweck, and James J. Gross. "Anger, Hatred, and the Quest for Peace: Anger Can Be Constructive in the Absence of Hatred." *Journal of Conflict Resolution* 55, no. 2 (2011): 274–291. doi: 10.1177/0022002710383670.

Shuman, Eric, Eran Halperin, and Michal Reifen Tagar. "Anger as a Catalyst for Change? Incremental Beliefs and Anger's Constructive Effects in Conflict." *Group Processes & Intergroup Relations* 21, no. 7 (2018): 1092–1106. doi: 10.1177/1368430217695442.

Silva, Laura Luz. "The Efficacy of Anger: Recognition and Retribution." In Ana Falcato and Sara Graca Da Silva (Eds), *The Politics of Emotional Shockwaves*, pp. 27–55. Cham, Switzerland: Palgrave Macmillan, 2021.

Culture & Anger

Allen, G. E., Hokule Conklin, and Davis K. Kane. "Racial Discrimination and Psychological Health among Polynesians in the US." *Cultural Diversity and Ethnic Minority Psychology* 23, no. 3 (2017): 416.

Chen, Rui Jun, Glenn Flores, and Rashmi Shetgiri. "African-American and Latino Parents' Attitudes and Beliefs Regarding Adolescent Fighting and Its Prevention." *Journal of Child and Family Studies* 25, no. 6 (2016): 1746–1754.

De Leersnyder, Jozefien, Michael Boiger, and Batja Mesquita. "Cultural Differences in Emotions." In Robert Scott and Stephen Kosslyn (Eds), *Emerging Trends in the Social and Behavioral Sciences: An Interdisciplinary, Searchable, and Linkable Resource*, pp. 1–15, New York: Wiley (2015): 1–15.

Dementia and Caregiving

Cooke, Heather A., Sarah A. Wu, Anna Bourbonnais, and Jennifer Baumbusch. "Disruptions in Relational Continuity: The Impact of Pandemic Public Health Measures on Families in Long-Term Care." *Journal of Family Nursing* 29, no. 1 (2023): 6–17.

Crespo, María, and Violeta Fernández-Lansac. "Factors Associated with Anger and Anger Expression in Caregivers of Elderly Relatives." *Aging & Mental Health* 18, no. 4 (2014): 454–462. doi: 10.1080/13607863.2013.856857.

Dimitriou, Tatiana, John Papatriantafyllou, Anastasia Konsta, Dimitrios Kazis, Loukas Athanasiadis, Panagiotis Ioannidis, Efrosini Koutsouraki, Thomas Tegos, and Magda Tsolaki. "Assess of Combinations of Non-Pharmacological Interventions for the Reduction of Irritability in Patients with Dementia and their Caregivers: A Cross-Over RCT." *Brain Sciences* 12, no. 6 (2022): 691. doi: 10.3390/brainsci12060691.

Fisher, Jane E., and Jeffrey A. Buchanan. "Presentation of Preferred Stimuli as an Intervention for Aggression in a Person with Dementia." *Behavior Analysis: Research and Practice* 18, no. 1 (2018): 33–40. doi: 10.1037/bar0000086.

Gimeno, Ignacio, Sonia Val, and María Jesús Cardoso Moreno. "Relation among Caregivers' Burden, Abuse and Behavioural Disorder in People with Dementia." *International Journal of Environmental Research and Public Health* 18, no. 3 (2021): 1263. doi: 10.3390/ijerph18031263.

Keene, Janet, Tony Hope, Christopher G. Fairburn, Robin Jacoby, Kathy Gedling, and Christopher J. G. Ware. "Natural History of Aggressive Behaviour in Dementia." *International Journal of Geriatric Psychiatry* 14, no. 7 (1999): 541–548.

Leonard, Ralph, Mary E. Tinetti, Heather G. Allore, and Margaret A. Drickamer. "Potentially Modifiable Resident Characteristics that Are Associated with Physical or Verbal Aggression among Nursing Home Residents with Dementia." *Archives of Internal Medicine* 166, no. 12 (2006): 1295–1300.

López, J., R. Romero-Moreno, M. Márquez-González, and A. Losada. "Anger and Health in Dementia Caregivers: Exploring the Mediation Effect of Optimism." *Stress and Health* 31, no. 2 (2015): 158–165.

McDermott, Cara L., and David A. Gruenewald. "Pharmacologic Management of Agitation in Patients with Dementia." *Current Geriatrics Reports* 8, no. 1 (2019): 1–11. doi: 10.1007/s13670-019-0269-1.

Moyle, Wendy, Jenny Murfield, Cindy Jones, Elizabeth Beattie, Brian Draper, and Tamara Ownsworth. "Can Lifelike Baby Dolls Reduce Symptoms of Anxiety, Agitation, or Aggression for People with Dementia in Long-Term Care? Findings from a Pilot Randomised Controlled Trial." *Aging & Mental Health* 23, no. 10 (2019): 1442–1450. doi: 10.1080/13607863.2018.1498447.

Ozcan, Munevver, and Imatullah Akyar. "Caregivers' Experiences of Patients with Moderate-Stage Alzheimer's Disease: A Qualitative Study." *Psychogeriatrics* 21, no. 5 (2021): 763–772. doi: 10.1111/psyg.12736.

Roberton, Terri, and Michael Daffern. "Improving the Assessment of Risk for Imminent Aggression in Older Adults in Residential Facilities." *Aggression and Violent Behavior* 51 (2020): 101364. doi: 10.1016/j.avb.2020.101364.

Van Dongon, Dorien H. E., Devi Havermans, Kay Deckers, Miranda Olff, Frans Verhey, and Sjacko Sobczak. "A First Insight Into the Clinical Manifestation of Posttraumatic Stress Disorder in Dementia: A Systematic Literature Review." *Psychogeriatrics* 22 (2022): 509–520.

Family

Crespo, María, and Violeta Fernández-Lansac. "Factors Associated with Anger and Anger Expression in Caregivers of Elderly Relatives." *Aging & Mental Health* 18, no. 4 (2014): 454–462.

Wand, Anne Pamela Frances, Carmelle Peisah, Brian Draper, and Henry Brodaty. "Carer Insights into Self-Harm in the Very Old: A Qualitative Study." *International Journal of Geriatric Psychiatry* 34, no. 4 (2019): 594–600.

Gender Differences (and Similarities)

Andrighetto, Luca, Paolo Riva, and Alessandro Gabbiadini. "Lonely Hearts and Angry Minds: Online Dating Rejection Increases Male (But Not Female) Hostility." *Aggressive Behavior* 45, no. 5 (2019): 571–581.

Archer, John. "Sex Differences in Aggression in Real-World Settings: A Meta-Analytic Review." *Review of General Psychology* 8, no. 4 (2004): 291–322.

Bartlett, Michelle L., Mitch Abrams, Megan Byrd, Arial S. Treankler, and Richard Houston-Norton. "Advancing the Assessment of Anger in Sports: Gender Differences and STAXI-2 Normative Data for College Athletes." *Journal of Clinical Sport Psychology* 12, no. 2 (2018): 114–128.

Blincoe, Sarai, and Monica J. Harris. "Status and Inclusion, Anger and Sadness: Gendered Responses to Disrespect." *European Journal of Social Psychology* 41, no. 4 (2011): 508–517.

Budziszewska, Magdalena, and Karolina Hansen. "'Anger Detracts From Beauty': Gender Differences in Adolescents' Narratives About Anger." *Journal of Adolescent Research* 35, no. 5 (2020): 635–664.

Campbell, Anne, and Steven Muncer. "Intent to Harm or Injure? Gender and the Expression of Anger." *Aggressive Behavior: Official Journal of the International Society for Research on Aggression* 34, no. 3 (2008): 282–293.

Carré, Justin M., Patrick M. Fisher, Stephen B. Manuck, and Ahmad R. Hariri. "Interaction between Trait Anxiety and Trait Anger Predict Amygdala Reactivity to Angry Facial Expressions in Men but not Women." *Social Cognitive and Affective Neuroscience* 7, no. 2 (2012): 213–221.

Ferrer, Rebecca A., Alexander Maclay, Paul M. Litvak, and Jennifer S. Lerner. "Revisiting the Effects of Anger on Risk-Taking: Empirical and Meta-Analytic Evidence for Differences between Males and Females." *Journal of Behavioral Decision Making* 30, no. 2 (2017): 516–526.

Fischer, Agneta H., and Catharine Evers. "The Social Costs and Benefits of Anger as a Function of Gender and Relationship Context." *Sex Roles* 65, no. 1 (2011): 23–34.

Gianakos, Irene. "Issues of Anger in the Workplace: Do Gender and Gender Role Matter?" *The Career Development Quarterly* 51, no. 2 (2002): 155–171.

González-Iglesias, Beatriz, José Antonio Gómez-Fraguela, and Mª Ángeles Luengo-Martín. "Driving Anger and Traffic Violations: Gender Differences." *Transportation Research Part F: Traffic Psychology and Behaviour* 15, no. 4 (2012): 404–412.

Harper, Felicity W. K., Amanda G. Austin, Jennifer J. Cercone, and Ileana Arias. "The Role of Shame, Anger, and Affect Regulation in Men's Perpetration of Psychological Abuse in Dating Relationships." *Journal of Interpersonal Violence* 20, no. 12 (2005): 1648–1662.

He, Zhenhong, Zhenli Liu, Ju Wang, and Dandan Zhang. "Gender Differences in Processing Fearful and Angry Body Expressions." *Frontiers in Behavioral Neuroscience* 12 (2018): 164.

Healey, Lindsay V., Vanessa Holmes, Susan Curry, Michael C. Seto, and Adekunle G. Ahmed. "Self-Reported Dysfunctional Anger in Men and Women at a Psychiatric Outpatient Clinic." *Journal of Rational-Emotive & Cognitive-Behavior Therapy* 37, no. 4 (2019): 395–410.

Ingram, Gordon P. D. "Evolutionary Developmental Explanations of Gender Differences in Interpersonal Conflict: A Response to Trnka (2013)." *Evolutionary Psychology* 11, no. 4 (2013): 787–790, 147470491301100402.

Kay, Jilly Boyce. "Introduction: Anger, Media, and Feminism: The Gender Politics of Mediated Rage." *Feminist Media Studies* 19, no. 4 (2019): 591–615.

Keck, Steffen. "Gender, Leadership, and the Display of Empathic Anger." *Journal of Occupational and Organizational Psychology* 92, no. 4 (2019): 953–977.

Krahé, Barbara. "Gendered Self-Concept and the Aggressive Expression of Driving Anger: Positive Femininity Buffers Negative Masculinity." *Sex Roles* 79, no. 1 (2018): 98–108.

Krems, Jaimie Arona, Steven L. Neuberg, Gabrielle Filip-Crawford, and Douglas T. Kenrick. "Is She Angry? (Sexually Desirable) Women "See" Anger on Female Faces." *Psychological Science* 26, no. 11 (2015): 1655–1663.

Kunst, Laura E., Judith de Groot, and A. J. van der Does. "Ambivalence Over Expression of Anger and Sadness Mediates Gender Differences in Depressive Symptoms." *Cognitive Therapy and Research* 43, no. 2 (2019): 365–373.

McDermott, Ryon C., Jonathan P. Schwartz, and Melissa Trevathan-Minnis. "Predicting Men's Anger Management: Relationships with Gender Role Journey and Entitlement." *Psychology of Men & Masculinity* 13, no. 1 (2012): 49.

Mermelstein, Ari. "Conceptions of Masculinity in the Scrolls and the Gendered Emotion of Anger." *Dead Sea Discoveries* 26, no. 3 (2019): 314–338.

Monaci, Maria Grazia, and Francesca Veronesi. "Getting Angry When Playing Tennis: Gender Differences and Impact on Performance." *Journal of Clinical Sport Psychology* 13, no. 1 (2019): 116–133.

Munar, Ana María. "Dancing between Anger and Love: Reflections on Feminist Activism." *Ephemera: Theory & Politics in Organization* 18, no. 4 (2018): 955–970.

Newman, Jody L., Dale R. Fuqua, Elizabeth A. Gray, and David B. Simpson. "Gender Differences in the Relationship of Anger and Depression in a Clinical Sample." *Journal of Counseling & Development* 84, no. 2 (2006): 157–162.

Parrott, Dominic J., and Amos Zeichner. "Effects of Trait Anger and Negative Attitudes Towards Women on Physical Assault in Dating Relationships." *Journal of Family Violence* 18, no. 5 (2003): 301–307.

Salerno, Jessica M., Liana C. Peter-Hagene, and Alexander C. V. Jay. "Women and African Americans are Less Influential When They Express Anger during Group Decision Making." *Group Processes & Intergroup Relations* 22, no. 1 (2019): 57–79.

Sharp, Shane, Deborah Carr, and Kathryn Panger. "Gender, Race, and the Use of Prayer to Manage Anger." *Sociological Spectrum* 36, no. 5 (2016): 271–285.

Shepherd, Gary, and Matthew Cant. "Difficult to Change? The Differences between Successful and Not-So-Successful Participation in Anger Management Groups." *Counselling and Psychotherapy Research* 20, no. 2 (2020): 214–223.

Simon, Robin W., and Kathryn Lively. "Sex, Anger and Depression." *Social Forces* 88, no. 4 (2010): 1543–1568.

Sloan, Melissa M. "Controlling Anger and Happiness at Work: An Examination of Gender Differences." *Gender, Work & Organization* 19, no. 4 (2012): 370–391.

Stewart, Andrew L. "Men's Collective Action Willingness: Testing Different Theoretical Models of Protesting Gender Inequality for Women and Men." *Psychology of Men & Masculinity* 18, no. 4 (2017): 372.

Sullman, Mark J. M., J. Paxion, and A. N. Stephens. "Gender Roles, Sex and the Expression of Driving Anger." *Accident Analysis & Prevention* 106 (2017): 23–30.

Weber, Hannelore, and Monika Wiedig-Allison. "Sex Differences in Anger-Related Behaviour: Comparing Expectancies to Actual Behaviour." *Cognition and Emotion* 21, no. 8 (2007): 1669–1698.

Intermittent Explosive Disorder (IED)

Coccaro, Emil F., Royce Lee, and Michael S. McCloskey. "Relationship between Psychopathy, Aggression, Anger, Impulsivity, and Intermittent Explosive Disorder." *Aggressive Behavior* 40, no. 6 (2014): 526–536.

Costa, Ana M., Gustavo C. Medeiros, Sarah Redden, Jon E. Grant, Hermano Tavares, and Liliana Seger. "Cognitive-Behavioral Group Therapy for Intermittent Explosive Disorder: Description and Preliminary Analysis." *Brazilian Journal of Psychiatry* 40 (2018): 316–319.

Fahlgren, Martha K., Alexander A. Puhalla, Kristen M. Sorgi, and Michael S. McCloskey. "Emotion Processing in Intermittent Explosive Disorder." *Psychiatry Research* 273 (2019): 544–550.

Fanning, Jennifer R., Jonah J. Meyerhoff, Royce Lee, and Emil F. Coccaro. "History of Childhood Maltreatment in Intermittent Explosive Disorder and Suicidal Behavior." *Journal of Psychiatric Research* 56 (2014): 10–17.
Krick, Lynette C., Mitchell E. Berman, Michael S. McCloskey, Emil F. Coccaro, and Jennifer R. Fanning. "Gender Moderates the Association between Exposure to Interpersonal Violence and Intermittent Explosive Disorder Diagnosis." *Journal of Interpersonal Violence* (2021): 15–16. 08862605211013951.
McCloskey, Michael S., K. Luan Phan, Mike Angstadt, Karla C. Fettich, Sarah Keedy, and Emil F. Coccaro. "Amygdala Hyperactivation to Angry Faces in Intermittent Explosive Disorder." *Journal of Psychiatric Research* 79 (2016): 34–41.
Medeiros, Gustavo C., Liliana Seger, Jon E. Grant, and Hermano Tavares. "Major Depressive Disorder and Depressive Symptoms in Intermittent Explosive Disorder." *Psychiatry Research* 262 (2018): 209–212.
Nickerson, Angela, Idan M. Aderka, Richard A. Bryant, and Stefan G. Hofmann. "The Relationship between Childhood Exposure to Trauma and Intermittent Explosive Disorder." *Psychiatry Research* 197, no. 1–2 (2012): 128–134.
Scott, K. M., C. C. W. Lim, I. Hwang, Tomasz Adamowski, A. Al-Hamzawi, E. Bromet, B. Bunting, M. P. Ferrand, S. Florescu, O. Gureje, H. Hinkov, C. Hu, E. G. Karam, S. Lee, J. Posada-Villa, D.J. Stein, H. Tachimori, M. C. Viana, M. Xavier, and R. C. Kessler. "The Cross-National Epidemiology of DSM-IV Intermittent Explosive Disorder." *Psychological Medicine* 46, no. 15 (2016): 3161–3172.

Measurements

Azevedo, Flávia, Scott G. Ravyts, Elliottnell Perez, Emily K. Donovan, Pablo Soto, and Joseph M. Dzierzewski. "Measurement of Aggression in Older Adults." *Aggression and Violent Behavior* 57 (2021): 101484. doi: 10.1016/j.avb.2020.101484.
Barros de, Yuan-Pang Wang, Alessandra Carvalho Goulart, Paulo Andrade Lotufo, and Isabela Martins Benseñor. "Application of the Spielberger's State-Trait Anger Expression Inventory in Clinical Patients." *Arquivos de Neuro-psiquiatria* 68 (2010): 231–234.
Culhane, Scott E., and Osvaldo F. Morera. "Reliability and Validity of the Novaco Anger Scale and Provocation Inventory (NAS-PI) and State-Trait Anger Expression Inventory-2 (STAXI-2) in Hispanic and Non-Hispanic White Student Samples." *Hispanic Journal of Behavioral Sciences* 32, no. 4 (2010): 586–606.
Furunes, Trude, and Reidar J. Mykletun. "Age Discrimination in the Workplace: Validation of the Nordic Age Discrimination Scale (NADS)." *Scandinavian Journal of Psychology* 51, no. 1 (2010): 23–30.
Schamborg, Sara, Ruth J. Tully, and Kevin D. Browne. "The Use of the State–Trait Anger Expression Inventory–II with Forensic Populations: A Psychometric Critique." *International Journal of Offender Therapy and Comparative Criminology* 60, no. 11 (2016): 1239–1256.
Shahsavarani, Amir Mohammad, Sima Noohi, Saeideh Jafari, Maryam Hakimi Kalkhoran, and Samira Hatefi. "Assessment & Measurement of Anger in Behavioral and Social Sciences: A Systematic Review of Literature." *International Journal of Medical Reviews* 2, no. 3 (2015): 279–286.

Marchiondo, Lisa A., Ernest Gonzales, and Shan Ran. "Development and Validation of the Workplace Age Discrimination Scale." *Journal of Business and Psychology* 31, no. 4 (2016): 493–513.

King, Scott P., and Fred B. Bryant. "The Workplace Intergenerational Climate Scale (WICS): A Self-Report Instrument Measuring Ageism in the Workplace." *Journal of Organizational Behavior* 38, no. 1 (2017): 124–151.

Snell, W. E., Jr., S. Gum, R. L. Shuck, J. A. Mosley, and T. L. Hite. (2013). The Clinical Anger Scale (CAS). Measurement Instrument Database for the Social Science. Retrieved from www.midss.ie

Miscellaneous

Binstock, Robert H. "From Compassionate Ageism to Intergenerational Conflict?" *The Gerontologist* 50, no. 5 (2010): 574–585. doi: 10.1093/geront/gnq056.

Bogdan, Smaranda Raluca. "Can Age, Sensation-Seeking and Impulsivity Predict Angry Thoughts of Romanian Drivers?" *Analele Științifice ale Universității» Alexandru Ioan Cuza «din Iași. Psihologie* 1 (2015): 53–69.

Kashdan, Todd B., Fallon R. Goodman, Travis T. Mallard, and C. Nathan DeWall. "What Triggers Anger in Everyday Life? Links to the Intensity, Control, and Regulation of These Emotions, and Personality Traits." *Journal of Personality* 84, no. 6 (2016): 737–749.

Perron, Rebecca. "The Value of Experience: AARP Multicultural Work and Jobs Study." *AARP Research* (2018).

Silton, Nava R., Kevin J. Flannelly, and Laura J. Lutjen. "It Pays to Forgive! Aging, Forgiveness, Hostility, and Health." *Journal of Adult Development* 20, no. 4 (2013): 222–231.

Stewart, Jesse C., Griffin J. Fitzgerald, and Thomas W. Kamarck. "Hostility Now, Depression Later? Longitudinal Associations among Emotional Risk Factors for Coronary Artery Disease." *Annals of Behavioral Medicine* 39, no. 3 (2010): 258–266.

Uzer, Tugba, and Sami Gulgoz. "Socioemotional Selectivity in Older Adults: Evidence from the Subjective Experience of Angry Memories." *Memory* 23, no. 6 (2015): 888–900. doi: 10.1080/09658211.2014.936877.

Narratives and Stories

Robertson, Sarah M. C., and Rhonda J. Swickert. "The Stories We Tell: How Age, Gender, and Forgiveness Affect the Emotional Content of Autobiographical Narratives." *Aging & Mental Health* 22, no. 4 (2018): 535–543.

Johnson, Dan R., Brandie L. Huffman, and Danny M. Jasper. "Changing Race Boundary Perception by Reading Narrative Fiction." *Basic and Applied Social Psychology* 36, no. 1 (2014): 83–90.

Kennedy, Maura, Jennifer Koehl, Christina L. Shenvi, Allyson Greenberg, Olivia Zurek, Michael LaMantia, and Alexander X. Lo. "The Agitated Older Adult in the Emergency Department: A Narrative Review of Common Causes and Management Strategies." *Journal of the American College of Emergency Physicians Open* 1, no. 5 (2020): 812–823. doi: 10.1002/emp2.12110.

Race and Racial Differences

Banks, Antoine J., and Melissa A. Bell. "Racialized Campaign Ads: The Emotional Content in Implicit Racial Appeals Primes White Racial Attitudes." *Public Opinion Quarterly* 77, no. 2 (2013): 549–560.

Banks, Antoine J., Ismail K. White, and Brian D. McKenzie. "Black Politics: How Anger Influences the Political Actions Blacks Pursue to Reduce Racial Inequality." *Political Behavior* 41, no. 4 (2019): 917–943.

Gibbons, Frederick X., Mary E. Fleischli, Meg Gerrard, and Ronald L. Simons. "Reports of Perceived Racial Discrimination among African American Children Predict Negative Affect and Smoking Behavior in Adulthood: A Sensitive Period Hypothesis." *Development and Psychopathology* 30, no. 5 (2018): 1629–1647.

Hayward, Lydia E., Linda R. Tropp, Matthew J. Hornsey, and Fiona Kate Barlow. "How Negative Contact and Positive Contact with Whites Predict Collective Action among Racial and Ethnic Minorities." *British Journal of Social Psychology* 57, no. 1 (2018): 1–20.

Huynh, Virginia W. "Ethnic Microaggressions and the Depressive and Somatic Symptoms of Latino and Asian American Adolescents." *Journal of Youth and Adolescence* 41, no. 7 (2012): 831–846.

Liang, Christopher T. H., and Carin M. Molenaar. "Beliefs In an Unjust World: Mediating Ethnicity-Related Stressors and Psychological Functioning." *Journal of Clinical Psychology* 72, no. 6 (2016): 552–562.

Mabry, J. Beth, and K. Jill Kiecolt. "Anger in Black and White: Race, Alienation, and Anger." *Journal of Health and Social Behavior* 46, no. 1 (2005): 85–101.

Magee, William, and Patricia Louie. "Did the Difference Between Black and White Americans in Anger-Out Decrease during the First Decade of the Twenty-First Century?" *Race and Social Problems* 8, no. 3 (2016): 256–270.

Outten, H. Robert, Michael T. Schmitt, Daniel A. Miller, and Amber L. Garcia. "Feeling Threatened about the Future: Whites' Emotional Reactions to Anticipated Ethnic Demographic Changes." *Personality and Social Psychology Bulletin* 38, no. 1 (2012): 14–25.

Pittman, Chavella T. "Getting Mad but Ending Up Sad: The Mental Health Consequences for African Americans Using Anger to Cope with Racism." *Journal of Black Studies* 42, no. 7 (2011): 1106–1124.

Rapoza, Kimberly A., Denise T. Wilson, Wendy A. Widmann, Michelle A. Riley, Thomas W. Robertson, Elizabeth Maiello, Nikisha Villot, Dana J. Manzella, and Alberto L. Ortiz-Garcia. "The Relationship between Adult Health and Childhood Maltreatment, as Moderated by Anger and Ethnic Background." *Child Abuse & Neglect* 38, no. 3 (2014): 445–456.

Saleem, Farzana T., and Sharon F. Lambert. "Differential Effects of Racial Socialization Messages for African American Adolescents: Personal versus Institutional Racial Discrimination." *Journal of Child and Family Studies* 25, no. 5 (2016): 1385–1396.

Tomfohr, Lianne M., Meredith A. Pung, and Joel E. Dimsdale. "Mediators of the Relationship between Race and Allostatic Load in African and White Americans." *Health Psychology* 35, no. 4 (2016): 322.

Williams, Janice E., David J. Couper, Rebecca Din-Dzietham, F. Javier Nieto, and Aaron R. Folsom. "Race-Gender Differences in the Association of Trait Anger with Subclinical Carotid Artery Atherosclerosis: The Atherosclerosis Risk in Communities Study." *American Journal of Epidemiology* 165, no. 11 (2007): 1296–1304.

Suicide and Anger

Alvarez, Pilar, Mikel Urretavizcaya, Luisa Benlloch, Julio Vallejo, and Jose Manuel Menchon. "Early- and Late-Onset Depression in the Older: No Differences Found Within the Melancholic Subtype." *International Journal of Geriatric Psychiatry* 26 (2011): 615–621.

Cooper, C., P. Bebbington, M. King, R. Jenkins, M. Farrell, T. Brugha, and S. McManus. "Happiness Across Age Groups: Results from the 2007 National Psychiatric Morbidity Survey." *International Journal of Geriatric Psychiatry* 26 (2011): 608–614.

Daniel, Stephanie S., David B. Goldston, Alaattin Erkanli, Joseph C. Franklin, and Andrew M. Mayfield. "Trait Anger, Anger Expression, and Suicide Attempts among Adolescents and Young Adults: A Prospective Study." *Journal of Clinical Child & Adolescent Psychology* 38, no. 5 (2009): 661–671.

Hirsch, Jameson K., Jon R. Webb, and Elizabeth L. Jeglic. "Forgiveness as a Moderator of the Association between Anger Expression and Suicidal Behaviour." *Mental Health, Religion & Culture* 15, no. 3 (2012): 279–300.

Richard-Devantoy, Stephane, Katalin Szsanto, Meryl A. Butters, Jan Kalkus, and Alexandre Y. Dombrowski. "Cognitive Inhibition in Older High-Lethality Suicide Attempters." *International Journal of Geriatric Psychiatry* 30 (2015): 274–283.

Wand, Anne Pamela Frances. Carmelle Peisah, Brian Draper, and Henry Brodaty. "Carer Insights into Self-Harm in the Very Old: A Qualitative Study." *International Journal of Geriatric Psychiatry* 34 (2019): 594–600.

Theories

Baltes, Paul B., and Jacqui Smith. "New Frontiers in the Future of Aging: From Successful Aging of the Young Old to the Dilemmas of the Fourth Age." *Gerontology* 49 (2003): 123–135. http://dx.doi.org/10.1159/000067946

Carstensen, Laura L., and Corinna E. Löckenhoff. "Aging, Emotion, and Evolution: The Bigger Picture." *Annals of the New York Academy of Sciences* 1000, no. 1 (2003): 152–179.

Coats, Abby H., and Fredda Blanchard-Fields. "Emotion Regulation in Interpersonal Problems: The Role of Cognitive-Emotional Complexity, Emotion Regulation Goals, and Expressivity." *Psychology and Aging* 23, no. 1 (2008): 39–51. https://doi.org/10.1037/0882-7974.23.1.39

Cohen, Marc A. "Against Basic Emotions, and Toward a Comprehensive Theory." *Journal of Mind and Behavior* 26, no. 4 (2005): 229–254.

Dalgleish, Tim. "The Thinking Person's Emotion Theorist: A Comment on Bartlett's Feeling, Imaging, and Thinking." *British Journal of Psychology* 100, no. S1 (2009): 199–201. doi: 10.1348/000712609X413683.

Deffenbacher, Jerry L., Eugene R. Oetting, Gregory A. Thwaites, Rebekah S. Lynch, Deborah A. Baker, Robert S. Stark, Stacy Thacker, and Lora Eiswerth-Cox. "State–Trait Anger Theory and the Utility of the Trait Anger Scale." *Journal of Counseling Psychology* 43, no. 2 (1996): 131.

Gross, James J. and Lisa Barrett. "Emotion Generation and Emotion Regulation: One or Two Depends on Your Point of View." *Emotion Review* 3, no. 1 (2011): 8–16. doi: 10.1177/1754073910380974.

Isom Scott, Deena A., and Zachary T. Seal. "Disentangling the Roles of Negative Emotions and Racial Identity in the Theory of African American Offending." *American Journal of Criminal Justice* 44, no. 2 (2019): 277–308.

Keltner, Dacher. "Expression and the Course of Life: Studies of Emotion, Personality, and Psychopathology from a Social-Functional Perspective." *Annals of the New York Academy of Sciences* 1000, no. 1 (2003): 222–243.

Kunzmann, Ute, Cathleen Kappes, and Carsten Wrosch. "Emotional Aging: A Discrete Emotions Perspective." *Frontiers in Psychology* 5 (2014): 380.

Labouvie-Vief, Gisela, Julie Hakim-Larson, Marlene DeVoe, and Steven Schoeberlein. "Emotions and Self-Regulation: A Life Span View." *Human Development* 32, no. 5 (1989): 279–299.

Labouvie-Vief, Gisela, Lisa M. Chiodo, Lori A. Goguen, and Manfred Diehl. "Representations of Self Across the Life Span." *Psychology and Aging* 10, no. 3 (1995): 404.

Levine, Linda. "The Anatomy of Disappointment: A Naturalistic Test of Appraisal Models of Sadness, Anger, and Hope." *Cognition & Emotion* 11, no. 4 (2010, July 1): 337–360. 10.1080/026999396380178.

Lewis, Marc D. "Bridging Emotion Theory & Neurobiology through Dynamic Systems Modeling." *Behavioral Brain Science* 28, no. 2 (2005, Apr): 169–194; discussion 194–245. doi: 10.1017/s0140525x0500004x.

Oatley, Keith, and Philip N. Johnson-Laird. "Towards a Cognitive Theory of Emotions." *Cognition and Emotion* 1, no. 1 (1987): 29–50.

Orgeta, Vasiliki. "Avoiding Threat in Late Adulthood: Testing Two Life Span Theories of Emotion." *Experimental Aging Research* 37, no. 4 (2011): 449–472.

Royzman, Edward, Pavel Atanasov, Justin Landy, Amanda Parks, and Andrew Gepty. "CAD or MAD? Anger (Not Disgust) as the Predominant Response to Pathogen-Free Violations of the Divinity Code." *Emotion* 14, no. 5 (2014, Oct): 892–907. doi: 10.1037/a0036829.

Shields, Stephanie A. "Magda B. Arnold's Life and Work in Context." *Cognition and Emotion* 20, no. 7 (2006): 902–919. https://doi.org/10.1080/02699930600615827

Tiedens, Larrisa Z. "Anger and Advancement versus Sadness and Subjugation: The Effect of Negative Emotion Expressions on Social Status Conferral." *Journal of Personality & Social Psychology* 80, no. 1 (2001): 86–94.

Weiner, Bernard. "An Attribution Theory of Achievement and Emotion." *Psychological Review* 92, no. 4 (1985): 548–573.

Wrosch, Carsten, Michael F. Scheier, and Gregory E. Miller. "Goal Adjustment Capacities, Subjective Well-Being and Physical Health." *Social and Personality Psychology Compass* 7, no. 12 (2013, Dec 1): 847–860. doi: 10.1111/spc3.12074.

Violence

Funk, Laura M., Rachel V. Herron, Dale Spencer, and Starr Lee Thomas. "Aggression and Older Adults: News Media Coverage Across Care Settings and Relationships." *Canadian Journal on Aging/La Revue canadienne du vieillissement* 40, no. 3 (2021): 500–511. doi: 10.1017/S0714980820000197.

Gerhart, James I., Bailey Seymour, Kim Maurelli, Krista Holman, and George Ronan. "Health and Relationships in Violence Reduction Participants: Indirect Effects of Angry Temperament." *Journal of Forensic Psychiatry & Psychology* 24, no. 2 (2013): 179–191.

Goldhagen, Renata F. S., and Jennifer Davidtz. "Violence, Older Adults, and Serious Mental Illness." *Aggression and Violent Behavior* 57 (2021): 101439. doi: 10.1016/j.avb.2020.101439.

Norlander, Bradley, and Christopher Eckhardt. "Anger, Hostility, and Male Perpetrators of Intimate Partner Violence: A Meta-Analytic Review." *Clinical Psychology Review* 25, no. 2 (2005): 119–152.

Payne, Jennifer Shepard, Frank H. Galvan, John K. Williams, Missy Prusinski, Muyu Zhang, Gail E. Wyatt, and Hector F. Myers. "Impact of Childhood Sexual Abuse on the Emotions and Behaviours of Adult Men from Three Ethnic Groups in the USA." *Culture, Health & Sexuality* 16, no. 3 (2014): 231–245.

Parrott, Dominic J., and Amos Zeichner. "Effects of Trait Anger and Negative Attitudes towards Women on Physical Assault in Dating Relationships." *Journal of Family Violence* 18, no. 5 (2003): 301–307.

Ravyts, Scott G., Elliottnell Perez, Emily K. Donovan, Pablo Soto, and Joseph M. Dzierzewski. "Measurement of Aggression in Older Adults." *Aggression and Violent Behavior* 57 (2021): 101484. doi: 10.1016/j.avb.2020.101484.

Roberton, Terri, and Michael Daffern. "Improving the Assessment of Risk for Imminent Aggression in Older Adults in Residential Facilities." *Aggression and Violent Behavior* 51 (2020): 101364. doi: 10.1016/j.avb.2020.101364.

Stripling, Ashley, and Natalie Dautovich. "Awareness and Answers for the Public Health Concern of Violence in Older Adults: An Introduction to Special Issue." *Aggression and Violent Behavior* 57 (2021): 101534. doi: 10.1016/j.avb.2020.101534.

Index

For the benefit of digital users, indexed terms that span two pages (e.g., 52–53) may, on occasion, appear on only one of those pages.
Tables and figures are indicated by t and f following the page number

Academic Search Ultimate, 161n.5
Achilles, 26
Achilles dragging the body of Hector around the walls of Troy (Testa), 23–24
activism, 123–33
   Chicago Seniors Together, 133
   choosing anger, 131
   constrained anger, 126–29
   de-legitimizing anger, 24f, 123–26
   Great Old Broads for Wilderness, 130
   Grey Panthers, 132
   Iaioflautas, 132, 133, 135
   importance, older activists, 131–33
   intellectual *vs.* emotional anger, 128
   productive anger, 126–29
   pros and cons of anger, 129–31
   Raging Grannies, 13, 17, 130–32, 136
adrenaline, 37, 59, 106, 148t
advice about anger, 121, 149t
Age Discrimination in Employment Act (ADEA), 9
aggrieved entitlement, 47, 101
aging, 136
   and divorce, 9
   mass, 1
   men, 53–54
   parents, 85
   physical, 35
   Canada's population, 118
   process, 1
   social, 4, 12, 126, 133
   stresses associated, 92
agitation, 118–19
altruists, amygdalae of, 36
Amanda and Larry were glad they didn't cancel the trip, 88f
American Cool: Constructing a 20th Century Emotional Style (Stearns), 120–21
American Cool emotional style, 119–21
Ames, Mark, *Going Postal*, 93, 102
amygdala, 36, 37, 38, 109
anger, 1–4
   advice about, to young person, 121, 149t

anger-in, 40, 41
anger-out, 6, 40
   as core emotion, 1–2
   culturally appropriate, 41
   de-legitimizing, 124
   disregarding, in older adults, 2
   embracing, 12
   expressed, 12, 40, 41, 128, 133
   extreme, as clarifying, 16
   gendered, 44–56 (*see also* gendered anger)
   internalized, 3, 4, 33, 40–41, 43, 128
   inward- *vs.* outward-directed, 6
   provocation of, 2
   reactions to, 2
   as state *vs.* trait, 6
   stifled, 4
   survival mode, 36, 111
   trigger, 2
   turned inward, 11
Anger and Forgiveness (Nussbaum), 56
Anger Becomes Her (Savage), 122
Anger in Love, 75–77, 76f
anger management, 105–15
   certification trainings, 108–9
   cognitive-behavioral therapy, 110
   Duluth Model, 109–10
   individual therapy, 112–14
   intermittent explosive disorder, 36–37, 38–39, 84–85, 107–8, 166n.4, 176n.3, 176n.4
   mandatory, 106
   program failures, 110
   self-help books, 112
   societal, 106
   succeeding in, 109
   survival mode, 36, 111
   veterans and PTSD, 110–11
   women, 111
      Black, referral to, 111
Anger Project, The, 3, 75–78, 76f, 139–46
   ethical approval, 139–40
   Facebook, 74–75, 76f, 77–78, 77f, 139, 140–42

198   INDEX

Anger Project, The, (cont.)
   Internet sample, 146
   Internet survey, 142–46, 143t, 145t, 147t, 148t, 149t
   interviews, 141–42
   results, 146
anger suppression, 6, 10–11, 13, 20–21
   American Cool, 119–21
   on health, 11–12
   in women vs. men, 54
Anger: The Struggle for Emotional Control in America's History (Stearns & Stearns), 120
"Angry by Design," (Munn), 70–71
"Angry Digital Silver in the Pandemic" (Oh), 74
Angry White Men (Kimmel), 47, 101
animal/animus, 46
antipsychotics, nursing home residents, 118
Aquinas, Saint Thomas, 32
Aristotle, 25–26, 33, 35
   Nicomachean Ethics, 25
   on revenge, 25, 26
   Rhetoric, 82
Aschbachers, Kirstin, 41
attention, anger attracting, 71

Baltes, Paul B., 2–3
Beyond Gender (Friedan), 46
Birditt, Kira, 54–55, 80
Black Lives Matter Movement, 57, 59
   demonstrations, 2020, 57, 59
Blackpast.org, 58
Blacks
   deaths
      COVID-19, 60
      maternal, 63
      youth, by police, 60–61
   life expectancy
      maternal deaths, 63
      men, 60
      men, young, 60–61
   women
      anger management referral, 111
      tiresomeness of it all, 61–64
Blanche-Tarrago, Daniel, 132
Blytheway, Bill, 8
bodies, angry, 35–43
   case study, 35–36, 37–38, 43
   context, 41–43
   late life variability, 38–39
   lizard brain, 36–37
   negative effects, 39–41
   survival circuit, 37–38

Boy Crisis, The (Farrell), 53
Boyd, Michelle R., *Jim Crow Nostalgia*, 64–65
Boylan, Jennifer Morozink, 42
Brady, William, 70
brain
   amygdala, 36, 37, 38, 109
   cerebral cortex, 38, 137
   orbital and medial prefrontal cortex, 38
   primitive, 36–37, 109
   seat of anger, 165n.2
   survival circuit, 37–38
Bright, Jennifer, 110
Brown, Susan, 9
Brown Berets, 59
Buchanan, Jeffrey, 119
Burtless, Gary, 8
Butler, Judith, *Undoing Gender*, 46

cantankerous, 21
caregiving, 9
Carol pointing a rifle, 125f
Carr, Emily, 13
Carroll, E. Jean, 47
Carstensen, Laura C., "Emotion and Aging: Experience, Expression, and Control," 2–3
Cassidy, Samuel James, 93–95, 100
catharsis, 16, 72
   mass, 10
cerebral cortex, 38, 137
character, anger building, 66–68
Chávez, César, 59, 170n.2
Chemaly, Sonya, *Rage Becomes Her*, 47
chemical restraint, 117–18
Cherelus, G., 39
Chewong, 19
Chicago Seniors Together, 133
Chicano identity, 170n.2
childrens' anger, towards/from parents, 84–86
child support, failure to pay, 50, 51–52
Chinese, 18–19
Christianity, 26, 29–31
   anger as sin, 32–33
   Jesus, 31–32, 33
Churchill, Winston, 136–37
Cicero, Marcus Tullius, 27
Citizen: An American Lyric (Rankine), 7, 59
Civilization and its Discontents (Freud), 106
Cixous, Helene, 46
code switching, 63
cognitive-behavioral therapy, for anger management, 110
conflict resolution, older couples, 80–81
constructive anger behavior, 41

context, 41–43
Cooper, Brittney, *Eloquent Rage: A black feminist discovers her superpower*, 63, 84
cortisol, 37–38, 40
Course of Love, The (de Botton), 83–84
COVID Lowers US Life Expectancy, 61f
COVID-19 pandemic
　anti-elderly rants, 72–73
　deaths, older adults, 72–74
Cozzolino, Elizabeth, 52
Craun, Sarah, James, "A Study of the Pre-Attack Behaviors of Active Shooters in the United States Between 2000 and 2013," 100–1
Crockett, Molly J., 70
crotchety, 21
Cullen, David, 104
culturally appropriate anger, 41
custody disputes, fathers in, 53
cyberranting, 71

Dante
　Divine Comedy, The, 33
　Inferno, The, 33
Darwin, C., *The Expression of Emotions in Man and Animals*, 4–5
Dead Sea Scrolls, gendered anger, 45
deaths, Black
　COVID-19, 60
　maternal, 63
　youth, by police, 60–61
deaths, older adults, 8
　COVID-19, 8
　Hurricane Katrina, 8
de Botton, Alain, *The Course of Love*, 83–84
Deffenbacher, Jerry, 54
De Ira (Seneca), 28–29
De Ira Dei (Lactantius), 30–31
de-legitimizing anger, 124
dementia, 120
　agitation, 118–19
demonstrations, 58–60
de Saussuer, Ferdinand, 16
despair, 90, 95, 96, 100, 118, 125
　Erikson's stage and, 136
　not giving in to, 131
Detail of Raging Medusa, 45f
Dewey, John, 5
Dexter, Miriam, 46
Diagnostic and Statistical Manual, 176n.4
Dimitrious, Tatiana, 119
disengagement theory, gero-transcendence, 15–16
disgruntled, beyond, 103–4
Divine Comedy, The (The Dante), 33

divorce, older Americans, 9
Dodd, C., 31
domestic violence
　false accusations, of men, 49–52
　victims, 173n.11
Dorr, Nancy, 42–43
Do you consider yourself an angry person? 150t
Duluth Model, 109–10

education, substandard, 66
Edwards, Jonathan, "Sinners in the Hands of an Angry God," 29
Eloquent Rage: A black feminist discovers her superpower (Cooper), 63, 84
embracing anger, 122
　advice, 121, 149t
　American Cool emotional style, 119–21
　antipsychotic use, nursing home residents, 118
　chemical restraint, 117–18
　example, 116–17
　stimulus for, preferred, 119
　treatments, hopeful, 118–19
　turning toward, 122
emotional intelligence
　age on, 80
　anger control, 26
emotional regulation
　older people, 114
　society and civilization, 106
"Emotion and Aging: Experience, Expression, and Control" (Gross, Carstensen, & Pasupathi), 2–3
emotions
　Darwin on, 4–5
　Dewey on, 5
　locus, 19
　suppressed, 4, 12 (*see also* anger suppression)
　survival circuit, 37–38
Ending Ageism (Gullette), 7
entitlement, aggrieved, 47, 101
Erikson, Eric, 136
exit strategies, 80
expressed anger, 12, 40, 41, 128, 133
Expression of Emotions in Man and Animals, The (Darwin), 4–5
Extinction Rebellion, 12–13
eye of the heart, 136

Facebook
　Anger Project, 74–75, 76f, 77–78, 77f, 139, 140–42
　rage, design favoring, 70–71

senior use, 74–75
Fair Share (Fine), 133
familicide, 98–99
family anger, 9–10
   love and, 81–82
Farrell, Warren, 52–53
   Boy Crisis, The, 53
fathers, custody disputes, 53
female anger
   vs. male, experiences vs. expression, 52–53
   Medusa, 44–45, 45f, 46
   #MeToo movement, 47
   suppression, 54
   in throats, 166n.6
   ugliness, 46–47
   unique issues, 115
Fernandez-Ardevol, Mireia, 132
Fine, Gary Alan, *Fair Share*, 133
Fingerman, Karen, 54–55, 80
fire disease, 10–11
Firestone, Robert, "The Simple Truth about Anger," 4
Fischer, Jane, 119
Flores, Abdiel, 41
Floyd, George, 59. See also Black Lives Matter Movement
Flutur, Randal H., "The Stranger Inside of Me," 18
Ford, Christine Blasey, 47
forgiveness
   Jesus, 31
   self-forgiveness, 40
Fox, Jackie, 132, 133
Freud, Sigmund, 11, 16
   Civilization and its Discontents, 106
Friedan, Betty, *Beyond Gender*, 46
fright, from others' anger, 119–20
Funk, Laura, 118

Gaelic, 19–20
Gardner, Richard, 50
gendered anger, 44–56
   Dead Sea Scrolls, 45
   female
      Medusa, 44–45, 45f, 46
      #MeToo movement, 47
      ugliness, 46–47
   female, self-criticism & rumination after anger, 55–56
   gender paradox, 55–56
   late life, freedom from binary rigidities, 46
   male
      angrier?, 47–49
      Men's Issues Movement, 52–53

      men's rights movement, 47–49
      men's rights movement, domestic abuse and rape, false accusations, 49–52
   male/female anger experiences vs. expression, 52–53
gero-transcendence, 15–16
Geun-hye, Park, 73–74
Going Postal (Ames), 93, 102
"going postal," 101–2
Golden, Bernie, *Overcoming Destructive Anger*, 112
grandchildren, legacy for, 64–65, 65f
Great Old Broads for Wilderness, 130
Grey Panthers, 132
Grief, 2, 31, 125
Gross, James J., "Emotion and Aging: Experience, Expression, and Control," 2–3
"Grumpy Old Men," 21
Guide for the Perplexed, A (Schumacher), 136
Gullette, M. M., 73
   Ending Ageism, 7
gun violence, 90–104. See also violence, mass
gynocentrism, 56

hahn, 11
Hance, Michael, 97, 100
Harris, Grace Gredys, 20
Harris, William V., 82, 87
health, anger on, 39–41
   African Americans, 42–43
   expressed vs. internalized, 128
   suppression of, 11–12
heat, of anger, 15–17
Hera, 82
Hirsch, Jameson K., 40
Ho, Judy Woon Yee, 19
Hofstra, Jori, 15, 18
home, anger at, 79–81
Homer, *The Illiad*, 26
How has your experience of anger changed with age? 147t
Huerta, Delores, 170n.2
Hurricane Katrina deaths, older adults, 8
hwa-byung, 10–11
hypothalamus-pituitary-adrenal (HPA) axis, 37–38

Iaioflautas, 132, 133, 135
idioms, disgusting, 17–18
Illiad, The, 26, 82
individuation, 46
Inferno, The (The Dante), 33
Injustice, 25, 28, 34, 57, 95, 101, 104, 111, 112, 118, 128

Instituto Nacional de Ciencias Medicas y Nutricion, 72
intermittent explosive disorder, 36–37, 38–39, 84–85, 107–8, 166n.4, 176n.3, 176n.4
internalized anger, 3, 4, 33, 40–41, 43, 128
Internet access and use, U.S. seniors, 74
Internet Sample Demographics, 145t
Internet survey, 142–46
    advice about anger, to younger person, 149t
    age on experience of anger, 147t
    angry person, self-evaluation, 150t
    body feelings, anger, 148t
    demographics, 145t
    incidents that made respondents angry, 150t
    instrument, 153–60
    pseudonyms, demographics & themes for interview respondents, 143t
    "really angry" incident, 148t
interviews, 141–42
    protocol, 151–18
intimate partner violence, victims, 173n.11

Jesus, 31–32, 33
Jim Crow Nostalgia (Boyd), 64–65
Jimenez-Sotomayor, Maria, 72
Jung, Carl, 46
Justice, 60, 132
    Anger's purpose 25
    Aquinas views, 32
    System, 51, 113–14

Karlsson, Linda, 99
Kashdan, Todd, 54
    Power of Negative Emotion, The, 54
Kay, Jilly Boyce, 47
Keeping, Joseph, 82
Kennedy, Maura, 118–19
Kessler, Ron, 107–8
kick the dog syndrome, 86–89, 88f
Kimmel, Michael, *Angry White Men*, 47, 101
Klabbers, Gonnie, 40–41
Klein, Ezra, 47
Kotzé, Zachiarias, 16–17
Kövecses, Zoltán, 17
Kuhn, Maggie, *No Stone Unturned: The Life and Times of Maggie Kuhn*, 12

Lactantius, Lucius Caecilius Firmianus, 30
    De Ira Dei, 30–31
language, on anger, 14–22
    articulating
        hesitance, 14–15
        "slant," 15

cantankerous, 21
catharsis, 16, 72
crotchety, 21
exploding, vignette, 15–16
explosion and heat, 15–17
"Grumpy Old Men," 21
idioms, disgusting, 17–18
metaphor, 15
metaphors, non-English, 18–20
suppression of expression, 20–21
terms, age-specific, 21–22
Lankenvich, Natalikea, "The Anger Project: Wisdom & Lessons for EMPATH," 141
Las Vegas mass shooting, 2017, 90, 91–93
LeDoux, Joseph E., 37
Le Guin, Ursula, 56
life expectancy
    Black men, 60
        young, 60–61
    Black women, maternal deaths, 63
    COVID on, 60, 61f
    global, 1
    Whites *vs.* Blacks, 60
Lin, I-Fen, 9
Lisak, David, 51
literary references, 23–24
Lively, Kathryn, 54
lizard brain, 36–37
Lord, Audre
    Sister Outside, 61
    Uses of Anger, The, 55
Lorenzini, Jasmine, 133
love, anger and, 79–89
    children, 84–86
    family, 81–82
    at home, 79–81
    kick the dog syndrome, 86–89, 88f
    lovers' quarrel, 82–83
    sulking, 83–84
lovers' quarrel, 82–83
loyalty strategies, 80

Magai, Carol, 41
Majid, Asifa, 17–18
male anger
    vs. female, experiences *vs.* expression, 52–53
    greater than female?, 53–55
    Men's Issues Movement, 52–53
    men's rights movement, 47–49
        false accusations, domestic abuse and rape, 49–52
    suppression, 54
marriage, anger in, 79–81

INDEX

Marsh, Abigail, 36
Martin, Ryan, 71–72
mass aging, 1
mass catharsis, 10
mass murder, 90–104. *See also* violence, mass
Mass Murders in America 1982-202, 95f
mass violence, 90–104. *See also* violence, mass
McCloskey, Michael, 36
Medea and Jason, 82–83
media, public, complaining about, 171n.2
medial prefrontal cortex, 38
Medusa's rage, 44–45, 45f, 46
Meisner, Brad, 72
Mendes, Wendy Berry, 41
Men's Issues Movement, 53
mens' rights, 53
    activists, 131–33
Mermelstein, Ari, *Power and Emotion in Ancient Judaism*, 45
metaphor
    for anger, 14–15, 17, 18, 19
metonym
    for anger, 16–18, 19
#MeToo movement, 47
microaggressions
    ageist, 6–7
    racist, 42, 44, 57, 59, 60, 63, 97
    sexist, 6–7
Moon, Kathryn, 9
Munn, Luke, "Angry by Design," 70–71
Munnell, Alicia, 9

National Anger Management Association, 108–9
Network, 10
New Testament, 31–32
Nicomachean Ethics (Aristotle), 25
No Stone Unturned: The Life and Times of Maggie Kuhn (Kuhn), 12
Nursing Home Bill of Rights, 118
Nussbaum, Martha, 2
    Anger and Forgiveness, 56

Oh, June, "Angry Digital Silver in the Pandemic," 74
Older adults can—and do—change the world, 137f
Older Women's League (OWL), 12
old old, 1
O'Meara, Carolyn, 17–18
"On the Physiologic Effects of the Indulgence in Anger," 39
orbital prefrontal cortex, 38
outrage, 12
Overcoming Destructive Anger (Golden), 112
Ovid, on Medusa's rage, 44–45

Paddock, Stephen Craig, 91–93, 95, 100
Parental Alienation Syndrome, 50
parental anger, towards/from children, 84–86
Park, Jiyoung, 41
passive-aggressive personality, aggressive type, 176n.4
Pasupathi, Monisha, "Emotion and Aging: Experience, Expression, and Control," 2–3
Pfeiffer, Rich, 108–9
Phillips, Linda Ree, 9–10
philosophical and theological traditions, Western, 23–34
    Achilles dragging the body of Hector around the walls of Troy (Testa), 23–24f
    Aristotle, 25–26, 33, 35
    Christianity, 26, 29–31
    anger as sin, 32–33
    Jesus, 31–32, 33
    literary references, 23–24
    Stoics, 26–29, 109
    vengeance, 29–31
Pierce, Chester M., 7
"pissed off," 17, 131
plasticity, brain, 37
Power and Emotion in Ancient Judaism (Mermelstein), 45
Power of Negative Emotion, The (Kashdan), 54
prefrontal cortex, 38
primitive brain, 36–37, 109
Pseudonyms, Demographics & Themes for Interview Respondents, 143t

Quinn, Sarah, 132, 133

race and anger, later life, 57–68
    anger builds character, 66–68
    anger in the streets, 58–60
    Antebellum and abolitionist movement, 58
    black enclaves, 64
    Black Lives Matter 2020, 57, 59
    César Chávez and Brown Berets, 59
    Chinese immigrant targets, 58–59
    code switching, 63
    COVID on life expectancy, 60, 61f
    education, substandard, 66
    grandchildren, legacy for, 64–65, 65f
    life expectancy, 60
    microaggressions, 42, 57, 59, 60, 63, 97
    race, origins, 57
    slave rebellions, 58
    tiresomeness of it all, female and Black, 61–64
    trauma, historical, 62–63
    unfairness, 66, 81
    violence from bigotry, 66
"Race is a fiction. Racism is real" (Williams), 44
Racism (Wilson), 57

INDEX

rage
  contagiousness, 70–71
  Medusa's, 44–45, 45f, 46
  pent-up, 11
  social media contagion, 70–71
  taming, 105–15 (see also anger management)
Rage Becomes Her (Chemaly), 47
rage-onomics, 101–2
Raging Grannies, 13, 17, 130–32, 136
Rankine, C., *Citizen: An American Lyric*, 7, 59
rants, cyberspace for, 71
rape, false accusations, 49–52
reductionism, psychological research, 5
Reflecting on what you did during the incident that made you "really angry," 148t
Regal Theater and Savoy Ballroom in Bronzeville, Chicago, IL, 65f
relationship conflicts, 80–81
research, 5–6
  FBI, 99, 101
  measuring anger 6
  on age-related changes, 96
  on agner management, 110
  on cortisol, 40
  on health effects of anger, 40, 41
  on hostility, 41
  on older activists, 132
  on trait anger, 40
  on age-related changes 3–4
  on microaggression 7
  on social media and loneliness, 78
restraint, chemical, 117–18
revenge, 23, 24
  Aquinas on, Saint Thomas, 32
  Aristotle on, 25, 26
  Barusch on, 33, 34
  "going postal," 102
  male, 44, 51, 52
  media portrayal, 176n.3
  murderers, 102, 104
  Seneca on, 28
  Theogony (Hesiod), 44
Rhetoric (Aristotle), 82
Rosset, Jan, 133
Ryan, Bill, 12–13

Sadler, G., 25
Sarton, May, 46
Savage, Allie, 18, 122
  Anger Becomes Her, 122
  "The Anger Project: Wisdom & Lessons for EMPATH," 141
  "Turning Towards Anger," 122
Savostina, Irina, 12

Schumacher, E. F., *A Guide for the Perplexed*, 136
Scott, Kate, 107–8
self-forgiveness, 40
Seneca, Lucius Annaeus, 27–29, 33
shootings, mass, 90–104. *See also* violence, mass
Silver, James, "A Study of the Pre-Attack Behaviors of Active Shooters in the United States Between 2000 and 2013," 100–1
Simon, Robin, 54
Simons, Andre, James, "A Study of the Pre-Attack Behaviors of Active Shooters in the United States Between 2000 and 2013," 100–1
"The Simple Truth about Anger" (Firestone), 4
sin, anger as, 32–33
"Sinners in the Hands of an Angry God" (Edwards), 29
Sister Outside (Lord), 61
slave rebellions, 58
social media, 69–78. *See also* Facebook
  Anger Project online, 75–78, 76f
  anti-elder posts, 69–70
  COVID-19 lockdown, 69–70
  cyberspace for rants, 71–72
  intergenerational tensions, 72–74
  rage, by design, 70–71
    Facebook, 70–71
    YouTube, 70, 71
  rage contagion, 70–71
  toxic communication, 70
  U.S.
    internet access, 74
    use, 74–75
  YouTube trap, South Korea, 74–75
socio-emotional selectivity, 2–3
Somers, Tish, 12
South Korea
  Taegukgi Squad, 74, 78, 136
  YouTube trap, 74–75
Spielberger, Charles Donald, 6
Spiro Agenda, 171n.2
State-Trait Anger Expression Inventory (STAXI), 6
Stearns, Carol, *Anger: The Struggle for Emotional Control in America's History*, 120
Stearns, Peter
  American Cool: Constructing a 20th Century Emotional Style, 120–21
  Anger: The Struggle for Emotional Control in America's History, 120
Stoics, 26–29, 109
  Cicero, Marcus Tullius, 27
  Seneca, Lucius Annaeus, 27–29, 33
Stott, J., 30

204 INDEX

Stout, Jeffrey, 132
"The Stranger Inside of Me" (Flutur), 18
"A Study of the Pre-Attack Behaviors of Active Shooters in the United States Between 2000 and 2013" (Silver, Simons, & Craun), 100–1
Sue, Derald W., 7
sulking, 83–84
suppressed anger, 6, 10–11, 13, 20–21
    American Cool, 119–21
    on health, 11–12
    in women *vs.* men, 54
suppressed emotions, 4, 12
survival circuit, 37–38
survival mode, 36, 111

Taafe, Julianne, 9
Taegukgi Squad, 74, 78, 136
taming rage, 105–15. *See also* anger management
Taylor, Melanie, 95
Taylor, Quintard, 58
Testa, Pietro, *Achilles dragging the body of Hector around the walls of Troy*, 23–24
"The Anger Project: Wisdom & Lessons for EMPATH," (Savage & Lankenvich), 141
theological traditions, 23–34. *See also* philosophical and theological traditions, Western
theory of socio-emotional selectivity, 2–3
therapeutic alliance, 178n.16
Thornton, Charles Lee "Cookie," 96–97, 101
threat, existential, 13
threat recognition, 36
    intermittent explosive disorder, 38, 107
tiresomeness, female and Black, 61–64
toxic communication, 70
Tran, Huu Can, 102–3
transcendence, 15–16
Tulsa Burning: The 1921 Race Massacre, 59
"Turning Towards Anger" (Savage), 122
Twitter, senior use, 74–75
Type of Incident that Made Respondents Angry, 150t

Undoing Gender (Butler), 46
unfairness
    mass shooters, 101
    race and anger, 66, 81
United Farm Workers, 170n.2
Uses of Anger, The (Lord), 55

Van Voorhees, Liz, 110–11
vengeance, 29–31
Vines, Anissa, 42
violence, mass, 90–104
    2023 incidents, 102–3

Cassidy, Samuel James, 93–95, 100
Columbine, 103–4
disgruntled, beyond, 103–4
familicide, 98–99
government, war on, 96
Hance, Michael, 97, 100
Las Vegas, 2017, 90, 91–93
lethality of, increased, 174n.1
Paddock, Stephen Craig, 91–93, 95, 100
rage-onomics/"going postal," 101–2
shooters, FBI study, 99–101
Thornton, Charles Lee "Cookie," 96–97, 101
Tran, Huu Can, 102–3
unfairness, nagging sense of, 101
U.S.
    age of shooters, 95–96
    frequency, trend, 95f
Wilkinson, Richard, 98–99, 100–1
Williams, Lee Roy, 96
Yazdanpanah, Azizolah "Bob," 98
Zhao, Chunli, 103

Walker, Julian, 110
Watt, Jennifer A., 119
Wesbecker, Joseph, 102
"What advice would you give to someone younger about anger?" 149t
What do you feel in your body when you get angry? 148t
"What makes you angry" post from The Anger Project, April 8, 2021, 76f
Wilkinson, Richard, 98–99, 100–1
Williams, Kimberlé, "Race is a fiction. Racism is real," 44
Williams, Leah, 80
Williams, Lee Roy, 97
Wilson, Carter A., *Racism*, 57
Wong, M. D., 60
Woodford, Jack, 171n.2
work, ageism at, 8–9
Wu, April, 9

Yardley, Elizabeth, 99
Yazdanpanah, Azizolah "Bob," 98
young old, 1
YouTube
    rage, design favoring, 70, 71
    senior use, 74–75
    trap, South Korea, 74–75

Zeus, 82
Zhao, Chunli, 103
Zulu, 18